Human-Computer Interaction and Beyond: Advances Towards Smart and Interconnected Environments (Part I)

Edited by

Nirmalya Thakur
Department of Electrical Engineering and Computer Science
College of Engineering and Applied Science
University of Cincinnati
Cincinnati, Ohio
United States

&

Parameshachari B.D.
Department of Telecommunication Engineering
GSSS Institute of Engineering & Technology for Women,
Mysuru
Affiliated to Visvesvaraya Technological University (VTU)
Belagavi, Karnataka
India

Human-Computer Interaction and Beyond: Advances Towards Smart and Interconnected Environments

(Part I)

Editors: Nirmalya Thakur and Parameshachari B.D.

ISBN (Online): 978-981-4998-81-9

ISBN (Print): 978-981-4998-82-6

ISBN (Paperback): 978-981-4998-83-3

Bentham Science Publishers Pte. Ltd.
80 Robinson Road #02-00
Singapore 068898
Singapore
Email: subscriptions@benthamscience.net

BENTHAM SCIENCE

CONTENTS

PREFACE

In this age of rapidly advancing technology, the future of living and functional environments would involve humans interacting, coordinating, and collaborating with computers, machines, robots, and various technology-laden systems in a multitude of ways. Examples of such smart and interconnected environments include Smart Homes, Smart Industries, Smart Workplaces, Smart Buildings, and Smart Cities, just to name a few. There are two parts of the edited book that presents discoveries, innovative ideas, concepts, theoretical findings, practical solutions, improvements, and novel applications in Human-Computer Interaction (HCI) aimed at developing trust, user acceptance, augmenting user performance, improving quality of life, and fostering human-technology partnerships in the future of technology-laden living and functional environments.

The topics covered in these books include the following:

- Applications of HCI for Smart Homes, Smart Cities, and Smart Vehicles
- Design of Technology for special user groups – elderly, disabled, *etc.*
- Prototypes of Interactive Systems with a focus on Human-Centered Design
- Applications of Artificial Intelligence, Machine Learning and Data Mining in HCI
- Computer Vision, Image Recognition and their applications in HCI
- Novel works in mobile or web development related to HCI for Smart Environments
- Applications of HCI in healthcare, education, entertainment, and games
- Applications of HCI and related technologies focusing on COVID-19

The current part of this book, Part 1, presents a unique and diverse collection of the global advancements in HCI in the above-mentioned application domains. It consists of chapters authored by experts and scientists in the field of HCI and its interrelated disciplines from 8 different countries – Chile, China, Croatia, India, Iran, Malaysia, Peru, and South Korea. This book is aimed at scientists, researchers, and developers in Academia and the Industry who wish to learn, design, implement, and apply the emerging technologies, concepts, and applications from the field of Human-Computer Interaction in different application domains, with a specific focus on the future of technology-laden living and functional environments. Each chapter has an abstract and keywords followed by the introduction, methodologies, and other sections. Readers can determine their interest level in any chapter quickly based on the keywords and the abstract.

ACKNOWLEDGEMENTS

We would like to acknowledge Bentham Science Publishers for this opportunity and for their professional support throughout this project. Finally, we would like to thank all the authors of the chapters in this book.

Nirmalya Thakur
Department of Electrical Engineering and Computer Science
College of Engineering and Applied Science
University of Cincinnati
Cincinnati, Ohio
United States

&

Parameshachari B.D.
Department of Telecommunication Engineering
GSSS Institute of Engineering & Technology for Women, Mysuru
Affiliated to Visvesvaraya Technological University (VTU)
Belagavi, Karnataka
India

List of Contributors

Abdulsalam S. Mustafa	College of Graduate Studies, University Tenaga Nasional, Selangor, Malaysia
A.K. Kureshi	MMANTC, Malegaon, India
A.N. Banubakode	MET Institute of Computer Science Bandra(W), Mumbai, Maharashtra, India
Andrej Bodrušić	Algebra University College, Zagreb, Croatia
Chhaya S. Gosavi	Department of Computer Engineering, Cummins College of Engineering for Women, Karvenagar, Pune, Maharashtra, India
Ganesh Bhutkar	Center of Excellence in Human-Computer Interaction, Vishwakarma Institute of Technology, Pune, India
Helena Bukovac	Algebra University College, Zagreb, Croatia
Hussain M.	ELTEC, College of Enginering, Ewha Womans University, Seoul, South Korea
José Reátegui	School of Architecture, Universidad Peruana de Ciencias Aplicadas, Lima, Peru
Kianoosh Karimi	Faculty of Management, University of Tehran, Tehran, Iran
Michael Hurtado	School of Architecture, Universidad Peruana de Ciencias Aplicadas, Lima, Peru
Mauricio Loyola	Faculty of Architecture and Urbanism, Universidad de Chile, Santiago, Chile
Muhammad Shoaib	Department of Computer Science, College of Science and Technology Wenzhou-Kean University, China
Mate G.S	JSPM's Rajarshi Shahu College of Engineering, Pune, India
Park S.K.	ELTEC, College of Enginering, Ewha Womans University, Seoul, South Korea
Pablo C. Herrera	School of Architecture, Universidad Peruana de Ciencias Aplicadas, Lima, Peru
Pranjali Deshpande	Department of Computer Engineering, Cummins College of Engineering for Women, Karvenagar, Pune, Maharashtra, India
Swapnil Pawar	Center of Excellence in Human-Computer Interaction, Vishwakarma Institute of Technology, Pune, India
Tiffany Ya Tang	Department of Computer Science, College of Science and Technology Wenzhou-Kean University, China
Xu Wei	Department of Computer Science, College of Science and Technology Wenzhou-Kean University, China

CHAPTER 1

A Survey of Approaches for Facilitating Rich User Experience in Healthcare Domain

Pranjali Deshpande[1] and **Chhaya S. Gosavi**[1,*]

[1] *Department of Computer Engineering, Cummins College of Engineering for Women, Karve-nagar, Pune, Maharashtra, India*

Abstract: HCI is a discipline concerned with designing, evaluating, and implementing interactive systems for human use. HCI focuses on the fact that "people should come first." The healthcare industry has more rapid influence and development with HCI in recent days. Healthcare systems with improved HCI would benefit the industry in terms of quality of service and throughput. In the healthcare domain, the Interaction possibilities are spread in a broad spectrum, *i.e.*, from tangible interfaces to wearable and implanted devices. The survey of the diverse device interactions in various healthcare systems from technological aspects is a significant area of research, useful to the medical fraternity and ordinary people. The presented survey will open up the doors for exploring novel approaches related to the rich User Experience in the healthcare domain for the benefit of society.

Keywords: Artificial Intelligent, DSS, Embodiment, HCI, Health Care, ICT, Implanted devices, Literature Review, Medical Services, Mobile Applications, Multidisciplinary, NLG, PRO, Quality Parameters, SHT, Tangible Interfaces, Ubiquitous Computing, User Experience, Voice Assistants, Wearable devices.

INTRODUCTION

Human-Computer Interface (HCI), also known as User Experience (UE), is the Computer science and engineering domain that focuses on the systems' Human-Centric Development. It influences and incorporates all the major Computer Science domains like Artificial Intelligence, Ubiquitous Computing, Database management, *etc*. With the tremendous advancement in these technologies, HCI has also flourished to enhance the user experience of almost all the systems used by human beings.

* **Corresponding author Chhaya Gosavi:** MKSSS's Cummins College of Engineering for Women, Karvenagar, Pune – 411052, Maharashtra, India; E-mail: chhaya.gosavi@cumminscollege.in

Nirmalya Thakur and Parameshachari B.D. (Eds)

HCI is also a multidisciplinary domain that facilitates human services in many fields like healthcare, gaming, social and organizational management systems, various tangible and auditory interfaces, *etc.*

HCI is a perfect reflection of how machines can make human beings' lives more comfortable and happier through various handy interfaces. Healthcare is an essential domain. It exploits all the different approaches, tools, and techniques in the medical field to help humans survive and cope with the various health problems arising from genetic issues, improper lifestyle, or health problems due to unforeseen and unavoidable accidents pandemics. As HCI systems are built keeping humans in the center, they prove to be a boon to humankind as right from motor organs to internal organs. Technology can be blended with medical techniques to create beneficial machines and tools. The use of HCI can be witnessed in the smooth functioning of almost all organs and senses. Various Information and Communication Technology (ICT) devices are built to handle multiple human feelings. Some of these ICT modalities include cameras for sight, various input/output devices like touch screens and keypads for touch, pointer devices for haptic control, microphones for hearing, different chemical sensors, and analyzers for smell taste. To enable human interaction with the outside world, different types of interfaces can be designed like gesture interfaces for expressing meaning or idea through various gestures by body parts like fingers, hands, arms, head, face, tangible interfaces, and organic interfaces to facilitate manipulation of object in three-dimension space, auditory and Natural Language interfaces, wearable and implanted device interfaces like pacemakers, *etc*. With this context, the importance of HCI to support healthcare services can be understood. The literature survey in this chapter encompasses the various possibilities and approaches of enhancement in medical facilities with the help of HCI. The survey considers the various health aspects, including the mental and physical health and use of various wearable and implanted devices for the well-being of humankind.

LITERATURE REVIEW

The literature review focuses on the approaches by researchers on various health aspects. Nowadays, we observe that people are getting more inclined towards a healthy lifestyle and diet due to awareness of junk and processed food. HCI can play a significant role in managing the dietary needs and constant monitoring of the patient. Luca Anselma and Alessandro Mazzei have designed an app, Multimedia Application for Diet Management (MADiMan), for diet management. MADiMan app focuses on two aspects. The first one studies users' dietary constraints and automatically adapts the users' diet through a numerical reasoner. The second part helps the user stick to a healthy diet by generating text messages through Natural Language Generation (NLG) system. The results generated by numerical reasoners are used for this purpose. The use of the reasoning module makes this app different from other commercial apps. The reasoning module generates a numerical representation of the diet and food consumed. This facilitates proper diet management through an app. Whereas the NLG module contains a document planner, sentence planner, and a realize module for providing customization of the messages. The CheckYourMeal app is used to evaluate the NLG module by considering the description of human-based simulation. Two experiments with two distinct groups of people are conducted, and the correctness of the app on various parameters is checked [1]

Franklin *et al.* categorized the important usability factors. They discussed some of the parameters that would make the interface practical and usable with specific quality parameters such as safety and reliability. The problems in the interfaces are analyzed from the clinical point of view, and the ways are figured out for usability improvement and for meeting the User Experience needs. They also planned to involve certain significant quantitative factors related to these qualitative factors to address the needs of next-generation healthcare systems to improve the usability of the interface [2]. There is less importance given to standardizing methods to collect and integrate Patient-Reported Outcomes (PROs) data in today's internet world. Deliya B *et al.* described a framework for understanding patients' usability and functional requirements collecting PRO data using applications (apps) and healthcare providers using these data at the point of care in ambulatory settings. The STS model asked the guided questions. Semi-structured interviews were conducted with eighteen patients and nine healthcare providers to elicit feedback about facilitators and barriers to the successful use of PRO apps and PRO data in ambulatory settings. The data were analyzed inductively to identify emergent themes. It was observed that younger patients were only interested in using a PRO app if they had an active health issue to track. The nine older patients preferred passive means of data collection to follow a health issue, selected direct contact with their healthcare provider and used office visits to share information. The app provides transparency and privacy. All patients desired optimal usability and emphasized bidirectional communication in an app. All healthcare providers agreed that PRO data would be most useful and relevant if key patient populations were targeted based on the specific measure [3].

In the case of Asthma, the patient's self-awareness and management of the clinical state of Asthma is beneficial. Otilia Kocsis *et al.* proposed a short-term prediction approach for asthma control status named myAirCoach, considering training multiple classification models for each monitored parameter and necessary pre-processing methods to enhance robustness and efficiency. The integrated sensors are used to understand physiological, behavioral, and environmental factors to monitor the increase in the symptoms. The work focuses on the prototype implementation of the Decision Support System (DSS) in the myAirCoach project. Various machine learning algorithms like Support Vector Machines, Random Forests, AdaBoost, and Bayesian Network are used. They concluded that the Random Forests and Support Vector Machines classifiers demonstrated overall superior performance for the case studies (models) considered. The dataset of asthma assessment tools of 76 patients was taken into consideration for experimenting. The experiments were conducted using the R language, and the performance of various algorithms was studied [4].

Erinc Merdivan *et al.* presented an overview of existing dialogue management methods and discussed their advantages and limitations. They also proposed a new image-based plan in Facebook bAbI Task 1 dataset in the Out of Vocabulary setting. They concluded that using dialogue as an image performs well and helps the dialogue manager expand out vocabulary dialogue tasks compared to Memory Networks [5]. Hayat Sedratia *et al.* [6] presented the review of the current development of mobile health applications for chronic and incapacitating diseases indicative of physical or mental disability in the patient, namely: brain injury, stroke, and spinal cord injury; psychoactive substance abuse and addiction, depression, stress, and anxiety. They searched various applications in both Android and Apple app stores. Based on these search results database is developed, and results are analyzed. They concluded that there is a need for healthcare professionals' involvement in the design and development of apps meant for diagnostic and treatment. They also observed the inequality of users' profiles in both mental and physical mobile apps. They evaluated the usefulness, efficiency, and suitability of the most relevant applications in the Moroccan context and performed a comparison and evaluation of the efficacy of these applications.

Ekaterina V. Bologvaa *et al.* used electronic medical records (EMR) by the Russian medical research center. They explored the challenges faced by HCI while handling this database. They observed that the quality of data stored in the database is affected by inadequate HCI. According to them, poor HCI design in EMR leads to some trivial mistakes. Possible consequences of such errors are discussed from clinical and data science perspectives. A specially designed Clinical Decision Support System (CDSS) is used to enhance HCI, resulting in a subsequent increase in EMR quality. Their study is a part of a larger project to develop complex CDSS on cardiovascular disorders for medical research centers [7].

Sustainability concerning reducing poverty, eliminating various diseases, and educating the entire population should always be the global level's topmost goals.

Jan Gulliksen *et al.* provided an overview of human-computer interaction (HCI) contribution to international development in different regions of the world. They addressed the fact that HCI needs to fulfill the contextual needs, develop digital innovations, and how it can be done. They used qualitative research methodology with an action research paradigm. The role of digitization is significant in the medical field. It helps in various aspects like the use of digital tools in spreading awareness of the symptoms and early detection of the disease, maintaining medical records, enhance the administration, facilitating symptom detection utilizing digital techniques like taking pictures of the patient in remote areas and sending them to doctor for reference and in the rehabilitation of the people in traumatic conditions like significant accidents. They concluded that digitalization is fundamentally changing society through the development and use of digital technologies and may profoundly affect the digital evolution of every country in the world [8].

Jarosław Kowalski *et al.* presented the results of an exploratory study examining the potential of voice assistants (VA) for some groups of older adults in the context of Smart Home Technology (SHT). The designed system consists of a speaker with a voice assistant agent, smartphone, and additional peripherals such as a TV set, an Android TV Set-Top Box, light controllers, Wi-Fi relays, *etc*. The authors suggested verifying the identified primary barriers and benefits, exploring the insights gathered and investigating their solution with different potential user groups to verify which insights may be group-specific and general. The results were found to be very promising when VA is blended with IoT [9].

Worldwide at least 50 million people are affected by Alzheimer's disease. The elderly population is impacted more by this disease. In the paper [10], a comprehensive HCI system named symbiosis is explained, which provides integrated solutions to various health problems arising due to Alzheimer's disease. Natural User Interface (NUI) is designed to facilitate physical and mental exercise. SymbioGames are designed to improve various skills like memory, attention, orientation, *etc*. SymbioSpace facility is constructed with auxiliary auditory and visual effects to facilitate a friendly environment for the patient through augmented reality. Similarly, SymbioMusic is designed for mood change, and SymbioEyes are built to track the patient through GPS. The system was tested on 20 patients, and the results were found to be very promising in terms of an increase in spatial perception, emotional and mental efficiency, *etc*.

Covid-19 pandemic has changed the perspective of socialism in society. Due to the norms of social distancing and the potential health risk due to Coronavirus, the prominent problem people face and will face in the future is the problem of loneliness. In the paper [11], the authors have tried to address this problem with the help of companion robots. The robots are designed for two purposes: to assist humans in domestic work and have social skills to interact with people. In the first step, data collection is done through various social media platforms to know the user experience of the people for the tiny robot named Vector. In the second phase, lexical and semantic analysis is done on the collected data. The posts are categorized as useful (*e.g.,* timer) or hedonic (*e.g.,* fun) depending on the contents. It is observed that the words like love, adore in the posts indicate the social intimacy of people with Vector during the quarantine period. The impact analysis of the use of companion robots is observed in the mitigation of loneliness. It can help the manufacturers enhance the features of a robot to provide a rich user experience to the users.

Shengzhi Wang *et al.* demonstrated the significant gap between the potential benefits offered by technologies such as AI and other AAI and the barriers that plague older adults in adopting these technologies. They mentioned that education is critical not only for older adults but also for technologists. They proposed to increase the "technology literacy" of older adults to provide meaningful improvements in helping these users. They added to build feedback loops that will help older adults to understand better their data and how these data are used to predict their healthcare needs [12]. Thakur *et al.* [13] have developed a human behavior-centric framework. The system provides a holistic approach, including studying, tracking, monitoring, and analyzing human behavior while performing various Activities of Daily Living (ADLs). It does this in two steps. In the first step, semantic analysis is done, catering to common behavioral patterns according to the complex activities involving extensive human interactions. Internet of Things (IoT) based environment is used for this purpose. In the second step, an intelligent decision-making algorithm is proposed for detecting the emergencies encountered during human interactions. For this purpose, the concept of 'zone' is proposed. Each 'zone' contains unique complex activities. Both these steps involve using recent technologies like HCI, IoT, Machine learning, and Ubiquitous Computing. The accuracy of 76.71% and 83.87% is observed in the above two steps, respectively.

SUMMARY OF THE LITERATURE REVIEW

The survey tries to cover some of the vital medical problems and approaches researchers have adopted to solve them. The whole world is experiencing different pandemics, sudden environmental changes, and lifestyle disorders, which are the potential threats humankind faces. The proposed survey highlights various tools and techniques in multiple computer science domains, such as machine learning, data analytics, pervasive computing, *etc.*, blended with HCI.

CONCLUSION

Humans have created various tools and technologies for their benefit. The evolution of computing systems has witnessed the gradual enhancement from many computers to tiny multifunctional wearable devices. To enhance people's living standards, improvements and innovations with rich and easy-to-use interfaces are a must. As the healthcare domain is crucial concerning the sustainability of humankind, the role of HCI in the healthcare domain is magnificent. A person is said to be healthy if he or she is clinically as well as psychologically healthy.

Catering to this, our work covers the broad spectrum of HCI possibilities in the welfare of humankind, right from the global perspective of the use of digital technologies to simple applications to help patients monitor and manage their illness. With the tremendous growth in artificial intelligence and ubiquitous and parallel computing domains, there is a need to promote multidisciplinary research. We can witness more precise and finely tuned systems for the accurate predictive analysis of diseases and pandemics in the future. User Experience plays a significant role in building automated systems to spread awareness regarding healthcare facilities and help the medical practitioners provide wholehearted support to the patient's right from early diagnosis of the disease until the maintenance of proper digital records and history.

CONSENT FOR PUBLICATION

Not Applicable.

CONFLICT OF INTEREST

The author confirms that this chapter contents have no conflict of interest.

ACKNOWLEDGEMENT

We want to thank the reviewers and the Cummins College of Engineering for Women, Pune.

REFERENCES

[1] L. Anselma, and A. Mazzei, "Building a persuasive virtual dietitian", *Informatics (MDPI),* vol. 7, no. 3, p. 27, 2020. [http://dx.doi.org/10.3390/informatics7030027]

[2] S. SathyaFranklin, and R. Sridaran, "Making human-computer interaction usable: Thinking from healthcare perspective", *Int. J. Comput. Appl.,* vol. 58, no. 1, pp. 34-40, 2012.

[3] D.B. Wesley, "A socio-technical systems approach to the use of health IT for patient-reported outcomes: Patient and healthcare provider perspectives", *J. Biomed. Inform. X,* vol. 4, no. 100048, p. 100048, 2019.

[http://dx.doi.org/10.1016/j.yjbinx.2019.100048]

[4] O. Kocsis, A. Lalos, G. Arvanitis, and K. Moustakas, "Multi-model short-term prediction schema for mHealth empowering asthma self-management", *Electron. Notes Theor. Comput. Sci.,* vol. 343, pp. 3-17, 2019. [http://dx.doi.org/10.1016/j.entcs.2019.04.007]

[5] E. Merdivan, D. Singh, S. Hanke, and A. Holzinger, "Dialogue systems for intelligent human-computer interactions", *Electron. Notes Theor. Comput. Sci.,* vol. 343, pp. 57-71, 2019. [http://dx.doi.org/10.1016/j.entcs.2019.04.010]

[6] H. Sedrati, C. Nejjari, S. Chaqsare, and H. Ghazal, "Mental and physical mobile health apps: Review", *Procedia Comput. Sci.,* vol. 100, pp. 900-906, 2016. [http://dx.doi.org/10.1016/j.procs.2016.09.241]

[7] E.V. Bologva, D.I. Prokusheva, A.V. Krikunov, N.E. Zvartau, and S.V. Kovalchuk, "Human-computer interaction in electronic medical records: From the perspectives of physicians and data scientists", *Procedia Comput. Sci.,* vol. 100, pp. 915-920, 2016. [http://dx.doi.org/10.1016/j.procs.2016.09.248]

[8] J. Gulliksen, "Institutionalizing human-computer interaction for global health", *Glob. Health Action,* vol. 10, no. sup3, 2017. [http://dx.doi.org/10.1080/16549716.2017.1344003] [PMID: 1344003]

[9] J. Kowalski, "Older adults and voice interaction: A pilot study with Google home", In: *Extended Abstracts of the 2019 CHI Conference on Human Factors in Computing Systems- CHI EA* , 2019. [http://dx.doi.org/10.1145/3290607.3312973]

[10] D. Mandiliotis, K. Toumpas, K. Kyprioti, K. Kaza, J. Barroso, and L.J. Hadjileontiadis, Symbiosis: An innovative human-computer interaction environment for Alzheimer's support.*Universal Access in Human-Computer Interaction. User and Context Diversity.* Springer Berlin Heidelberg: Berlin, Heidelberg, 2013, pp. 123-132. [http://dx.doi.org/10.1007/978-3-642-39191-0_14]

[11] G. Odekerken-Schröder, C. Mele, T. Russo-Spena, D. Mahr, and A. Ruggiero, "Mitigating loneliness with companion robots in the COVID-19 pandemic and beyond: an integrative framework and research agenda", *J. Serv. Manag.,* vol. 31, no. 6, pp. 1149-1162, 2020. [http://dx.doi.org/10.1108/JOSM-05-2020-0148]

[12] S. Wang, K. Bolling, W. Mao, J. Reichstadt, D. Jeste, H.C. Kim, and C. Nebeker, "Technology to support aging in place: Older adults' perspectives", *Healthcare (Basel),* vol. 7, no. 2, p. 60, 2019. [http://dx.doi.org/10.3390/healthcare7020060] [PMID: 30974780]

[13] N. Thakur, and C.Y. Han, "An ambient intelligence-based human behavior monitoring framework for ubiquitous environments", *Information (Basel),* vol. 12, no. 2, p. 81, 2021. [http://dx.doi.org/10.3390/info12020081]

CHAPTER 2

Conducting Digital Product Usability Tests with Children who have Atypical Development

Helena Bukovac[1] and **Andrej Bodrušić**[1,*]

[1] *Algebra University College, Zagreb, Croatia*

Abstract: When creating digital products, it is essential to validate design decisions through user testing. Ensuring a digital product meets targeted user groups and personas' needs, all sorts of design decisions need to be carefully evaluated and adjusted, including informational architecture, navigation, selections, control patterns, feedback, colors, typography, iconography, and many more. Every testing session is unique and needs to be personalized according to the testing persona. When working with special needs persons, atypical development, or visual impairments, special care and preparation are required. These circumstances of user testing are even more challenging when the targeted audience is children with said disabilities. In preparation for testing, it is essential to understand the type of disability a child has and inform their legal guardian or medical caretaker. Considering all these things, conducting user testing can still prove challenging because of a child's unpredictable behavior. They might seem interested; they might lose focus or generally not be in the mood. With research skills, clear set goals, and preparation, a healthy dose of empathy and human understanding must gather valuable testing session's insights. Insights that will help inform further design decisions.

Keywords: ASD, Atypical development, Atypical users, Autism, Cognitive bias, Developmental disabilities, Digital design, Digital products, Human-computer interaction, Product design, Sensory integration, Specialized design, UI design, Usability testing, User experience, User interface, User research, User testing, UX research, UX/UI.

INTRODUCTION

A digital product is an application, a website, software, or any product in a digital form and requires interaction with users. To create a perfect experience for the desired user, it is necessary to define user requirements. According to Baxter *et al.,* "User requirements refer to the features/attributes a product should have or

* **Corresponding author Helena Bukovac:** Algebra University College, Zagreb, Croatia;
E-mail: helena.bukovac@racunarstvo.hr

Nirmalya Thakur and Parameshachari B.D. (Eds)

how it should perform from the users' perspective. User-centered design (UCD) is an approach for collecting and analyzing these requirements." [1].

User research enables teams and companies to define who they are making a product and ask their desired user if the product works for them. The purpose of user research is a faster product development process. Speeding up the development process lowers the cost for companies that are funding the operation. As Kuniavsky *et al.* define it – "User research provides a consistent, rapid, controlled, and thorough method of examining the users' perspective." [2]. The users' perspective guides the way the product should be created and defines the result's success.

Product development should not be a linear process. Relying on the design thinking process enables fast problem detection and creates a means to solve the problems in an educated way – based on research results. The design thinking process is an iterative, non-linear process that goes through empathizing, defining, ideating, prototyping, and testing [3]. The main benefit of design thinking is that goals can be adjusted according to previous research findings through the iterative process. This way, everything is moving faster, and products are built in a better way – more fitting for the end-users.

THE VALUE OF USER TESTING

Before conducting a user testing session, much preparation is needed. First and foremost, goals need to be determined. These goals depend on what the current task at hand is. They can either be a business goal or a user-centered goal. Business goals usually define a benefit the research might bring, and these goals, in the majority, have a unique value connected to them. User-centered plans bring value to the users themselves, such as ease of use or an experience that brings satisfaction.

User testing is done in several stages: planning, setting user tasks, recruiting testers, and facilitating the testing [4]. In all these stages, a provisional persona is kept in mind. Provisional personas are generalized perfect users based on assumptions about who might use the product or its target. These hypothetical personas need to be validated so that actual target users can be recruited for user testing [5]. A good determination of the user base can affect successful goal achievement because business and user-centered goals are similar. Considering that user (customer) satisfaction is an essential factor in user (customer) retention, it is necessary to ensure that users encounter minimal service failure [6]. Service failure usually means that users did not successfully finish a task or encountered frustrating situations that created negative emotions attached to the product.

According to [7], to ensure better user experiences in different contexts, it is necessary to analyze user interactions and understand their expectations to provide a positive affective state. The real value of user testing is the ability to funnel research data into manageable information that can be used to influence design decisions. Design elements such as informational architecture, navigation, selections, control patterns, feedback, colors, typography, iconography all need to be carefully considered and selected to serve the users as required.

APPROACHING THE USER BASE

Using provisional personas serves as a guideline in recruitment. Usually, these personas are idealistic and much generalized. Problems arise when the end-users or the target group are not ideal. A perfect example of a non-typical user group is children. Adapting the user testing style is necessary and desired. Children have different needs and require a different approach [8]. Barendregt and Bekker provide a set of guidelines that include best practices for approaching children from ages 5-7. According to these guidelines, children should be educated and eased in the testing as a game. They should also be lightly guided and find support in the researcher [8].

There are not many research papers that focus on testing with children but focusing primarily on children with atypical development. Adding another layer of difficulty to user testing would be testing with children that have atypical development. Children with atypical development have a good grasp of their emotions. They learn that their feelings wane over time and that they should think before they act. Children with atypical development sometimes have problems with regulating emotions, which results in unexpected reactions. These results can be manifested in anger or depression [9].

PREVIOUS EXPERIENCE

The authors have conducted several user testings' which included children that have atypical development. During those researches, they applied techniques that were usual and aligned with their training so far. However, due to the users' specifics, much modification was needed during the research. One research was conducted for a mobile application that teaches sign language to children with atypical development. Preparation for the user testing session was accompanied by a short educational lesson by the expert accompanying the research. The research itself had a few specifics that are out of the scope of this Chapter. However, the main conclusion was that approaching children on their level is vital — appearing as non-threatening, fun to work with and lighthearted provided better cooperation from the children joining in the research.

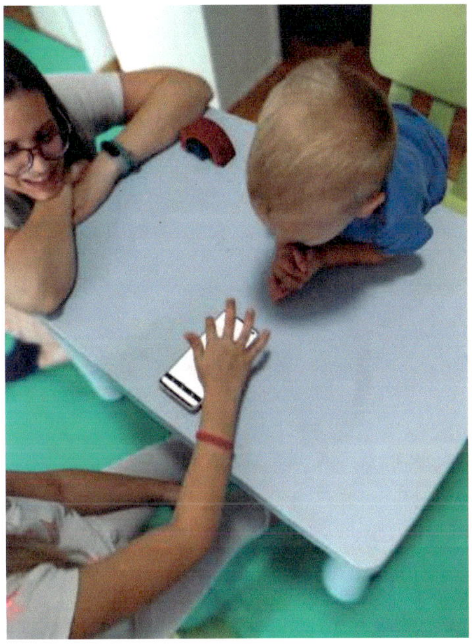

Fig. (1). One of the authors researching with children.

As seen in Fig. (**1**), which was taken during that specific research, the author joined the children by sitting on the floor, not something the children expected from the adult stranger. Also shown in Fig. (**1**) is a modification that was done during the testing. Usually, the children went in one by one accompanied by adults. However, this child felt more comfortable in the presence of their young sibling, which provided extra comfort to a strange situation. Considering that many modifications were needed during this research, the authors continued to work with the experts on defining specifics and finding out how to approach specific users.

METHODS

To better understand adults and what they expect when they encounter a child they have not previously met, we conducted a survey. The survey was created to put the subjects in a specific situation and asked for their opinions and reactions. Most of the survey was measured in qualitative data, while essential characteristics were measured in quantitative data. To further strengthen the hypothesis that extra education is needed before conducting user research, an expert interview was conducted. The questions correlated to the ones asked in a survey for ease of conclusion.

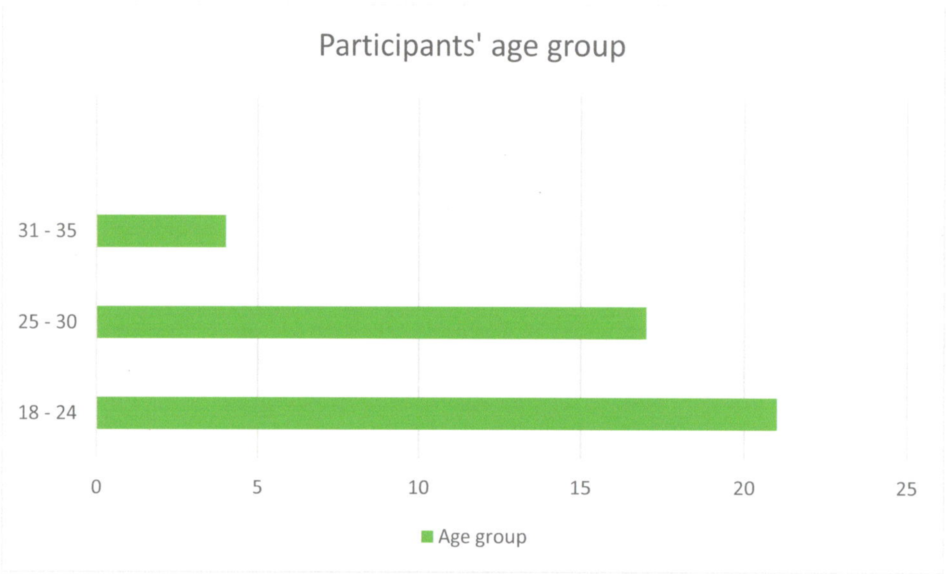

Fig. (2). Participants' age group.

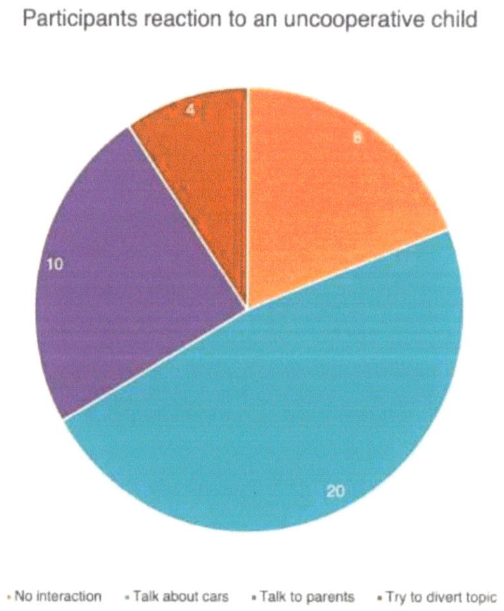

Fig. (3). Participants reaction to an uncooperative child.

RESULTS OF THE SURVEY

The survey was conducted on 42 participants *via* an online survey tool called Typeform. Most of the participants (50%) were in 18-24, as shown in Fig. (**2**).

The participants were relatively evenly distributed regarding gender (52% female). While being anonymous, the group was still controlled, with subjects ranging from medical students to UX designers and IT experts. The survey consisted of three role-play questions and several follow-up questions. The problems will be cited, along with several highlighted replies.

1. The situation is this: You are at a birthday party; you need to greet a child with their parents. You come up, say hi, gimme 5! The child looks away from you and starts talking about cars. What would you think about the situation, and what would you do?
   As shown in Fig. (**3**), most participants (47.6%) would try to continue the conversation with the child talking about cars. The next biggest group (23.8%) would continue talking with the child's parents, turning their attention. Some of the participants (19%) would give up on interaction and leave the scene. The least number of participants (9.5%) would try to divert to a different topic.
   "I'd probably have a confused face, get up to the parents, and have a small laugh, probably asking them how come the kid is on ignore mode. What I'd think is that the kid is either shy, rude, or uninterested (probably depending on the age!)."
   This reply was interpreted as continuing to talk with the child's parents.
   "I would say to the child that is not very nice and ask him/her why he/she didn't say hi."
   This reply is a bit more aggressive than the others and the most extreme straightforward comment directed to the child.
2. Moving on from that situation, you ask the kid what their name is. The child looks at the floor and stays silent. What do you think is going on?
   Most of the participants concluded that the child is either shy or scared. Only one reply highlighted that the child might be autistic.
   "The child may be timid or have some sickness like autism. "
   "The child is uncomfortable around me, or maybe just uncomfortable in this space (unknown house, lots of people, *etc.*). I would ask the child what's their name again and smile and look relaxed and positive. "
   "He/she is shy and just needs some time to relax in a new environment. "
3. You will not give up! The child's parents are your friends, and you will make your best effort to interact. Giving it one last shot, you do your cheesiest "put em up partner" and make a shooting cowboy gesture. The child, as always, looks away. What are your thoughts this time?
   As shown in Fig. (**4**), most participants (28.9%) would not have pushed the situation further. There were several rebukes to the authors for bullying a child with an aggressive approach.
   "I believe that if the child does not want interaction, it should be respected. No

matter what my relationship with their parents is."
"Leave him alone."
The next big group of respondents (23.7%) believed there was an issue with them. That they might scare the child, their approach was wrong, they were threatening, and others. Most of them searched for internal problems in this situation.
"The child has a fear, and I shouldn't push it. Maybe it's socially anxious, or maybe I'm just a stranger danger type."
Some of the respondents thought there was an issue with the child (18.4%) or that the child was just timid (15.8%). Some respondents (13.2%) expressed concern that the child might have some difficulties or not properly socialized.

4. We were finishing our scene, time for questions. At which point would you have given up on the interaction with the child?
   As shown in Fig. (**5**) – most of the participants would have given up on the second try (36.6%), while the first (24.4%) and third (26.8%) try are evenly measured. Only a minority of participants would not have given up at all (12.2%).
5. Did it cross your mind that the child might have special needs? (such as autism, hearing issues, other mental disabilities)
   As shown in Fig. (**6**), the majority (30) of the participants assumed that the child has some difficulties.
6. If you knew the child had special needs, would you act differently? If yes, please explain in the "other" section.
   From Fig. (**7**), we see that the majority (26) of the participants would have acted differently if they knew that the child had some difficulties. Some claimed they would not have changed their approach (14). Two of the participants chose not to reply to this question.
   Some of the participants chose to explain how they would act differently and adapt to their approach (13).
   "If I knew that this child has special needs, I would probably change the way I'm trying to interact with him/her. If the kid is deaf, I would never try to talk to him because I know he can't hear me. Or if this child has autism, I will probably try to talk to him in a way he can understand me, and I would try to be on his "level."
   "I would approach it more carefully and with less energy. I wouldn't be as assertive towards the child."
   "I would first ask the parents how to initiate a conversation with the child."
   Concluding the survey results, the expert interview will relate to some of the survey questions.

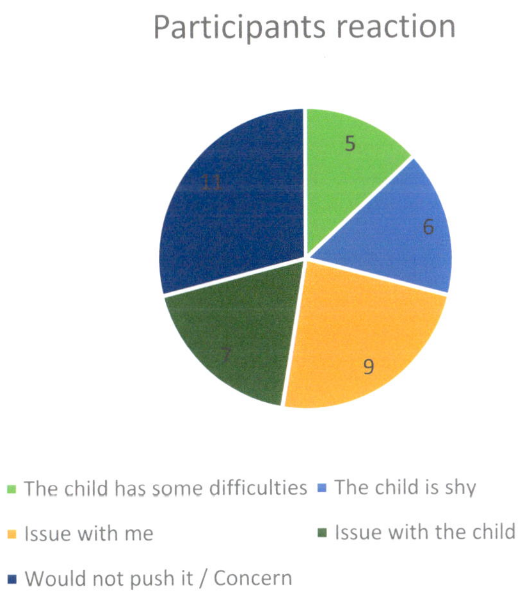

Fig. (4). Participants reaction after failing multiple tries of interaction.

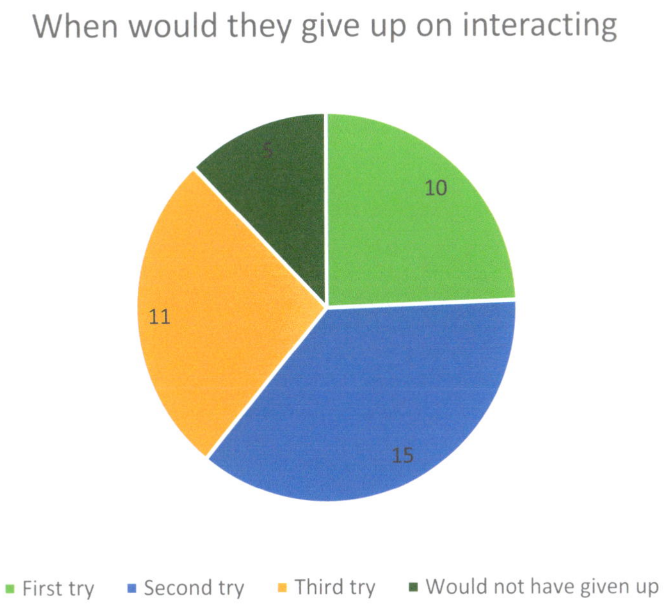

Fig. (5). When would participants give up on interacting.

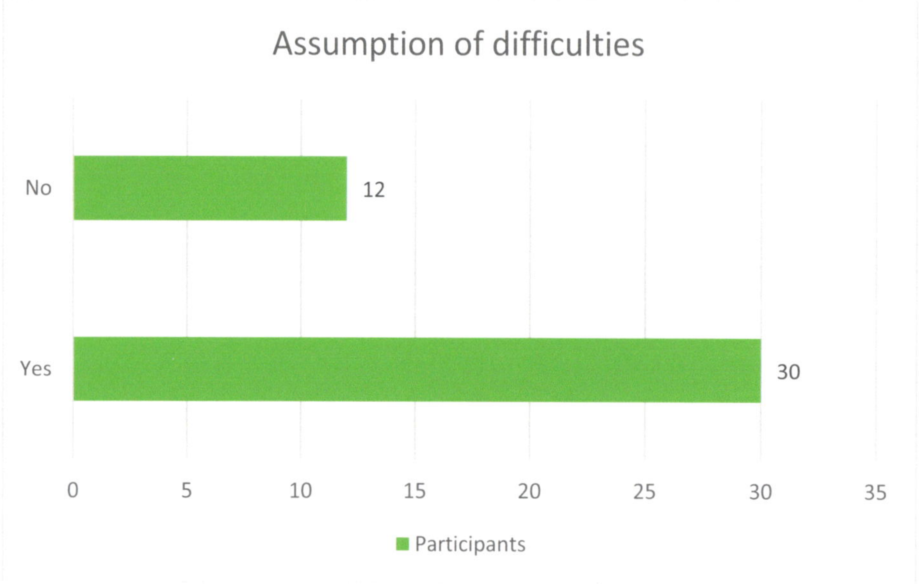

Fig. (6). Did the participants assume that child has difficulties?.

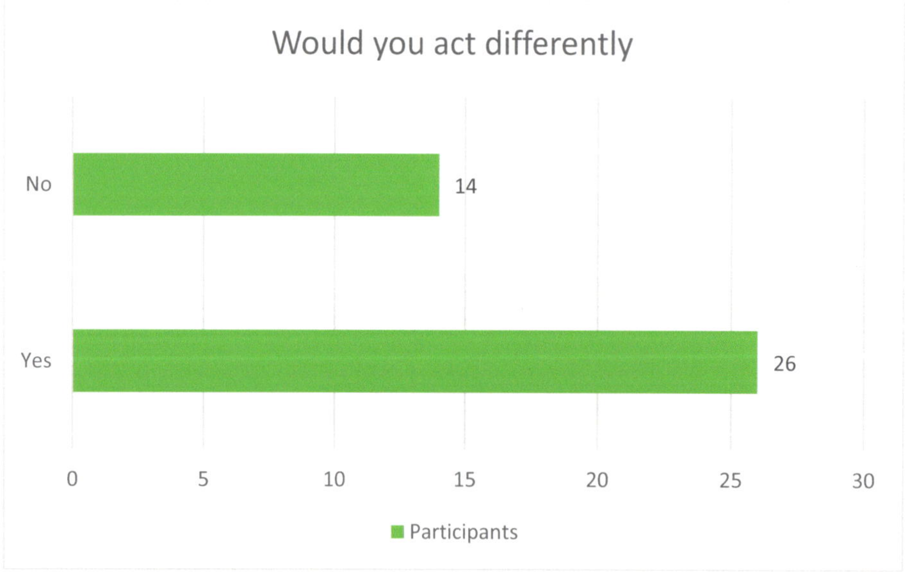

Fig. (7). Would the participants act differently?.

EXPERT OPINION

To get a better idea of approaching children with atypical development, the authors interviewed an expert who works daily with atypical development children. Lina Daxini is a B.Sc. in psychology, a sensory integration specialist for infants, and a Baby Signs instructor. She is the founder and president of the iLab Center. The iLab Center offers social services for early intervention and psychosocial support. In Croatia, families can receive prevention, habilitation, counseling, and education services. In other words, children with atypical development may apply for certain services such as speech therapy or sensory integration treatment with iLab.

The most common disabilities Lina encounters daily are of the sensory integration kind, autism, intellectual disabilities, communication difficulties, or undiagnosed issues. When asked if there is a typical adult reaction when meeting a child with atypical development for the first time, Lina stated that adults who had previous experience with such children would adapt more quickly. While on the other hand, adults with no prior experience will often ignore such children, creating an even more difficult situation. According to Lina, adults turn to the child's parent when not receiving a child's response and expect a reply from them.

When asked about prejudice and biases concerning children with atypical development, Lina replied that most inappropriate reactions come from lack of education. Adults are used to instant gratification and instant replies to their questions. This collides with the children's perception of the situations; sometimes, they need more time to process what is happening and choose an appropriate reaction. Frequently, by the time they choose their course of action, the adult has already given up on them, and they are flagged as "slow."

To ease the first contact for the adult, Lina advises patience. Patience to allow children to react. She also suggests open-mindedness and acceptance. This comes along hand in hand with education and working on our behavior. Often, we expect the children to adapt their behavior without adapting ours in return.

About easing the same situation for the child, Lina advises educating adults primarily. After the adults know how to act in this situation, it will be much easier because there will not be much pressure. To prepare children for this encounter, Lina advises explaining what to expect; this includes verbal and visual preparation, to whichever the child reacts in a better way. A verbal explanation means that we will explain the situation broken down into smaller parts while explaining what to expect in every step. A visual description includes using cue cards the child is familiar with to describe the same things and what might happen at which "chapter." Another approach is using social stories of similar situations while emphasizing acceptable behavior — this way, the child will know what to expect and how it is expected to act.

DISCUSSION

Conducting a survey that consisted of a role-play scenario enabled a more focused questioning. The scenes were vivid enough but left room for imagination. Each of the participants could have filled the rest of the stage with their own life experiences, but the main actors remained the same. The results showed that most participants wanted to give a more humane approach than the one suggested with the scene. Also, the vast majority of the participants suspected that something was wrong with the child. The exciting part was cross-checking most participants' opinions *versus* the expert opinion. Indeed, most of the adults would at some point turn to their parents for guidance on how to act. Depending on the way that is done, it can do more damage than good things. If done at an early stage, without giving the child enough time to react, it can harm. If done after giving it enough time, it can be beneficial because the child may feel relieved to be out of the spotlight.

A thing that the expert highlights are the need for education. Most "negative" reactions came from a lack of knowledge about a child's condition and proper handling of the situation. Learning about every state is not feasible. However, learning before conducting user research about a specific diagnosis and sharing personal experiences with other researchers should become a norm. Empathy is a necessary skill for every researcher because it enables the understanding of their users. Detachment from what users are feeling but caring enough to solve their problems objectively is a difficult skill to acquire. It is essential to ask the right questions, what they need, what they want, how they behave and think, *etc* [10]. This thinking directly applies to the design thinking methodology. Most of the survey participants were not ux researchers, but they represented the layman's approach to an unusual situation. This approach to the target base was chosen with the hypothesis in mind that ux researchers are humans. Their success with conducting similar research would depend equally on their experience and previous interaction with atypical users.

CONCLUDING REMARKS

Applying a type of experience prototyping, we managed to perceive how researchers, this time in the role of an unassuming person that found themselves in a new situation, would react. Bucheneau and Fulton Suri define experience prototyping as any representation of engagement with the product, space, or system we design [11]. This type of experience was extended to a user scenario [12], in which our users (survey participants) participated in an imaginary scene. They were to interact with an unknown child and explain their thought process. As anticipated, most of the participants did not think the child would be of atypical development. What was not expected was that most participants wanted to give up on the imaginary situation and not push the child into an uncomfortable interaction. While cross-referencing the participants' actions with an experts' opinion, we concluded that lack of education is the culprit in many businesses that would result in an undesirable way. That is why the idea that additional education after creating the provisional personas is needed to conduct a successful user testing session with atypical users was confirmed.

When conducting user testing, having a good set of research skills, crafting an exact list of goals, and preparing a healthy dose of empathy and human understanding must gather valuable testing sessions' insights. Insights that will help inform further design decisions.

CONSENT FOR PUBLICATION

Not Applicable.

CONFLICT OF INTEREST

The author confirms that this chapter contents have no conflict of interest.

ACKNOWLEDGEMENTS

The authors would like to thank Lina Daxini for her time and efforts. Lina went above and beyond to be able to participate in this research. We would also like to thank iLab for enabling us to do the research that made us curious about this topic.

REFERENCES

[1] Elsevier, "Understanding your users", [Online]. Available: https://Elsevier.com. [Accessed: 10-Ma--2021]

[2] M. Kuniavsky, *Observing The User Experience.* Morgan Kaufmann, 2010.

[3] B. Cuthbert, T. Vaugh, and F.C. Chambers, *"What is Design Thinking?" in Learning to Mentor in Sports Coaching.* Routledge, 2018, pp. 24-54. [http://dx.doi.org/10.4324/9781315172279-2]

[4] *What is Usability Testing?*. [Online]. Available: https://Interaction-design.org.[Accessed: 10-Ma--2021]

[5] J. Levy, *UX strategy: How to devise innovative digital products that people want.* O'Reilly Media: Sebastopol, CA, 2015.

[6] C. Ranaweera, and J. Prabhu, "On the relative importance of customer satisfaction and trust as determinants of customer retention and positive word of mouth", *J. Target. Meas. Anal. Mark.,* vol. 12, no. 1, pp. 82-90, 2003. [http://dx.doi.org/10.1057/palgrave.jt.5740100]

[7] N. Thakur, and C.Y. Han, "Methodology for forecasting user experience for smart and assisted living in affect aware systems", In: *Proceedings of the 8th International Conference on the Internet of Things,*

2018.
[http://dx.doi.org/10.1145/3277593.3277630]

[8] W. Barendregt, and M.M. Bekker, "Guidelines for user testing with children", [Online]. Available: http://Undesigning.nl. [Accessed: 10-Mar-2021]

[9] G.T.M. Stegge, and M. Meerum Terwogt, *Awareness and Regulation of Emotion in Typical and Atypical Development; in Handbook of Emotion Regulation.* Guilford Press: London, England, 2007, pp. 269-286.

[10] "Empathy", [Online]. Available: https://Interaction-design.org. [Accessed: 10-Mar-2021]

[11] K. Keane, V. Nisi, and L. Ciolfi, "Experience prototyping: Gathering rich understandings to guide design", In: *IADIS International Conference Interfaces and Human-Computer Interaction 2012 (part of MCCSIS 2012)*, 2012, pp. 115-122.

[12] B. Verplank, *Observation and Invention: The use of Scenarios in Interaction Design.,* 1993.

CHAPTER 3

Assistive Technologies and Artificial Intelligence for Visually Impaired: Investigating Ongoing Issues and Challenges

Xu Wei[1], **Muhammad Shoaib**[1,*] and **Tiffany Ya Tang**[1]

[1] *Department of Computer Science College of Science and Technology Wenzhou-Kean University, China*

Abstract: Nowadays, assistive technologies facilitate visually impaired people a lot. However, they still face many challenges in their daily lives, such as the perception of rich visual information around their adjacent environment. Several assistive technology-based solutions have adopted Artificial Intelligence (AI) which offers instant information of nearby visible things, objects, and persons to visually impaired people. Visually impaired people can also easily access online communication with emerging solutions using AI and perform numerous daily routine tasks. This paper presents a review of AI's role in visually impaired and solving their everyday life problem intelligently. A detailed analysis of assistive technologies and smartphone-based solutions for the visually impaired is presented, highlighting the need for technological enrichments and AI-based interventions for them. Furthermore, some challenges were addressed which faced by the visually impaired during the use of AI-based solutions. Additionally, the usefulness and limitations of the recent assistive solution are presented. Lastly, future research endeavors are introduced, which may help researchers and developers propose some innovative solutions.

Keywords: Adaptive feedback, Artificial Intelligence, Assistive, Auditory, Character recognition, Development, Emerging solution, Environment, Finger-sized, Information, Interventions, Innovation, Interfaces, Learning, Navigation, Smartphone, Technologies, Training, Visual, Visually impaired.

INTRODUCTION

The World Health Organization (WHO) reported approximately 738 million people globally, with about 285 million visually impaired people [1]. Technology innovation can be support visual impairment more proficiently. Assistive technology and Artificial Intelligence can facilitate visually impaired persons.

* **Corresponding author Muhammad Shoaib:** Department of Computer Science, College of Science and Technology, Wenzhou-Kean University, China; E-mail: mshoaib@wku.edu.cn

Nirmalya Thakur and Parameshachari B.D. (Eds)

Assistive technology is used during the development of products, equipment, systems, and mobile applications to enhance learning, escalate work capabilities, and daily routine task performance in visual impairment. It can alleviate the effects of disabilities that limit the ability to perform activities of daily living and enhance the independence factor. Assistive technology provides simple interactions with technology, enabling visually impaired users to perform complicated tasks efficiently. It is difficult for blind users to interact with the nearby environment without using assistive technology. The early study has shown that independent navigation is a real challenge for the visually impaired [2].

The visually impaired construct a spatial map according to two information channels. One is they can adjust their direction by tracking the sources according to their surroundings or sounds. The other is to sense the information of the surrounding environment according to the sense of touch and adjust the direction through tactile feedback.

On the other hand, AI refers to the simulation of human intelligence in a machine programmed to think like a human and imitate its behavior. As technology continuously improves, the benchmarks that previously defined AI have become obsolete. The goals of AI include learning, reasoning, and perception [3]. For example, the face recognition technology of mobile phones has been widely used and gradually inherent new functions and features.

Typically, people can obtain environmental information through multiple information channels, such as hearing, vision, touch, *etc*. But the visually impaired mainly depend on pictures for information acquisition, which leads to their perception of the surrounding environment significantly reduced. Some earlier studies [4 - 6] have shown that visual impairment brings inconvenience to life, and it is even more challenging to walk independently in a strange and complex environment. Several devices based on AI help the visually impaired walk alone improve walking independence for the visually impaired.

With the rapid development and popularization of information technology, people use digital devices to perform various activities. These digital devices have many automated features, *i.e.*, brightness control, temperature control, and screen display. But there is a lack of such kind of interface which provides support to visually impaired people. Additionally, human beings still have various obstacles. Vision impairment is a prominent aspect, although innovation in digital devices has made a lot of progress [7]. There are still many challenges for human beings to solve vision impairment to interact with digital devices.

Assistive technology and AI play an essential role in introducing new and innovative interaction mechanisms with the digital device to facilitate visual impairment. This paper has reviewed the earlier studies that have used assistive technology and AI to help visually impaired persons.

The remaining sections of the paper mentioned as section 2 provide a detailed overview of the previous studies conducted for visually impaired people. Section 3 summarizes the earlier researchers and summarizes Assistive Technologies and AI interventions for the visually impaired. In section 4, we have a discussion and conclusion of the topic, and finally, section 5 has the future direction for the researchers.

RELATED WORK

Many AI and Assistive Technology researchers are trying to improve the independence of the visually impaired. They are trying to design a more advanced and intelligent AI system and devices. The work related to this area is outlined as follows.

More and more wearable devices [4 - 6] help the visually impaired overcome many difficulties in their daily life. Chang *et al.* [4] proposed that wearable assistive devices based on AI edge computing assist the visually impaired zebra crossing walking. The device consists of a pair of smart glasses, a walking cane, and a waist-mounted box. When the visually impaired cross a zebra-crossing, the device can provide traffic signal information. If there is a deviation during zebra-crossing, the visually impaired will be reminded by voice, and Bluetooth provides the voice guidance service. To lighten the burden of the visually impaired, Kamal *et al.* [5] proposed a kind of glasses that can help the visually impaired get information about the surrounding environment while walking to avoid falling. Their proposed system used RGB data from microcontrollers and smartphones to calculate surface smoothness during the day and in the dark. The system estimated the highest surface smoothness of 96.341% in the daytime and 98.683% at night.

This system helped the visually impaired walk efficiently and find and evade obstacles without holding any sticks or other heavy objects. In terms of navigation and tracking the trajectories of the visually impaired, Shandu *et al.* presented the design of an intelligent walking stick for blind users using Raspberry Pi 3 b+ as a central microcontroller, Ultrasonic sensors, and Global Positioning System (GPS) [6]. Ultrasonic sensors are used to scan the environment of sidewalks and sides at a defined distance using sound waves, while GPS modules are used for real-time direction and navigation. For the safety of the visually impaired, the GPS position coordinates of the visually impaired are sent to the nursing staff through the SMS subscription account connected to the GPIO pin of Raspberry Pi. In this way, it is convenient for the nursing staff to track emergencies for the visually impaired.

This colorful world has always been a great attraction for the visually impaired. One of the challenges for the visually impaired is to recognize colors. Mungkaruna *et al.* proposed a prototype of an affordable talking color identifier for visually impaired individuals [8]. The talking color identifier of the device supports 27 standard colors. It is lightweight, portable, and safe to use. The device uses a TCS230 color sensor because it is cheaper and accurate. More people with visual impairment can afford it in the same technology area to support color perception visually impaired. Tapson *et al.* developed a sensory enhancement system designed to provide color to the visually impaired [9]. This is a hardware system consisting of gloves, in which a short distance optical color sensor is mounted on the fingertip. The color sensor detects the color of the object, and then each fingertip is mapped to four colors, namely red, green, blue, and yellow, using pulse-code representation. Auditory interfaces are beneficial for visually impaired people in the absence of vision. Shoaib *et al.* proposed adaptive auditory feedback for desktop assistance of visually impaired people. With adaptive auditory feedback, task completion time and action awareness are enhanced in auditory interfaces, and visually impaired people feel satisfied with adaptive auditory feedback [10, 11].

EXISTING RESEARCH SUMMARIES ONGOING ISSUES AND CHALLENGES

This section will further categorize some earlier works into different applications on which they applied to highlight the significant challenges and obstacles that are still left unsolved.

Accessing Web Content

Websites have become one of the most important information sources in the world. Most of the information on the website needs to be obtained in graphical form. So it is challenging for the visually impaired to access the visual content of the websites. Web Content Accessibility Guide 2.0 (WCAG 2.0) provides recommendations on Web content accessibility. It was developed by the World Wide Web Consortium (W3C) and available for all web designers. Web content introduced some guidelines and benefits for the visually impaired [12]. There are two kinds of web access tools that have been used to help blind and visually impaired people and search the relevant information. One is a screen-reader, and another is BrookesTalk. Nowadays, the information on websites is becoming more and more complex, so the usability of screen readers is facing significant challenges.

Borodin *et al.* [13] put forward the challenges and improvement strategies for screen readers. In screen-reading technology, the problem is not accessibility but usability. When a screen reader accidentally browses a web page with a large number of links, the screen reader will interrupt the information currently being read [13, 14]. Zajicek *et al.* [15] proposed a prototype application called BrookesTalk, a web navigation tool that combines a web browser and a screen reader. It displays the results of the search information in audio form. The application does not depend on another web browser that provides visual rendering, so it cannot work like a plug-in application or a web browser extension [14, 15].

Entertainment

Entertainment can attract the participants, grab their attention, and make them feel happy and satisfied. Typically, an entertainment platform is developed according to the general needs of the participants. Simultaneously, the visually impaired people required some additional features because the visually impaired cannot see the colorful and exciting world like ordinary people. Therefore, it is imperative to develop such platforms for the visually impaired to access the entertainment content easily. The visually impaired usually cannot play mainstream video games because the game content contains graphics. Game accessibility refers to the ability of players to experience the game under limited conditions [16]. Torre and Khaliq [16] proposed the current situation of technology and design a practical solution to provide game support for the visually impaired. Donggil *et al.* [17] designed a mobile learning game for children with visual impairment. They developed two audible mobile games and tested them named Cardinal Direction and modified Tower of London. Testing results indicate that the visually impaired enjoy the fun.

Navigational Support

The design and implementation of the navigation tool can help the visually impaired navigate independently and reach the destination quickly and safely [18]. Kumar *et al.* [18] proposed a new navigation aid tool, which is very useful for people with visual impairment. The visually impaired can navigate quickly and safely through the navigation tools' voice-oriented output with the aid of their navigation stick. But their navigation tools have some disadvantages, *i.e.*, the system needs to be operated on a specific building. In the field of navigation for the visually impaired, there are continuous breakthroughs in technology. Divya *et al.* [19] proposed an ultrasonic-based blind and visually impaired user walking stick with Arduino.

The device can measure the distance between the obstacle and the intelligent walking stick by the ultrasonic sensor. When the block enters the range of the ultrasonic sensor, the visually impaired can understand the barrier by hearing the sound produced by the buzzer. Navigation field and can meet the daily life requirements of visually impaired.

Social Activities Assistance

Visual impairment is the optical system's functional limitation, and it limits the individual from carrying out many social activities [20]. Sumanasekera *et al.* [20] proposed to solve the problem of social isolation of the visually impaired by implementing voice-based smartphone applications to overcome social issues.

Learning Enhancement

Technology innovation provides opportunities for the visually impaired to learn and enhance their knowledge. Courseware is a kind of multimedia application program, which can improve students' performance in the learning process. But Roseli *et al.* [21] found no courseware designed for the visually impaired. So, they proposed auxiliary courseware for the visually impaired. To let the visually impaired, learn and enjoy ordinary people's courses, the auxiliary courseware adopts unique teaching methods and provides particular elements for the visually impaired. Noha *et al.* [22] proposed a tool that can help math teachers provide accessible learning materials for linear equations in the form of 3D models. This tool generates 3D models of linear equation maps printed in predefined boards with appropriate Braille captions. For linear equations, teachers usually explain their concepts in theory without actually drawing them. One way to enhance the teaching of this concept to visually impaired students is to use 3D Printing.

For a decade, the software is helping to encourage people to learn more attractively [23 - 27]. Blind people use it happily because most of them feel pleasure during the use of mobile devices [27 - 29]. Different audio base virtual environments helpful for blind people to learn, develop and improve their skills [30]. Audio Nature [31] is software which is works on mobile devices for learning. Design software like ecosystems using high color contrasts to deal with challenges and learn how to solve them. Due to the design of the interface of high color determines users can interact residual vision. The interaction of the blind user with AudioNature makes through mobile touch screens and buttons when they interact audio feedback is generated, which helps realize the effect of actions and state of the ecosystem. The above is summarized in Table **1**.

Table 1. Summary of Assistive Technologies interventions.

Intervention	Category	Output Response	User Interaction Platform	Purpose	Contribution	Future Work
Voice over [23]	Interaction with screen contents	Voice	Smartphone	Voice over facilitate visually impaired user to read UIs contents and labels easily.	Accessible to blind users offer a simple interaction, and the user feels comfortable with this application.	Usability can be enhanced by using a virtual application-independent key, tactile point of reference, and vibrotactile feedback.
Smart Assistive Navigation System [24]	Obstacle recognition	Voice	Vest	Successfully meets the safety, comfort, and independent navigation needs of the visually impaired.	Secure safe and low-cost navigation.	Data-fusion obtained by the new generation Kinect v. two contains a light filter that tolerates the sunlight, hence facilitating outdoor navigation.
Mg Sys Visi [25]	Transformation of text, speech, and Braille.	Voice; Braille	Internet	Provide a better web browsing experience for the visually impaired.	Mg Sys Visi, designed for blind learners, can also be used for other special needs users, *i.e.*, the elderly and physically impaired persons.	The system design concept can be applied to applications, not just for browsers.

(Table 1) cont.....

Intervention	Category	Output Response	User Interaction Platform	Purpose	Contribution	Future Work
CCNY Smart Cane [26]	Plan indoor route to destination	Voice; Haptic	CCNY Smart Cane system, a robotic white cane, and mobile device navigation software	Help the blind and visually impaired navigate indoors.	Implement indoor navigation software for Google Tango devices. The SmartCane, an enhanced white cane, can communicate with the Tango software and guide a BVI user to a destination. Demonstrate the effectiveness of the SmartCane system in aiding visually impaired users in navigating indoors.	Further research is required when weighing one pathfinding technique and line fitting algorithm over another.

DISCUSSION AND CONCLUSION

Commercial Products in the Market

Besides research efforts in adopting AI for the population, many large companies have unveiled products that could assist people daily. For example, Microsoft's iOS app *Seeing AI*™ [32] can serve as navigational 'channels' for the visually impaired during daily encounters with everyday objects. The app can recognize short text, documents, products, currency, *etc*. *Office Lens* from Microsoft is another free application that offers optical character recognition (OCR) capabilities; however, unlike *Seeing AI*™, *Office Lens* is also available for the computer. AiServe provides a portable and wearable solution to the visually impaired and blind to navigate independently and gracefully [33]. Horus and

MyEye are two other companies that mainly work with wearable AI technology for the population. For example, Horus's shape acts as reminiscent of an MP3 player, while, in *OrCam MyEye2^{TM}*, a typically looking eyeglass with the finger-sized device that magnetically attached, could recognize faces and text [34].

Table 2. Summary of Artificial Intelligence-based interventions.

Intervention	Category	Output Response	User Interaction Platform	Purpose	Contribution	Future Work
iSee [27]	Object Recognition	Voice	Smartphone	Narrate the surrounding environment of the visually impaired.	Identify objects in an image and provide results to visually impaired people through the text to speech synthesizers.	Can introduce more technical features in this app to provide a better experience during the daily routine task performance of blind people.
Wearable Medicines Recognition System [28]	Object Recognition	Voice	Wearable smart glasses; Wearable waist-mounted drug pills recognition device; A mobile device application; A cloud-based management platform	Helping visually impaired identify pills.	Identify the pill, match the shape of the medicine on the cloud platform, and tell the visually impaired to take the correct medication through voice.	Can simplify the device and reduce the burden for the visually impaired.
Automatic digit recognition [29]	Digital recognition	Voice	Smart PC and a hat embedded with two webcams	Providing reliable bus route information for the visually impaired without others' help.	Can detect and recognize 11 classes of digit and non-digit (noise) images for bus route information from natural scenes.	Add more sorts of buses such as yellow, red and green bus to provide a wide range of services.

(Table 2) cont.....

Intervention	Category	Output Response	User Interaction Platform	Purpose	Contribution	Future Work
Bionic Kinect device [30]	Obstacle and person identification	Haptic and voice	Kinect sensor, NUC (Next Unit of Computing) board, and haptic feedback	Helping visually challenging persons to move freely without any external assistance.	The bionic Kinect device is portable, which is also cheap and can be used directly without training.	Replace NUC with android, implement OCR (Optical Character Recognition), detect uneven surface and stairs detections.

Major Challenges and Concluding Remarks

Visually impaired persons cannot be ignored in the development of artificial intelligence and assistive technology. They can perform the daily routine task with the help of innovative technologies. Thakur *et al.* [35] introduced a framework for monitoring human behavior, which significantly improved the quality of life in the aging population to perform the daily routine task efficiently. This paper provides a detailed overview of previous studies related to the visually impaired and summarized the experimental findings used to improve their quality of life. Several researchers introduced technological solutions for the visually impaired and tried to reduce the issues of their lives.

Currently, there are still some challenges that exist in providing technical assistance to the visually impaired. We found that visually impaired people presently using various assistive technology-based solutions, *i.e.*, navigational support, learning support, and accessing the contents. Still, some challenges need to be overcome, like enhancing auditory feedback mechanisms, introducing the simplified design, and adding more functionalities. Most technological-based solutions provide auditory feedback based to the visually impaired. The user-centric design (UCD) based studies are beneficial for designing the application for to visually impaired. Haptic-based interactions and vibrotactile feedback can also be used to develop artificial intelligence and assistive technology-based solutions. We should pay more attention to people with multiple disabilities, provide scientific and technological assistance for such people, and improve their quality of life by using artificial intelligence and assistive technology. Many studies offer technical support to the visually impaired. We can provide more help to the visually impaired based on the existing research and make their life more convenient.

In the future, we can try to overcome the various challenges of the visually impaired, *i.e.*, introduce large screen touch screens, the text representation of visual information, and virtually explore the needs of the visually impaired. Additionally, we can enhance the design of the gesture-based system. Lastly, we can develop universal user interfaces for visually impaired people on smartphones.

CONSENT FOR PUBLICATION

Not Applicable.

CONFLICT OF INTEREST

The author confirms that this chapter contents have no conflict of interest.

ACKNOWLEDGEMENT

The authors would like to thank all their colleagues who supported in improving the chapter.

REFERENCES

[1] "Blindness and vision impairment", [Online]. Available: http://www.who.int. [Accessed: 10-Ma--2021]

[2] M. Dascalu, A. Moldoveanu, O. Balan, R.G. Lupu, F. Ungureanu, and S. Caraiman, "Usability assessment of assistive technology for blind and visually impaired", In: *2017 E-Health and Bioengineering Conference*. EHB, 2017, pp. 523-526.

[3] J. Frankenfield, *Artificial Intelligence (AI)*. 08-Mar-2021. [Online]. Available: http://Investopedia.com [Accessed: 10-Mar-2021]

[4] W-J. Chang, "An AI edge computing-based Wearable assistive device for visually impaired people zebra-crossing walking", In: *2020 IEEE International Conference on Consumer Electronics (ICCE)*, 2020.
[http://dx.doi.org/10.1109/ICCE46568.2020.9043132]

[5] M.M. Kamal, A.I. Bayazid, M.S. Sadi, M.M. Islam, and N. Hasan, "Towards developing walking assistants for the visually impaired people", In: *2017 IEEE Region 10 Humanitarian Technology Conference (R10-HTC)*, 2017, pp. 238-241.
[http://dx.doi.org/10.1109/R10-HTC.2017.8288947]

[6] N.E. Shandu, P.A. Owolawi, T. Mapayi, and K. Odeyemi, "AI-based pilot system for visually impaired people", In: *2020 International Conference on Artificial Intelligence, Big Data, Computing, and Data Communication Systems (icABCD)*, 2020, pp. 1-7.
[http://dx.doi.org/10.1109/icABCD49160.2020.9183857]

[7] M. Bousbia-Salah, M. Bettayeb, and A. Larbi, "A navigation aid for blind people", *J. Intell. Robot. Syst.*, vol. 64, no. 3–4, pp. 387-400, 2011.
[http://dx.doi.org/10.1007/s10846-011-9555-7]

[8] P. Mungkaruna, P. Piyawongwisal, K. Ropkhop, and U. Hatthasin, "The talking color identifying device for the visually impaired", In: *2016 13th International Conference on Electrical Engineering/Electronics, Computer, Telecommunications and Information Technology (ECTI-CON)*, 2016, pp. 1-5.

[http://dx.doi.org/10.1109/ECTICon.2016.7561405]

[9] J. Tapson, "The feeling of color: A haptic feedback device for the visually disabled", In: *2008 IEEE Biomedical Circuits and Systems Conference.*, 2008, pp. 381-384. [http://dx.doi.org/10.1109/BIOCAS.2008.4696954]

[10] M. Shoaib, I. Hussain, A. Ishaq, A. Wahab, A. Bashir, and M. Tayyab, "Adaptive auditory feedback: A new method for desktop assistance of the visually impaired people", In: *Proceedings of the 2018 ACM International Joint Conference and 2018 International Symposium on Pervasive and Ubiquitous Computing and Wearable Computers*, 2018. [http://dx.doi.org/10.1145/3267305.3267654]

[11] M. Shoaib, I. Hussain, and H.T. Mirza, "Automatic switching between speech and non-speech: adaptive auditory feedback in desktop assistance for the visually impaired", *Univers. Access Inf. Soc.,* vol. 19, no. 4, pp. 813-823, 2020. [http://dx.doi.org/10.1007/s10209-019-00696-5]

[12] H. Iwata, N. Kobayashi, K. Tachibana, J. Shirogane, and Y. Fukazawa, "Web accessibility support for visually impaired users using link content analysis", *Springerplus,* vol. 2, no. 1, p. 116, 2013. [http://dx.doi.org/10.1186/2193-1801-2-116] [PMID: 23667799]

[13] Y. Borodin, J.P. Bigham, G. Dausch, and I.V. Ramakrishnan, "More than meets the eye: A survey of screen-reader browsing strategies", In: *Proceedings of the 2010 International Cross-Disciplinary Conference on Web Accessibility (W4A) - W4A '10*, 2010. [http://dx.doi.org/10.1145/1805986.1806005]

[14] F. Kusumaningayu, and M.A. Ayu, "A web accessing tool for blind and visually impaired people using Bahasa Indonesia", In: *2017 2nd International Conference on Informatics and Computing (ICIC)*, 2017, pp. 1-6. [http://dx.doi.org/10.1109/IAC.2017.8280605]

[15] M. Zajicek, C. Powell, and C. Reeves, "A Web navigation tool for the blind", In: *Proceedings of the 3rd International ACM Conference on Assistive Technologies - Assets '98*, 1998. [http://dx.doi.org/10.1145/274497.274534]

[16] I. Dela Torre, and I. Khaliq, "A study on accessibility in games for the visually impaired", In: *Media Conference (GEM)*, 2019, pp. 1-7. [http://dx.doi.org/10.1109/GEM.2019.8811534]

[17] D. Song, A. Karimi, and P. Kim, "Toward designing mobile games for visually challenged children", In: *Proceeding of The International Conference on e-Education, Entertainment and e-Management*, 2011, pp. 234-238. [http://dx.doi.org/10.1109/ICeEEM.2011.6137794]

[18] J.R. Babu, C. Sekharaiah, and G.M. Kumar, "A navigation tool for visually impaired persons", In: *2015 2nd International Conference on Computing for Sustainable Global Development (INDIACom)*, 2015, pp. 938-940.

[19] S. Divya, S. Raj, M. Praveen Shai, A. Jawahar Akash, and V. Nisha, "Smart assistance navigational system for visually impaired individuals", In: *2019 IEEE International Conference on Intelligent Techniques in Control, Optimization and Signal Processing (INCOS)*, 2019, pp. 1-5. [http://dx.doi.org/10.1109/INCOS45849.2019.8951333]

[20] K. Sumanasekera, S. Mihilar, C. Wickramasinghe, and S. Arunathilake, "kawulu': A voice-based social network using smart mobile devices for the visually impaired community in Sri Lanka", In: *2018 International Conference on Information and Communication Technology Convergence (ICTC)*, 2018, pp. 228-233. [http://dx.doi.org/10.1109/ICTC.2018.8539569]

[21] N.H.M. Roseli, N. Aziz, and A.A. Mutalib, "The enhancement of assistive courseware for visually impaired learners", In: *2010 International Symposium on Information Technology*, 2010, pp. 1-6. [http://dx.doi.org/10.1109/ITSIM.2010.5561368]

[22] N. Al-Rajhi, A. Al-Abdulkarim, H.S. Al-Khalifa, and H.M. Al-Otaibi, "Making linear equations accessible for visually impaired students using 3D printing", In: *2015 IEEE 15th International Conference on Advanced Learning Technologies*, 2015, pp. 432-433. [http://dx.doi.org/10.1109/ICALT.2015.46]

[23] B. Leporini, M.C. Buzzi, and M. Buzzi, "Interacting with mobile devices *via* VoiceOver: Usability and accessibility issues", In: *Proceedings of the 24th Australian Computer-Human Interaction Conference on - OzCHI '12*, 2012. [http://dx.doi.org/10.1145/2414536.2414591]

[24] M. Owayjan, A. Hayek, H. Nassrallah, and M. Eldor, "Smart assistive navigation system for blind and visually impaired individuals", In: *2015 International Conference on Advances in Biomedical Engineering (ICABME)*, 2015, pp. 162-165. [http://dx.doi.org/10.1109/ICABME.2015.7323277]

[25] B.Z. Halimah, A. Azlina, P. Behrang, and W.O. Choo, "Voice recognition system for the visually impaired: Virtual cognitive approach", In: *2008 International Symposium on Information Technology*, 2008, pp. 1-6. [http://dx.doi.org/10.1109/ITSIM.2008.4631738]

[26] Q. Chen, "CCNY Smart Cane", In: *2017 IEEE 7th Annual International Conference on CYBER Technology in Automation, Control, and Intelligent Systems (CYBER)*, 2017, pp. 1246-1251. [http://dx.doi.org/10.1109/CYBER.2017.8446303]

[27] M. Thomas et, "ISee: Artificial intelligence-based android application for visually impaired people", *Journal of the Gujarat Research Society,* vol. 21, no. 6, pp. 200-208, 2019.

[28] W-J. Chang, "A deep learning-based wearable medicines recognition system for visually impaired people", In: *2019 IEEE International Conference on Artificial Intelligence Circuits and Systems (AICAS)*, 2019, pp. 207-208. [http://dx.doi.org/10.1109/AICAS.2019.8771559]

[29] D. Lee, H. Yoon, C. Park, J. Kim, and C.H. Park, "Automatic number recognition for bus route information aid for the visually-impaired", In: *2013 10th International Conference on Ubiquitous Robots and Ambient Intelligence (URAI)*, 2013, pp. 280-284. [http://dx.doi.org/10.1109/URAI.2013.6677367]

[30] F. Ahmad, I. Tanveerulhaq, F. Ahmad, Tanveerulhaq I. Ishaq, D. Ali, and M. F. Riaz, "Bionic Kinect device to assist visually impaired people by haptic and voice feedback", In: *2016 International Conference on Bio-engineering for Smart Technologies (BioSMART)*, 2016, pp. 1-4.

[31] J. Sánchez, and H. Flores, "Virtual mobile science learning for blind people", *Cyberpsychol. Behav.,* vol. 11, no. 3, pp. 356-359, 2008. [http://dx.doi.org/10.1089/cpb.2007.0110] [PMID: 18537508]

[32] "Seeing AI app from Microsoft", Microsoft.com. [Online]. Available: https://www.microsoft.com/en-us/ai/seeing-ai [Accessed: 10-Mar-2021]

[33] "AiServe", Aiserve.co. [Online]. Available: https://www.aiserve.co/ [Accessed: 10-Mar-2021]

[34] "Glasses for the blind: These glasses change it all - OrCam", Orcam.com, 01-Jun-2017. [Online]. Available: https://www.orcam.com/en/article/new-lease-sight-glasses-blind-see/ [Accessed: 10-Ma--2021]

[35] N. Thakur, and C.Y. Han, "An ambient intelligence-based human behavior monitoring framework for ubiquitous environments", *Information (Basel),* vol. 12, no. 2, p. 81, 2021. [http://dx.doi.org/10.3390/info12020081]

CHAPTER 4

Usability Testing of Twitter App with Indian Users

Swapnil Pawar[1] and **Ganesh Bhutkar**[1,*]

[1] *Center of Excellence in Human-Computer Interaction, Vishwakarma Institute of Technology, Pune, India*

Abstract: This research paper presents a usability testing of the Twitter app with Indian Twitter users for identifying usability problems, especially for the new users or beginners. This usability test mainly focuses on a normal usage context and subject of observations, which significantly affects the user experience with the Twitter app. Various Twitter functionalities/features have been explored during usability testing, and ten frequently used tasks were selected. The selected users have been ten Indian college students in the age group of 21-23 years but are not using Twitter now or have not used Twitter before. It is directly affected by usability problems related to the app like Twitter. Therefore, several usability problems have been identified during usability testing. These problems include the ambiguous design of icons, faulty design of buttons, hidden options inside the menu, information overload, and inefficiency with functions. Few remedies are also proposed for dealing with identified usability problems with the Twitter app. It is believed that the design updates based on identified usability problems and remedies will improve the user experience of Indian Twitter users, boosting the popularity of the Twitter app among Indian youths.

Keywords: Android Smartphone, Artificial Intelligence, Bookmarking, Content Localization, HCI, Indexical Icons, Indian Users, Interface Simplicity, Laboratory Testing, Lists, Micro Blog, Mobizen App, Section Navigation, Social Media, Time Efficiency, Trends, Twitter App, Usability Problems, Usability Testing, Walkthroughs.

INTRODUCTION

Twitter is a popular microblogging and social networking site that allows users to send messages of up to 280 characters, called tweets, to groups of listeners referred to as followers [1]. Twitter has about 883 million users globally and, out of which 330 million users are monthly active users as per Global Digital. Report 2019 [2] and according to the article of Business Insider [3].

* **Corresponding author Ganesh Bhutkar:** Center of Excellence in Human-Computer Interaction, Vishwakarma Institute of Technology, Pune, India; E-mail: ganesh.bhutkar@vit.edu

Nirmalya Thakur and Parameshachari B.D. (Eds)

The users access Twitter through its website interface, through a short message service, or mobile application (App). The registered users with Twitter can tweet or post and retweet or share, but unregistered users can only read the tweets or posts. Usually, Twitter users utilize this platform to express themselves and give opinions to anyone about anything. Each user can choose to follow people and organizations with similar interests to him/her. If a Twitter user follows some other users, he/she can see their tweets in his/her Twitter timeline. Users have found many different uses for Twitter, including communication with friends and family, a way to publicize an event or a memory, and/or as a tool to communicate with the customers for a company.

India has around 34 million Twitter users, and among them, 7.6 million users are monthly active users as per India Digital Report 2019 [4]. These Indian users are curious about Twitter as a social networking site, but it differs from other social networking sites such as Facebook and Instagram. Twitter co-founder and CEO Jack Dorsey want young Indians to tweet their hearts out. Still, the micro-blogging website doesn't appear to be the most popular social media platform for his target group, the 18-to-30-year-olds, and there is some reason like don't know what Twitter or character limit is [5]. The majority of Indian users have never heard of Twitter or only know its name and rarely use Twitter. India has fewer active monthly Twitter users compared to the total Indian Twitter users. Gartner's Asheesh Raina says that Twitter is a 'Literate' tool and is more textual, unlike Facebook, Instagram, and Snapchat. These social networking sites have too much usage, especially with Facebook and WhatsApp. Indian people fail to understand what's the real benefit of Twitter [6]. This research paper is focused on usability testing of Twitter – its UI with the Indian student community. This usability testing is focused on identifying parts of Twitter UI, which is complex and needs improvement in terms of usability in the future.

LITERATURE REVIEW

Several research papers have been identified during the literature study related to usability evaluation of Twitter and usability testing of other Social Networking Sites (SNS) as desktop and mobile applications. These research papers are discussed widely in this section. The first study is a usability testing of Twitter for elderly Arab users using the usability evaluation tool – Morae. This study focuses on usability tests with only elderly people and has used Morae for recording the user's behavior *via* Mobizen software. These users are observed in real-time. The main aim of this study includes analyzing the response of first-time Twitter users and the retention of existing users. This research has provided some suggestions for customizing icon sizes, caption fonts, related hints, and color schemes for elderly users [7]. This study has selected vital tasks such as account creation, composing a tweet, replying tweet, and deleting a tweet. These tasks are rigorously investigated during the usability testing process conducted during this research work.

A study on usability evaluation of messenger apps of Android phones using cognitive walkthrough has provided several usability issues with these apps. This usability evaluation is carried out with three messenger apps - WhatsApp, Skype, and Go SMS Pro. During this study, vital usability issues include the absence of legends for the message, overuse of uncommon indexical icons, and longer textual instructions for users [8]. These types of problems can be found on various social networking sites including in the Twitter app. There is a plan of investigation for similar kinds of usability issues during the usability testing of Twitter.

The next research paper studied is about the usability testing of Tweet-Caster third-party applications for Twitter on Android and Blackberry. Tweet-Caster is a simplified version of the Twitter platform for those who have difficulty or don't like the official Twitter UI. This study includes some tasks that need to be performed by the participants, like composing a tweet, replying to a friend's tweet, visiting the user's profile, and finding trending topics. The mean time spent on each of these tasks is calculated to estimate efficiency [9]. This research paper has been used as a vital guideline for usability testing for Twitter.

There is an interesting study focusing on heuristic evaluation on Twitter with the participation of 100 users. These users have responded through web-based e-questionnaires that cover every part of Twitter in a heuristic manner. In this study, professional/expert users are considered along with naive users. This study has utilized the combination of five attributes out of Nielsen's attributes of usability, such as Learnability (Ease of Learning), Efficiency of Use, Memorability, Errors (Accuracy), and Subjective Satisfaction. A related questionnaire covers every Twitter module and needs to evaluate for better user satisfaction and completion of goals, which Twitter intends to do [10]. The questionnaire used in this paper has been useful in designing questionnaires for usability testing of Twitter.

Another study deals with usability testing of selected tasks performed with mobile apps. It is focused on a comparison between laboratory and field testing. The test participants are given some tasks to perform with the application. And for the difference between laboratory and field testing, they used equipment like a camera and tripod to study outdoor testing environments and participants' performance [11]. Their research concluded with the result of different types of advantages in laboratory testing. This study improves the understanding of the effect on the work environment in usability testing. In the next paper, usability testing of ten social messaging apps on iOS is conducted. These apps specifically are chosen with the most downloaded apps on the Apple App Store. In this study, participants need to perform five tasks with selected apps. Important tasks include sending an instant message, replying to an incoming message and, deleting or blocking a contact. The number of user interactions for every task is measured to calculate mean values. Based on these values, the best usable apps are identified [12]. This study improves the understanding of possible approaches to usability testing.

A research paper related to usability testing of three different SNS - Orkut, Facebook, and Myspace. This testing has 10 participants, including eight females and two males, with an average age of 27. Some of these participants have hardly any knowledge about these sites. In this research, participants need to perform the same set of tasks on these three websites, such as adding new information to their profile, changing privacy settings, making a comment, and joining a group. During the execution of these tasks, few parameters, such as the percentage of successful tasks, user ratings for navigation efficiency, and user satisfaction, have been calculated [13].

RESEARCH METHODOLOGY

The motivation for this research work has been to identify the usability issues through usability testing of the Twitter app. Usability testing has been conducted through a field study involving several stages. These stages include – Features / Facilities in Twitter, Selection of Participant Users, Selection of Tasks, and Benchmark Duration for Tasks.

Features / Facilities in Twitter

There are several major features or facilities available with Twitter. These features or facilities are discussed herewith:

1. User Profile –This feature with Twitter is highly customizable. Users display their information such as personal information, profile picture, own background, users followed, users following, tweets, replies, likes, and unique personal view A user profile on Twitter is vital, as it reflects the user persona, presented it to the SNS world.
2. Search Option -The search option is displayed on the top of the Twitter app's home screen. A user can find other users, topics, pages, images, videos, and trends through the search option. The search option makes the Twitter app more relevant to users.
3. Timeline / News Feed – In this section, users can see the posts, news, and some unique content posted by other users. At the timeline, other users can

provide their opinions about the selected user or any related topic. This timeline or news feed can be customized as per user preferences. The timeline for the user profile can be seen on the main home screen of Twitter.

4. Following / Friends–This section contains a list of Twitter users with whom the user wishes to communicate, know them, or follow them. The users can see their followers as well as followers of other users through their profile section.
5. Communication -This facility is one of the core features of Twitter. Using this facility, the user can exchange text, media privately or publicly with other users or various groups. Each user can enable or disable communication on Twitter.
6. Privacy -A user can post his / her comment or provide an opinion on any topic that is meant to be seen by other users publicly. Twitter has provided privacy to choose who or what type of users can see tweets posted. Privacy is an important feature of Twitter.
7. Comment / Response - user can post his / her comment or provide an opinion on any topic that is meant to be seen by other users publicly. The main objective of this feature is to create and build social relationships with other users. Like-minded users can recognize each other *via* comments.
8. Bookmark / Save- This facility provides an option for the users to save anything posted on Twitter for later access.
9. Tweet function - A Tweet function is the primary function of Twitter. Users can tweet a limited amount of text along with images, videos, or a voting pole. Also, one can communicate *via* tweet publicly with the option of mentioning or tagging other users. One can even share their own or related location. Currently, the maximum limit on the length of a tweet is 280 letters. A user has several options along with tweets. The tweet option is available at multiple locations, such as on the home screen, trending page, or notification.
10. Retweet -This option provides the user an opportunity to share another user's tweet posted. A user can simply reshare the related Tweet with his name. The retweet option is placed under every tweet on Twitter.
11. Trends -This section displays current trends of what is happening worldwide with customizable options with their category options. A user can set preferences for customized trends and can get related trends based on the location selected.
    1. List Option -A list option enables the user to create a list of users from whom he/she desires to get updates on Twitter. A user can also create a list of desired topics or people. One can add other user's lists in their list and can also share their list with other users. This list option is located on the main menu of Twitter.
    2. Content Localization -Twitter has provided an option to see the trends and

tweets from other places. Users can change a content location to a specific country. It's a state, region, or city. Using this feature, users can get to know the happenings in that selected town, city, region, state, or country.

Selection of Participant Users

Participant users are required for usability testing of any IT application. Ten naive users are selected for usability testing, including eight boys and two girls. The selected users are Indian college students in the age group of 21-23 years, and they use social networking sites – Facebook, WhatsApp, or Instagram on their mobile phones. Most of them have heard about Twitter but are not using Twitter now or have not used Twitter before. These college students have actively participated in performing the selected tasks with Twitter during the usability testing process.

Selection of Tasks

Users perform several tasks with Twitter as a social networking application. The vital tasks are selected based on their frequency as well as their importance to the users. These tasks utilize almost all features and facilities available with Twitter and are used during the usability testing process. These ten selected tasks with the assessment of their frequencies are discussed ahead.

Task 1: - Make a tweet - type a message - 'Good Morning.'
The task – 'Tweet a text' is a primary function of Twitter and users perform this task regularly with high frequency.
Task 2: - Find an account/user profile - '@Dstrokes2020'.
The 'Search an account is a necessary option, occasionally used on Twitter. It is used less frequently in real-time.
Task 3: - Follow @Dstrokes2020 user.
The task - 'Follow a user' is a primary function of Twitter, helping users build social relationships. The users perform this task regularly with high frequency.
Task 4: -Send a direct message - 'Hello, Follow me back.' to @Dstrokes2020 user.
The task - 'Send a message' is also the primary function of Twitter and is performed with high frequency.
Task 5: - Retweet user @Dstrokes2020's any tweet.
The task - 'Retweet a tweet' is a primary and unique Twitter function, and its frequency is high in real-time.
Task 6: -Bookmark the tweet that you previously retweeted.

The task - 'Bookmark a tweet' is a simple and frequently used Twitter function, and its frequency is high in real-time.
Task 7: -Create a Twitter list and name it 'Friends.'
The task - 'Create a list - is an important and unique function of Twitter. The users perform this task regularly with high frequency.
Task 8: - Add user @Dstrokes2020 to the Twitter list called 'Friends.'
The task – 'Add user to a list is an extension of the list function of Twitter, and its frequency is high in real-time.
Task 9: - Find Trending Topic section.
The task – 'Find a trending topic section' is an important and unique function of Twitter. The users perform this task regularly with high frequency.
Task 10: -Change your content/trend location from 'India' to 'Worldwide.'

The task – 'Change content/trend location' is a necessary option, occasionally used on Twitter, and its frequency is low in real-time.

Benchmark Duration for Tasks

In IT applications, the task duration or time is taken by the user to complete the task, which is an important factor in the usability evaluation of that application. Users usually don't prefer prolonged tasks with lengthy steps or time-consuming functionalities. They expect to consume minimum time to perform or complete given tasks. Table **1** provides the benchmark times that we are comparing with our results.

Table 1. Benchmark duration for selected tasks with the Twitter.

Task Number	Selected Task	Benchmark Duration (In Sec)
1	Tweet a text	06
2	Search an account	08
3	Follow a user	02
4	Send a message	07
5	Retweet a tweet	02
6	Bookmark a tweet	04
7	Create a list	05
8	Add user to a list	05
9	Find a trending topic section	02
10	Change content location	04

RESEARCH METHODOLOGY AND RESULTS ANALYSIS

Usability testing of Twitter has been performed with chosen Indian participants. Usability testing is the testing of software, website, or mobile app by real users or customers. It evaluates how well end-users can use software or mobile app. The main goal of usability testing is to collect or identify usability problems, functionality problems, and every minor detail that affects any functionality. It can give unbiased, accurate, and detailed evaluation results. It lets the evaluator address simple as well as complex issues affecting application reputation. It gives more room for improvement with identifying problems fixing early issues saving both development time and cost.

In a usability testing session, the researchers give a specific set of tasks to the participant users and ask them to complete each task with or without guidance and instructions. The researcher's responsibility is to observe or record their sessions and give participants hints or suggestions if they are stuck in any task.

Usability testing of Twitter has been performed with the chosen participants. During usability testing, every participant's session has been analyzed for a better understanding of UI, task difficulties, and UI problems. For every session, the time required (In Sec) to complete the selected task has been recorded for each participant, and all such timings have been noted, as seen in Table **2**. The columns are related to participants - A to J for displaying completion timings of tasks. The rows depict completion timings for each of the selected ten tasks. The first entry in Table **2** is 15 and, it suggests that a participant 'A' has completed the first task - 'Tweet a text' in 15 seconds.

Table 2. Task completion times for selected tasks with Twitter for each participant user.

Task Number & Task Name	Completion Time for Participants (In Sec)									
	A	B	C	D	E	F	G	H	I	J
1. Tweet a text	15	09	14	09	15	08	26	12	08	11
2. Search an account	18	20	13	16	13	24	21	20	24	12
3. Follow a user	03	05	04	02	03	02	04	02	03	02
4. Send a message	22	10	16	10	14	20	19	14	12	11
5. Retweet a tweet	30	40	12	10	04	56	27	59	04	03
6. Bookmark a tweet	14	16	26	24	31	53	42	63	47	18
7. Create a list	23	20	23	09	08	42	38	42	41	13
8. Add user to list	40	23	23	28	14	17	52	33	16	26

(Table 2) cont.....

Task Number & Task Name	Completion Time for Participants (In Sec)									
	A	B	C	D	E	F	G	H	I	J
9. Find a trending section	03	02	03	02	02	02	03	03	02	02
10. Change content / trend location	20	07	15	03	13	06	34	06	05	05

The analysis for each of the ten selected tasks, as seen in Table **2**, is discussed ahead. All participants complete all tasks. Some tasks took more time than benchmark time, and some tasks took less time than benchmark time. For this analysis, we created a timeline for each task for all participants. After the breakdown of the timeline, we identified several usability problems.

Task 1: - Make a tweet-Type 'Good Morning.'

In this task, each participant has typed 'Good Morning' and has tweeted it. The related action sequence is depicted in Table **3** as a walkthrough for task 1. A participant has to locate and click a button for composing tweets for typing the desired message as per in Fig. (**1a**). This message is tweeted by clicking a button – 'Tweet,' as seen in Figs. (**1b** and **1c**).

Table 3. Walkthrough of an action sequence for task 1.

Step	Action
1	Locate and click a button - 'Compose Tweet'
2	Type a message - 'Good Morning.'
3	Click a button - 'Tweet' for tweeting a message

In task 1, each participant has made a simple tweet typing - 'Good Morning.' This simple task has a benchmark of 6 seconds, as seen in Table **1**. Fig. (**2**) depicts the completion times of all 10 participants for task 1. All participants have taken more time than the benchmark time of 6 seconds. Participants - A and G took more time locating and identifying the compose button required for typing a text and tweeting it. The timeline breakdown of task 1 is depicted in Table **4** for the next level of detailed analysis.

Table 4. Timeline breakdown of task 1.

Participant	Stepwise Completion Time (In Sec)			Task Completion Time (In Sec)
	Step 1	Step 2	Step 3	
A	05	09	01	15
B	02	06	01	09
C	02	11	01	14
D	01	07	01	09
E	03	11	01	15
F	01	06	01	08
G	05	15	06	26
H	01	10	01	12
I	01	06	01	08
J	03	07	01	11

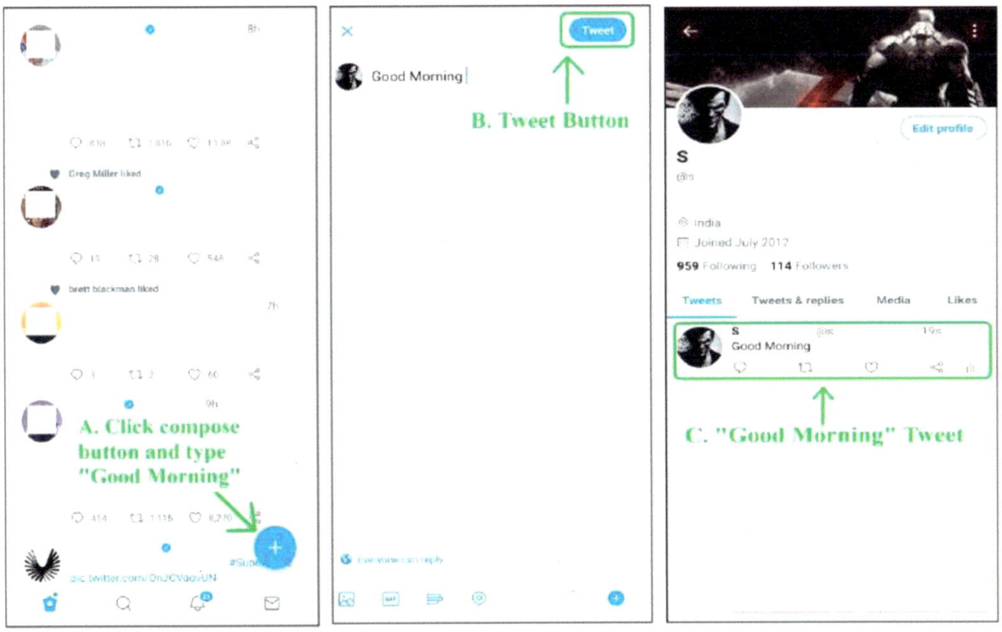

Fig. (1). Task 1 – making a tweet (a), (b), and (c).

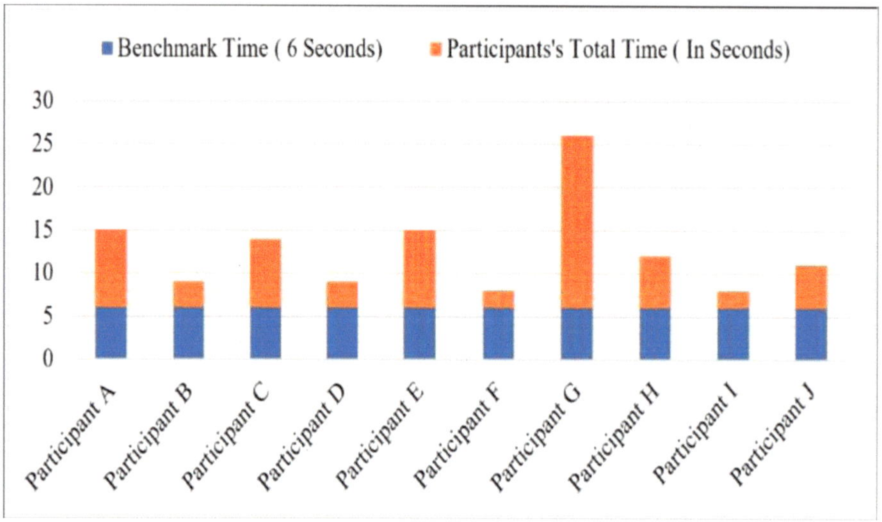

Fig. (2). Graph depicting completion times for task 1.

From Table **4**, it can be observed most of the participants have taken 1-3 seconds for step 1, which is locating and clicking a button - 'Compose Tweet.' But, participants - 'A' and 'G' have taken about 5 seconds to complete step 1.

As seen in Fig. (**1a**), the 'Compose Tweet' button is a round button, with an icon showing a bird feather and a plus sign together. The bird feather indirectly refers to a Tweet, and a plus (+) sign refers to the process of adding or composing, just like adding a friend or a bookmark on SNS. This is an index type of iconic representation, in which its meaning is conveyed indirectly [14 - 16]. Such an ambiguous visual representation of a button can confuse the naive users of Twitter. So, two participants have ignored this button, looking for it elsewhere for a couple of seconds.

During step 2, each participant has typed 'Good Morning.' These participants have taken different durations from 6-15 seconds. For typing as each participant has a different speed of typing. And, their delay in typing messages is sure, not an app issue.

During step 3, the participants need to click the 'Tweet' button. For this step, all participants have taken a second only, except participant - G, who has taken much more time than 6 seconds. A 'Tweet' button is located at the top-right position on the text window in Fig. (**1b**). But participant G has been confused and has misunderstood the 'Tweet' button as a labeled name - 'Tweet.' It has taken a few more seconds for the participants to select the 'Tweet' button after a neat observation.

Thus, during task analysis of task 1 based on completion time, two major usability problems have been identified. These usability problems are –the ambiguous visual representation of the button - 'Compose Tweet' with an index type of icon and misinterpretation of the 'Tweet' button as the labeled name.

Task 2: - Find an account/user profile – '@Dstrokes2020.'

In this task, each participant searched for another user account. The related action sequence is depicted in Table **5** as a walkthrough for task 2. A participant needs to locate the search icon to open its text box and type the desired user's account name, starting with '@' or his custom name.

Table 5. Walkthrough of an action sequence for task 2.

Step	Action
1	Locate the search icon and open its text box.
2	Click text box and type account name - @Dstrokes2020
3	Click an account named @Dstrokes2020 to open his profile

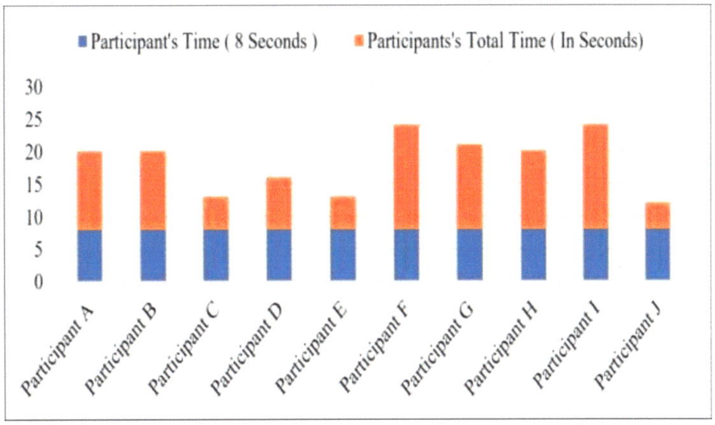

Fig. (3). Graph depicting completion times for task 2.

In task 2, each participant has located the search icon, and then a text box appears. All participants type the desired account name - '@Dstroke2020' and clicked on the name to visit that profile. This simple task has a benchmark of 8 seconds, as seen in Table **1**. All participants have taken more time than the benchmark time, as seen in Fig. (**3**). The timeline breakdown of task 2 is depicted in Table **6** for the next level of detailed analysis.

Table 6. Timeline breakdown of task 2.

Participant	Stepwise Completion Time (In Sec)			Task Completion Time (In Sec)
	Step 1	Step 2	Step 3	
A	01	18	01	20
B	01	18	01	20
C	01	11	01	13
D	01	14	01	16
E	01	11	01	13
F	01	22	01	24
G	01	19	01	21
H	01	18	01	20
I	01	22	01	24
J	01	10	01	12

From Table **6**, it can be observed that all participants have taken minimum time – just 1 second for steps 1 & 3. In step 2, all participants have taken 10-22 seconds for typing, and their delay in typing is sure, not an app issue.

Task 3: - Follow an account/user profile – '@Dstrokes2020.'

Each participant has followed an account in this task, found in the previous search task 2. The related action sequence is depicted in Table **7** as a walkthrough for task 3. A participant has to locate the button – 'Follow' and click that button to follow the selected user profile. After following, the button label will change into a new label called 'Following' as seen in Figs. (**4a** and **4b**).

Table 7. Walkthrough of an action sequence for task 3.

Step	Action
1	Locate a button - 'Follow.'
2	Click a button – 'Follow.'

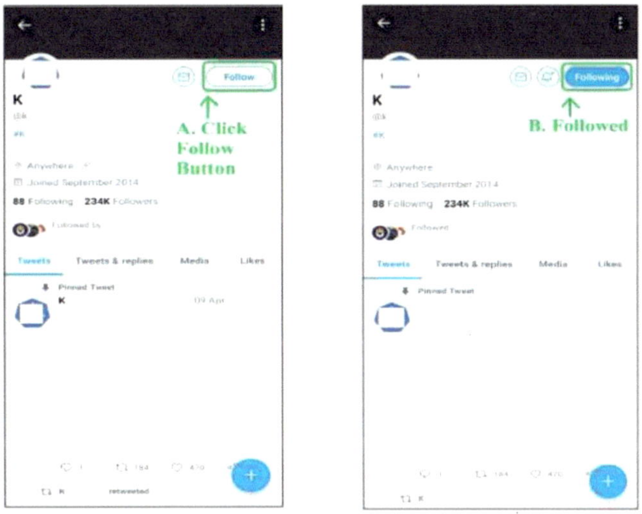

Fig. (4). Task 3 – follow an account (a) and (b).

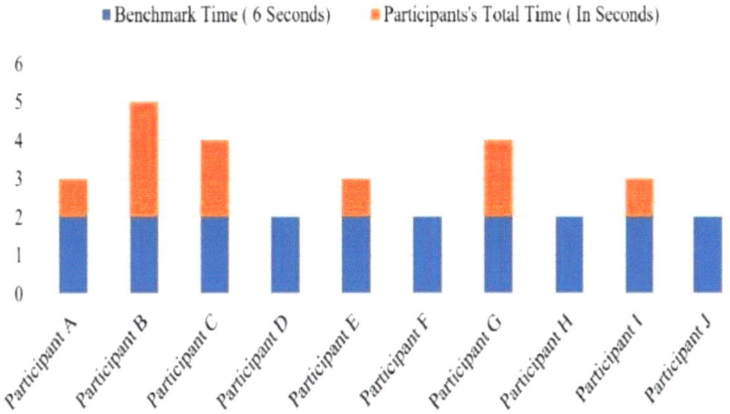

Fig. (5). Graph depicting completion times for task 3.

In task 3, each participant has followed a user account found in the previous task. This task has a benchmark time of 2 seconds. Fig. (**5**) depicts completion times of all 10 participants for task 3. Some participants took more time than the benchmark time of 2 seconds. Participants A, B, C, E, G, and I, took 3-5 seconds, that is, more time. This time is taken to locate and identify the button - 'Follow' or understand that the button - 'Follow' is required to follow that user's account. The timeline breakdown of task 3 is depicted in Table **8** for next-level detailed analysis.

Table 8. Timeline breakdown of task 3.

Participant	Stepwise Completion Time (In Sec)		Task Completion Time (In Sec)
	Step 1	Step 2	
A	02	01	03
B	04	01	05
C	03	01	04
D	01	01	02
E	02	01	03
F	01	01	02
G	03	01	04
H	01	01	02
I	02	01	03
J	01	01	02

From Table **8**, it can be observed that most of the participants have taken 2-4 seconds for step 1, which is locating a button – 'Follow.' As seen in Fig. (**4a**), the button - 'Follow' is shaped like a rectangle with rounded corners located at the top-right position on the profile. Most participants have taken 3-5 seconds, which is more time to locate & click a button – 'Follow.' Some of these participants have failed to understand that it's a labeled button to follow. Few of the participants even have thought that when they have searched and opened the account as in task 2, they have automatically followed that account because after they visited the searched user profile, they have seen the labeled option - 'Follow' on the profile. They have failed to recognize that the 'Follow' labeled option is a button, and they have ignored it. But, after prompting, they have completed this task of following a user account. The completion of task 3 is indicated with a change in the label of the button - 'Follow' to a label - 'Following.' These participants have no idea about the button – 'Follow.' They looked surprised after the user profile is followed.

Thus, during task analysis of task 3 based on completion time, a major usability problem has been identified. The misinterpretation of the 'Follow' button is the labeled name. Follow button has a lack of recognizability and example of solid *vs.* hollow icons [18].

Task 4: - Send direct message - 'Hello, Follow me back' to @Dstrokes2020 user.

In this task, the participant has sent a message to the user followed in the previous task. The related action sequence is depicted in Table **9** as a walkthrough for task

4. A participant has to locate and click the message icon for sending a desire text message.

Table 9. Walkthrough of an action sequence for task 4.

Step	Action
1	Locate and click a 'Message' icon.
2	Type and send a text - 'Hello, Follow me back.'

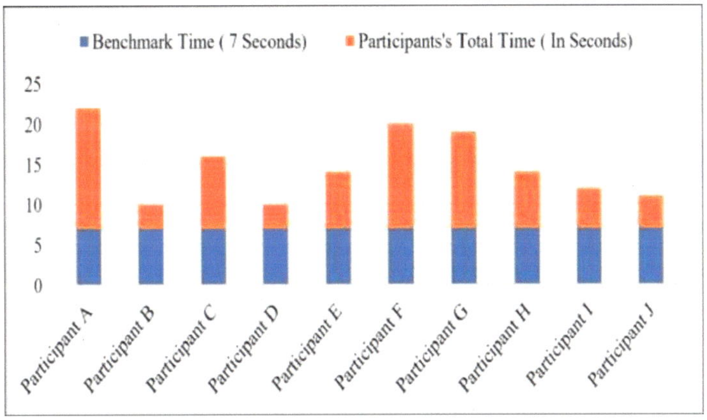

Fig. (6). Graph depicting completion times for task 4.

In task 4, each participant has located and clicked the message icon to send a text. After clicking the message icon, a new window appeared with a text box where each participant has typed a text message – 'Hello, Follow me back.' This task has a benchmark time of 7 seconds, as seen in Table **1**. All participants have taken more time than the benchmark time, as seen in Fig. (**6**). The timeline breakdown of task 4 is depicted in Table **10** for the next level of detailed analysis.

Table 10. Timeline breakdown of task 4.

Participant	Stepwise Completion Time (In Sec)		Task Completion Time (In Sec)
	Step 1	Step 2	
A	01	21	22
B	01	09	10
C	01	15	16
D	01	09	10
E	01	13	14
F	01	19	20

(Table 10) cont.....

Participant	Stepwise Completion Time (In Sec)		Task Completion Time (In Sec)
	Step 1	Step 2	
G	01	18	19
H	01	13	14
I	01	11	12
J	01	10	11

From Table **10**, it can be observed that all participants have taken minimum time – just 1 second for step 1. In step 2, a time of 10-22 seconds has been taken by users for typing, and this delay in typing is sure not an app issue.

Task 5: - Retweet user @Dstrokes2020's any tweet.

In this task, participants have retweeted @Dstrokes2020 user's tweets from their profile section. The related action sequence is depicted in Table **11** as a walkthrough for task 5. Participants have to click the retweet icon to retweet a tweet. After clicking the retweet icon, they will get three options - the first option is a 'Retweet,' the second is a 'Quote a tweet,' and the third is a 'React with a tweet.' Participants have to click on the retweet to proceed through this task. The retweet icon indicates a successful retweet turned into green in color. In task 5, each participant has located the retweet icon. After clicking, they have presented three options, and they have chosen the retweet option to retweet a tweet. This simple task has a benchmark of 2 seconds, as seen in Table **1**. All participants have taken more time than the benchmark time, as seen in Fig. (**8**). The timeline breakdown of task 5 is depicted in Table **12** for the next level of detailed analysis.

Table 11. Walkthrough of an action sequence for task 5.

Step	Action
1	Locate and click a 'Retweet' icon.
2	Choose the retweet option to retweet a tweet.

Table 12. Timeline breakdown of task 5.

Participant	Stepwise Completion Time (In Sec)		Task Completion Time (In Sec)
	Step 1	Step 2	
A	28	01	29
B	39	01	40
C	11	01	12

(Table 12) cont.....

Participant	Stepwise Completion Time (In Sec)		Task Completion Time (In Sec)
	Step 1	Step 2	
D	09	01	10
E	03	01	04
F	55	01	56
G	26	01	27
H	58	01	59
I	03	01	04
J	02	01	03

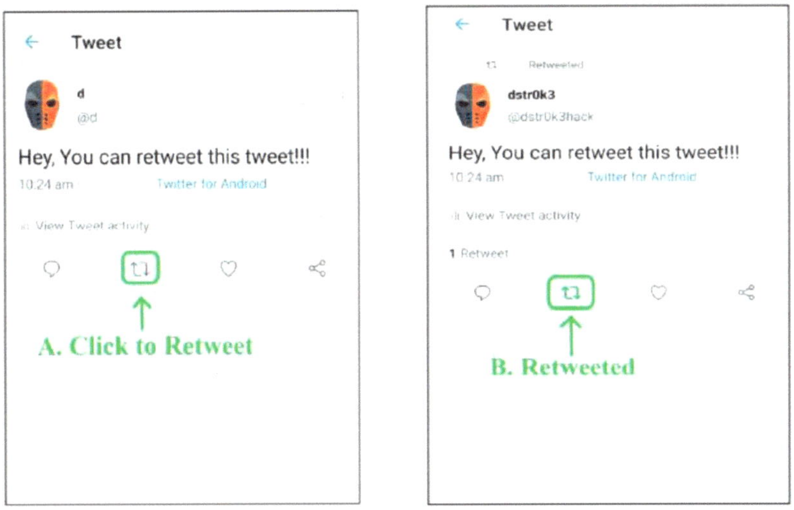

Fig. (7). Task 5 – retweet a tweet (a) and (b).

From Table **12**, it can be observed that all participant has taken more time to locate a simple retweet icon. Only participants E, I, and J had a possible good time locating the retweet icon. All other participants have taken 11-56 seconds for a simple step. As seen in Figs. (**7a** and **7b**), the retweet icon is shaped as two arrows pointing to each other in a rectangular form. It's a simple icon, but many participants have failed to know its retweet function. Before proceeding with this task, the participant has asked the observers - what is the retweet function? They have misunderstood retweets with the share function. Some participants did simply navigate in various sections and wasted time. Some participants simply have clicked blindly, trying all other icons on the screen, and eventually have found the retweet icon. Participants conveyed that retweeting a tweet is a whole new function that they have discovered. Thus, during task analysis of task 5 based on completion time, a major usability problem has been identified.

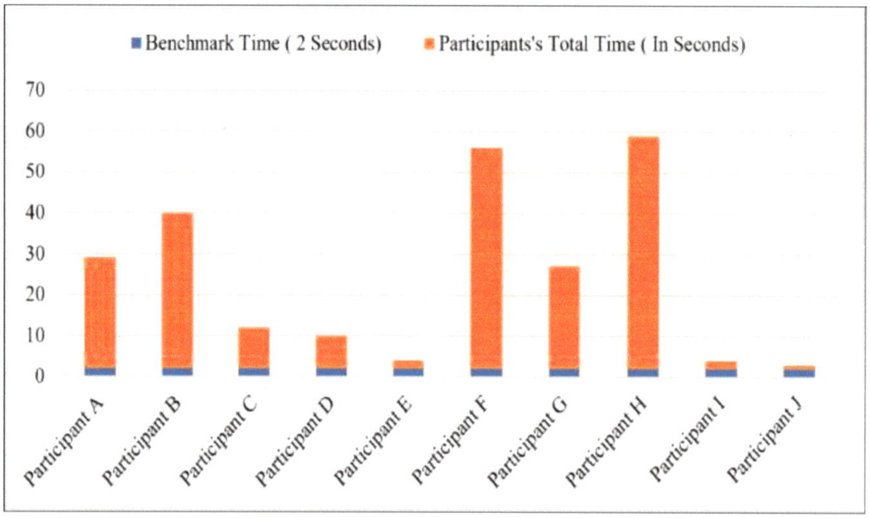

Fig. (8). Graph depicting completion times for task 5.

Lack of Consistency with the used icon a retweet on Twitter.

These icons are hard to interpret by users in the context of the Twitter app. These icons are symbols, which have a confusing function. As seen in Fig. (**7a**), the retweet icon also has other possible meanings like repost, refresh, repeat, transfer, or swap. The users have expected one outcome and have got another one. These little problems have delayed or prevented the user's actions due to a poor understanding of these icons.

Task 6: - Bookmark a tweet that you previously retweeted. In this task, each participant has bookmarked a tweet that he/she retweeted in the previous task 5. The related action sequence is depicted in Table **13** as a walkthrough for task 6. A participant has to locate the Bookmark icon and need to click the icon to bookmark a tweet. If the tweet is successfully bookmarked, then the message - 'Tweet added in the bookmark' pops up on the screen as seen in Figs. (**9a** and **9b**).

Table 13. Walkthrough of an action sequence for task 6.

Step	Action
1	Locate and click a 'Bookmark' icon.
2	Choose the bookmark option to bookmark a tweet.

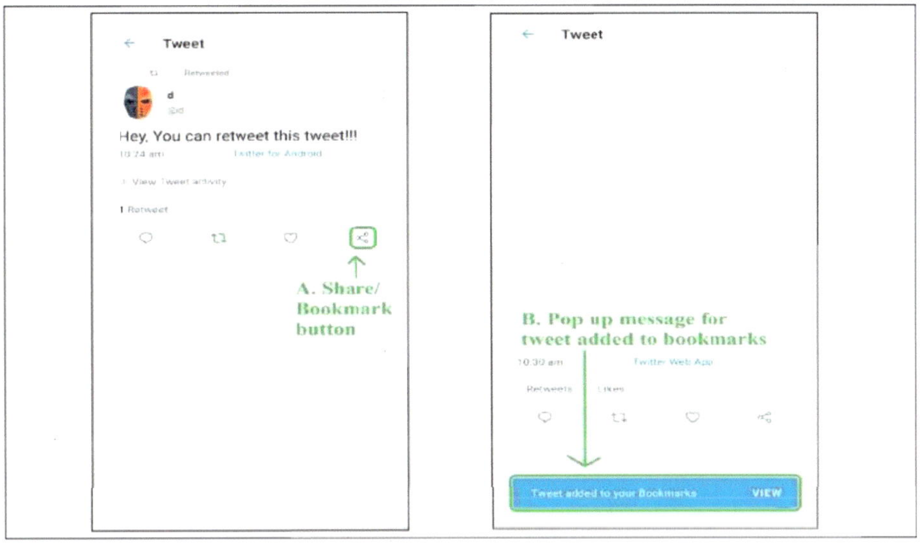

Fig. (9). Task 6 – add the tweet to the bookmark.

In task 6, each participant has bookmarked a tweet that he retweeted in task 5. This task has a benchmark time of 4 seconds, as seen in Table **1**. Fig. (**10**) depicts the completion time of all 10 participants for task 6. All participants took more time than the benchmark time of 4 seconds. The timeline breakdown of task 6 is depicted in Table **14** for the next level of detailed analysis.

Table 14. Timeline breakdown of task 6.

Participant	Stepwise Completion Time (In Sec)		Task Completion Time (In Sec)
	Step 1	Step 2	
A	13	01	14
B	15	01	16
C	25	01	26
D	23	01	24
E	30	01	31
F	52	01	53
G	41	01	42
H	62	01	63
I	46	01	47
J	17	01	18

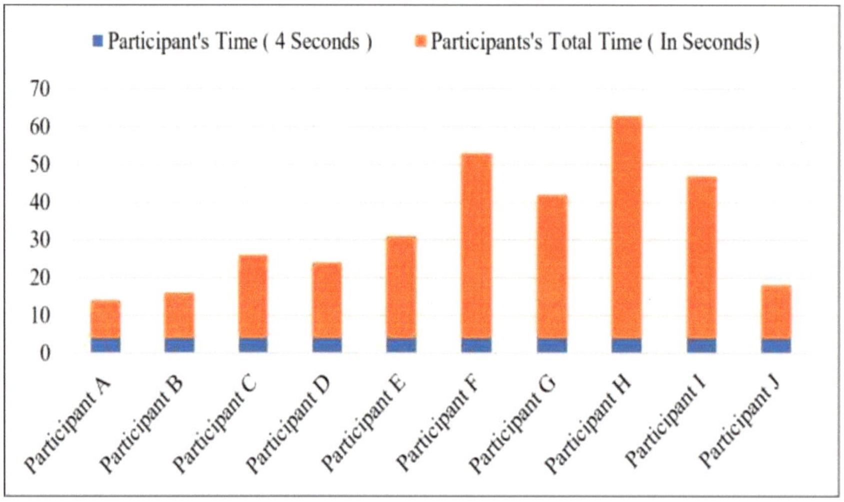

Fig. (10). Graph depicting completion times for task 6.

From Table **14**, it can be observed that most of the participants have taken 13 – 62 seconds for step 1, which locate and click the bookmark icon.

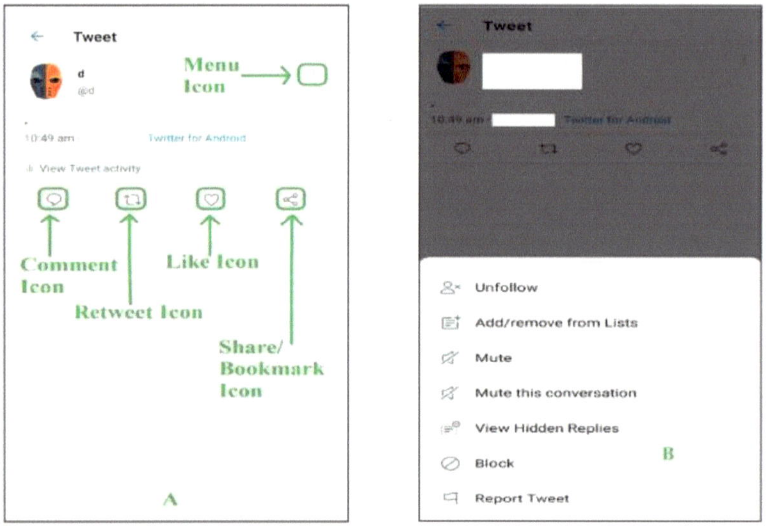

Fig. (11). Tweet page.

As seen in Fig. (**11a**), there are various icons on the tweet page. These icons include icons for comment, retweet, like, menu, camera, *etc*. Some of them are not known to the participants.

Participants - B and J did stare at the entire profile page. After a few seconds, they directly clicked the share icon without knowing that the bookmark option was hidden there. Thus, they bookmarked that tweet successfully but unknowingly.

Participants - A and C clicked the 'Like' icon and then thought they completed this task. They were informed that they did not complete this task. After staring at the screen for a few more seconds, they clicked the share button as a last resort. They also found the bookmark option and successfully bookmarked that tweet.

Participants - D, E, F, G, and I did stare at the entire screen for some seconds after they clicked the menu icon as seen in Fig. (**11a**), and this prompted various menu options as seen in Fig. (**11b**). They tried to find a bookmark option in that menu, but they failed to find one. After some time, they clicked the share icon as a curiosity and eventually found the bookmark option, and they completed this task successfully.

Participant H clicked the 'Like' icon and thought that he completed this task. After prompting, he checked the menu options, but he failed to find the bookmark option. After staring for a long time at the screen, he clicked the share icon out of curiosity and found the bookmark option and completed this task successfully.

Thus, during task analysis of task 6 based on completion time, a major usability problem has been identified. A major problem is a lack of consistency and standard for the bookmark option. The share icon in the Twitter app has been responsible for both the share and bookmark functions. As per real-world convention, a share icon is not an option used for the bookmark function. The bookmark option is not properly visible to a user, and there is no shortcut for bookmarking.

Task 7: - Create a Twitter List and name it 'Friends.'

In this task, each participant has created a list named - 'Friends' in which he/she can add personal favorite users to receive their tweets and updates from them. The related action sequence is depicted in Table **15** as a walkthrough for task 7. Each participant has to locate the 'Lists' option on Twitter. After creating a list, the participants give the name - 'Friends' to the list, as seen in Figs. (**12a** and **12b**).

Table 15. Walkthrough of an action sequence for task 7.

Step	Action
1	Locate and click a 'Lists' option.
2	Create a list and give the name - 'Friends.'

In task 7, each participant has created a list named 'Friends.' This task has a benchmark time of 5 seconds, as seen in Table **1**. Fig. (**13**) depicts completion times of all 10 participants for task 7. All participants took more time than the benchmark time of 5 seconds. Some Participants took 5-40 seconds for step 1 is to locate the list option. The timeline breakdown of task 7 is depicted in Table **16** for the next level of detailed analysis.

Table 16. Timeline breakdown for task 7.

Participants	**Stepwise Completion Time (In Sec)**		**Task Completion Time (In Sec)**
	Step 1	**Step 2**	
A	20	03	23
B	16	04	20
C	20	03	23
D	06	03	09
E	05	03	08
F	40	02	42
G	35	03	38
H	39	03	42
I	38	03	41
J	10	03	13

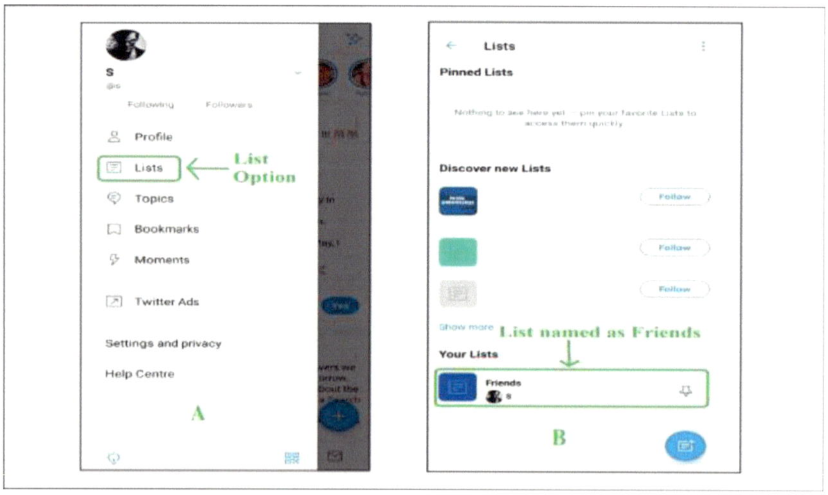

Fig. (12). Task 7 – make a list (a) and (b).

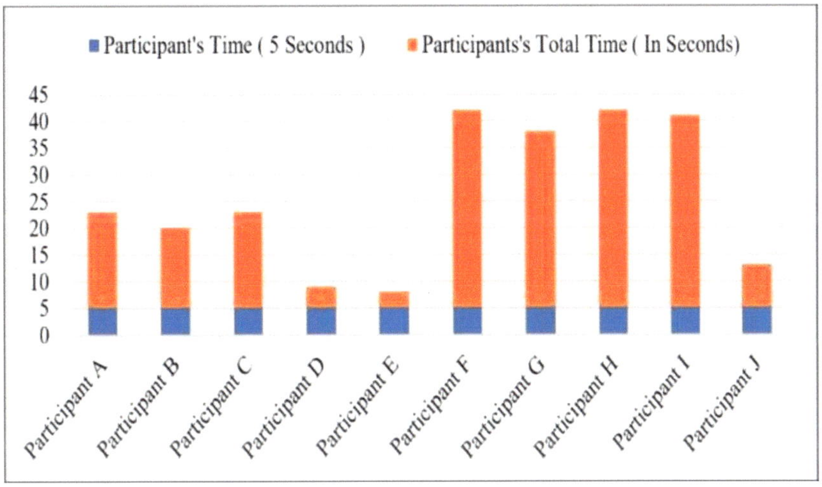

Fig. (13). Graph depicting completion times for task 7.

From Table **16**, it can be observed that most participants have taken 6-40 seconds for step 1, which is locating the 'Lists' option. All participants took more time for task 7 than the benchmark. As seen in Fig. **(14)**, there are multiple options to look at profile/main menu option, location option, and trend settings. The list option is in the main menu option. The participants clicked first the location option because its icon exactly looks like the setting icon.

Fig. (14). Trending section.

The participants didn't find the list option there. Then, some participants clicked the trend settings option because the trend settings icon also looks like the minimize option icon. But they didn't find the list option there also. The participants also switched to the home screen and looked for the 'List' option there. But, after wasting too much time, they clicked on the profile picture, and they found the list option in the main menu. For step 2, all participants took the time to type the list name.

Thus, during task analysis of task 7 based on completion time, a major usability problem has been identified. The major problems are an information overload issue on the trending page and a lack of simplicity in designing the main menu option. Participant's seeing several settings and options icons with their variants icon, cause of that, some participants may be confused or not able to process these options to gain a view of the system of Twitter. This may cause any user to overlook or skip the desire options.

Task 8: - Add user @Dstrokes2020 to the Twitter list called 'Friends.'

In this task, each participant has added a user to a list. The related action sequence is depicted in Table **17** as a walkthrough for task 8. A participant has to add '@Dstrokes2020' in a newly created list called 'Friends' that he/she has created in the previous task. After adding the user to a list, the list will show newly added users on the screen, as seen in Fig. (**15**).

Table 17. Walkthrough of an action sequence for task 8.

Step	Action
1	Add '@Dstrokes2020' user in the list called 'Friends.'

In task 8, each participant has added a user named '@Dstrokes2020' to a list called 'Friends,' created in task 7. This task has a benchmark time of 5 seconds, as seen in Table **1**. Fig. (**16**) depicts the completion time of all participants for task 8. All participants have taken more time than the benchmark time of 5 seconds. The timeline breakdown of task 8 is depicted in Table **18** for the next-level detailed analysis. From Table **18**, it can be observed that all participants have taken 14-52 seconds just for adding a user to the list.

Table 18. Timeline breakdown of task 8.

Participant	Task Completion Time (In Sec)
A	40
B	23
C	23
D	28
E	14

(Table 18) cont.....

Participant	Task Completion Time (In Sec)
F	17
G	52
H	33
I	16
J	26

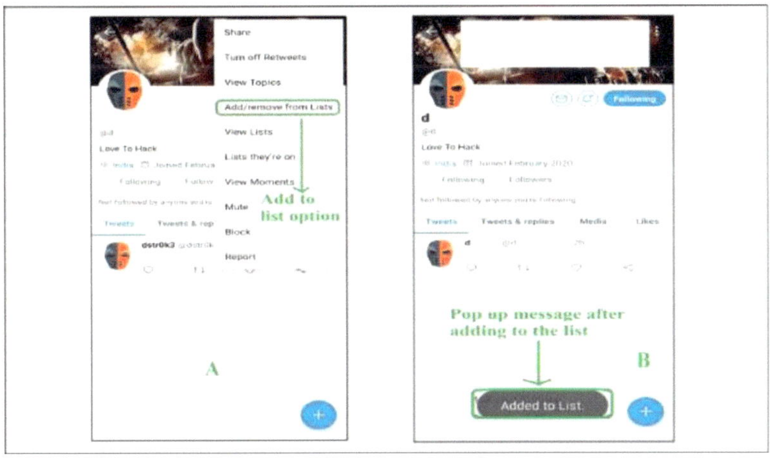

Fig. (15). Task 8 – add a user to the list.

All participants know that the list option is located on the main menu. So, they visited the list section to add the user to the list. The participants looked at every option in the list section, as seen in Fig. (**12b**), and tried everything like edit list name, delete list name. But they didn't find the option to add a user to the list and wasted too much time in the list section.

After some time, they navigated to the user profile of the user they were supposed to add to the list. They clicked the profile menu option and saw the 'Add to list option in the menu. Thus, the participants added the user to the list and completed task 8 successfully. Some of the participants were frustrated, and some were even confused after completing this particular task. Most of the participants got the idea of this functionality. Some of them felt that if they need to add ten users to the list, they have to navigate those ten user profiles to add them individually.

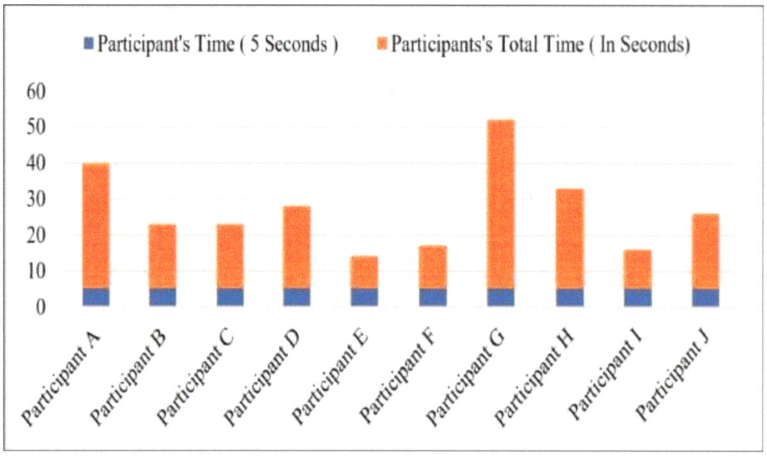

Fig. (16). Graph depicting completion times for task 8.

Thus, during task analysis of task 8 based on completion time, a major usability problem has been identified. The major problem is the lack of simplicity in UI options. No shortcut or option is provided in the list section for adding a user to the Twitter list. Because of the lengthy or hidden process, time efficiency also decreases. In this context, the current Twitter design has failed due to its complexity. To a workload reduction and not supportive of the automation, the design makes sure that there is a need to facilitate user interaction in a much easier, simple, and faster way.

Task 9: - Find Trending topic section.

In this task, each participant has found the trending topic section on Twitter. The related action sequence is depicted in Table **19** as a walkthrough for task 9. A participant has to locate the 'Trending topic' section.

Table 19. Walkthrough of an action sequence for task 9.

Step	Action
1	Find a 'Trending' topic section on Twitter.

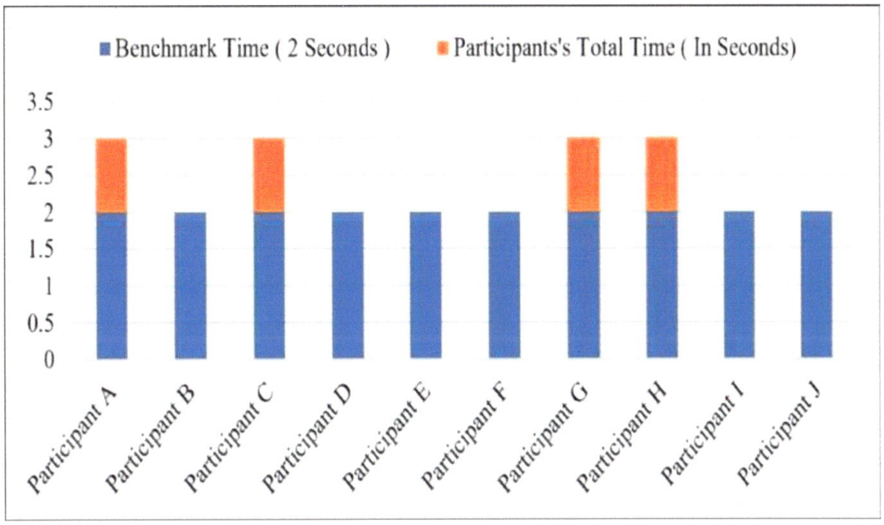

Fig. (17). Graph depicting completion times for task 9.

In Task 9, each participant has found the 'Trending section.' This task has a benchmark time of 2 seconds, as seen in Table **1**. Fig. (**17**) depicts the completion times of all 10 participants for task 9. All Participants completed this simple task at a very good time of 3 seconds (maximum). Most Twitter users frequently visit the trending section, and their next action depends on the 'Trending section.' In this task, each participant has changed the content location from settings. The related action sequence is depicted in Table **21** as a walkthrough for task 10. A participant has to locate the setting icon or setting option or appropriate option on the trending section to change the content location 'India' to 'Worldwide.' After changing the location, the trending section shows worldwide tweets and updates Fig. (**18**).

Table 20. Timeline breakdown of task 9.

Participant	Task Completion Time (In Sec)
A	03
B	02
C	03
D	02
E	02
F	02
G	03
H	03

(Table 20) cont.....

Participant	Task Completion Time (In Sec)
I	02
J	02

Task 10: - Change your content/trend location 'India' to 'Worldwide'.

Table 21. Walkthrough of an action sequence for task 10.

Step	Action
1	Locate the setting icon or setting option or the appropriate option.
2	Change content location 'India' to 'Worldwide.'

In Task 10, each participant has changed the content location from the settings. This task has a benchmark time of 4 seconds, as seen in Table **1**. Fig. (**19**) depicts the completion time of all 10 participants for task 10. Participants A, C, E, and G took more time than the benchmark time of 4 seconds. The timeline breakdown of task 10 is depicted in Table **22** for the next level of detailed analysis. From Table **22**, it can be observed that most of the participant has taken 6-20 sec for step 1, which is locating the setting icon or setting option or the appropriate option. As seen in Fig. (**18**), the location option is located right upper side of the trending section. Reading the given task, participants visited the trending section and looked at 'Trending in India, which is in the trending section as seen in Fig. (**14**).

Table 22. Timeline breakdown of task 10.

Participant	Stepwise Completion Time (In Sec)		Task Completion Time (In Sec)
	Step 1	Step 2	
A	19	01	20
B	06	01	07
C	14	01	15
D	02	01	03
E	12	01	13
F	05	01	06
G	33	01	34
H	05	01	06
I	04	01	05
J	04	01	05

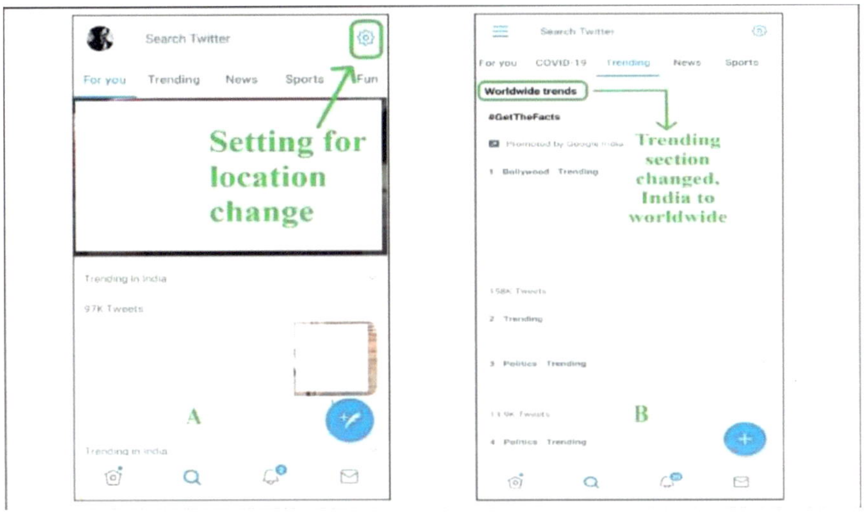

Fig. (18). Task 10 – change content location 'India' to 'Worldwide' (a) and (b).

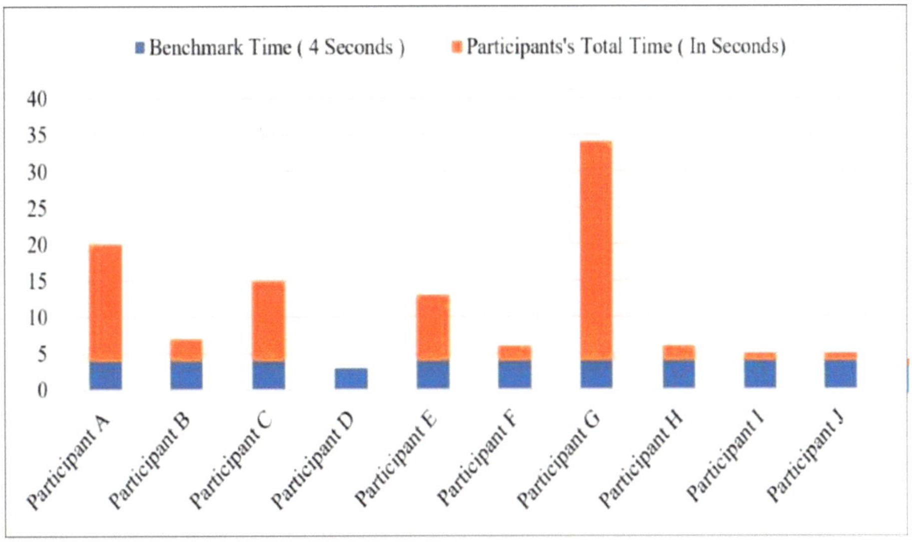

Fig. (19). Graph depicting completion times for task 10.

They clicked near trend settings to change a location next to the 'Trending in India' mini section. After failing, they thought worldwide tweets and content were available in the list of trends. So, they navigated downward, but they didn't find any worldwide label, tweet, or content. In these activities, they wasted too much time. After some time, participants tried the location option and completed this task successfully.

Participants B, D, F, H, I, and J have tried the location option in the first attempt to complete this task successfully. Thus, during task analysis of task 10 based on completion time, a major usability problem has been identified. F

or this task, participants had a problem with information overload on the trending section. There are too many settings and options for different purposes in the trending section of Twitter.

IDENTIFIED USABILITY PROBLEMS AND REMEDIES

Users identify several major usability problems during usability testing of the Twitter app. These are summarized in Table **23**. The following remedies or solutions for the usability problems discussed in Table **23** are proposed for the Twitter app's future design.

Table 23. Identification of usability problems from the Twitter mobile application.

Sr. No.	Usability Problem Identified	Usability Problem Description	Relevant Task(s) performed	Affected Functions in Twitter
1	Ambiguous or inconsistent visual representation of icons	The buttons used for 'Composing a Tweet' and 'ReTweet' represent an index type of icons [15] and [16]. Users find the meaning of related icons (to compose a tweet) somewhat ambiguous and difficult to understand. Similarly, a 'Retweet' icon looks ambiguous and has other meanings like repost, refresh, reload, repeat, transfer, or swap.	Task 1: Make a tweet - type a message - 'Good Morning.' Task 5: Retweet user @Dstrokes2020's any tweet.	'Compose' & 'ReTweet'
2	Misinterpretation of the button as a label	A 'Follow' button in the profile section has a hollow representation. It is confusing for users as it looks more like a label.	Task 3: Follow@Dstrokes2020 user.	'Follow'
3	Hidden options inside the menu / option	A frequently used 'Bookmark' option is hidden under the iconic option - 'Share.' Twitter bookmark is a sub-category of share function, difficult to understand for many users.	Task 6: Bookmark the tweet that retweeted in task 5	'Bookmark'

(Table 23) cont.....

Sr. No.	Usability Problem Identified	Usability Problem Description	Relevant Task(s) performed	Affected Functions in Twitter
4	Information Overload	The main trending section has too many settings and options presented to the users, creating information overload. Many of these iconic options are used for trend settings, locations, and user profiles. Multiple settings and options may be confusing to many users.	Task 7: Create a Twitter list and name it 'Friends.' Task 10: Change content/trend location from 'India' to 'Worldwide.'	'List' & 'Trends'
5	Lack of simplicity and efficiency	There is no simple and efficient way to use a list function, which users frequently use. If a user wishes to add ten users to the list, then he/she has to navigate to those ten user profiles to simply add them individually.	Task 8: Add user @Dstrokes2020 in the Twitter list called 'Friends.'	'List'

Design of Icons

Designs of two icons are proposed, and these icons include - 'Compose' and 'Retweet' icons.

(a) Compose icon

Some users have a hard time recognizing the 'Compose' button for a tweet. During usability testing, the participant took extra time to recognize the 'Compose' button. In the proposed design, a 'Pencil' icon with the 'Plus' symbol is used on a 'Compose' button, as seen in Fig. (**20**). With a proposed 'Compose' icon, users can understand better and also compose Tweets easily.

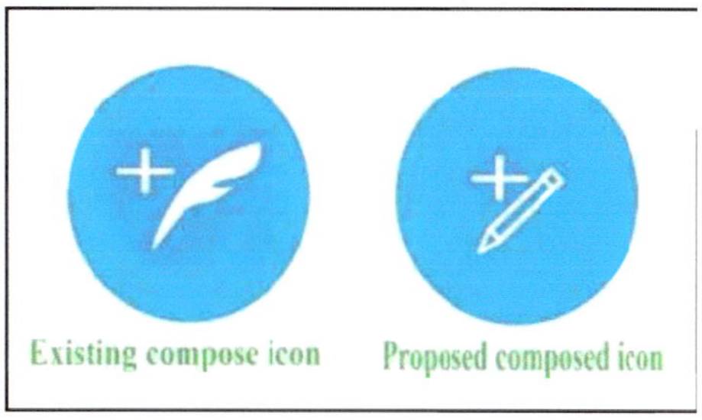

Fig. (20). Proposed 'Compose' icon.

(b) Retweet icon

During usability testing, it was found that most of our participants did not identify the 'Retweet' icon. Twitter's Retweet icon currently has an alternate meaning: refresh, repost, reload, repeat, transfer, or swap. To retweet means the user simply shares a tweet with his name. But as seen in Fig. (**21**), a 'Share' icon also exists with the retweet icon that shares a tweet with third-party apps and direct messages. Both 'Retweet' and 'Share' icons are used for sharing. The only difference is that the 'Retweet' icon works within Twitter, and the 'Share' icon works both insides (direct message to other users) and outside (third party apps) of Twitter.

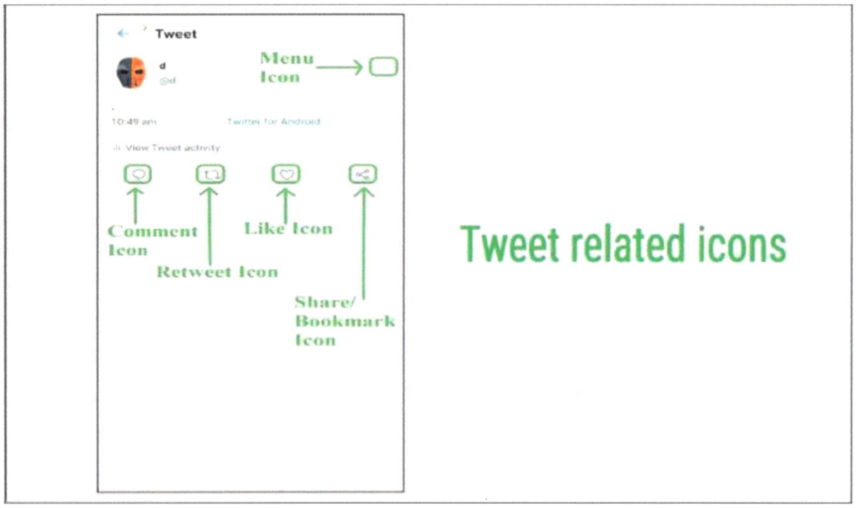

Fig. (21). Tweet related icons on Twitter.

As seen in Fig. (**22**), an alternate icon has been proposed with an outline of a bird, an official 'Twitter' icon, and an arrow from left to right, indicating a function as a share. The user can know or can get the idea about retweeting or sharing a tweet from the proposed icon. If the user wants to share a tweet with third-party apps or as a direct message, they can choose the 'Share' icon instead.

Fig. (22). Proposed 'Retweet' Icon.

Design of Button

Follow button

The 'Follow' button in the Twitter app has been misinterpreted as a label as it is currently hollow, as seen in Fig. (**23**). So, in this context, many users took the time to recognize that button. Instead of using such a hollow button, a solid 'Follow' button, as seen in Fig. (**23**), can be designed, quickly recognized by even the new users.

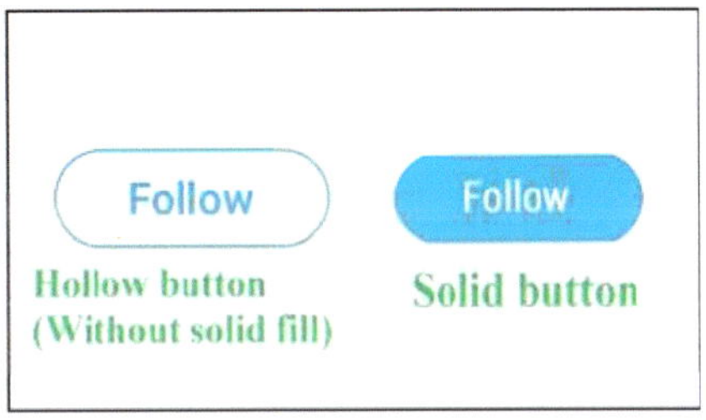

Fig. (23). Proposed 'Follow' button.

Shortcut for Bookmark

The 'Bookmark' option is hidden under the iconic option of the 'Share' icon. A bookmarking is a sub-category of the Twitter share function, difficult to understand for many users. Therefore, a shortcut option with a 'Bookmark' icon can be added alongside tweet settings, as seen in Fig. (**24**). Users can simply bookmark the desired tweet with one click without exploring other options unnecessarily with this shortcut.

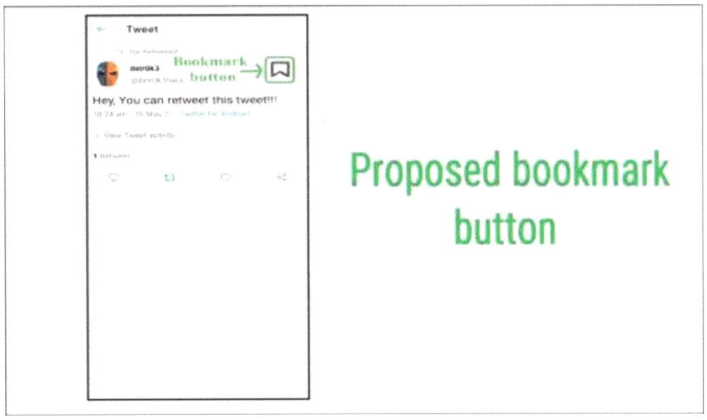

Fig. (24). Proposed 'Bookmark' shortcut.

Reduction in Information Overload

The problem of information overload has been identified during tasks – 7 and 10.

(a) List section

The multiple setting options are confusing users to use the most regular section/function like the 'List.' The 'List' section contains the user's favorite and saved profiles, which he/she desires to connect the most. Therefore, the 'List' section deserves a place in the main section of Twitter. In the proposed design, the 'List' section is added among the main of Twitter, as seen in Fig. (**25**). From the main home screen, the user can access the list without delay in time.

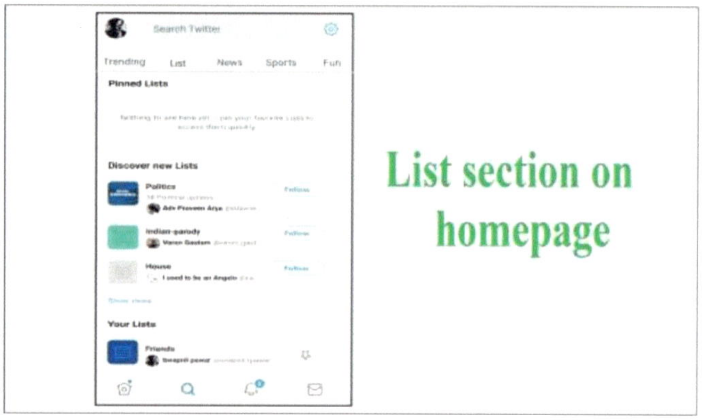

Fig. (25). Proposed 'List' Section.

(b) Location option

There are multiple settings on Twitter while changing location, as seen in Fig. (**26a**). The participants got confused among these options while getting to the 'Location' option. A standard 'Location' icon can be proposed as a localization option on the main screen of Twitter, as seen in Fig. (**26b**).

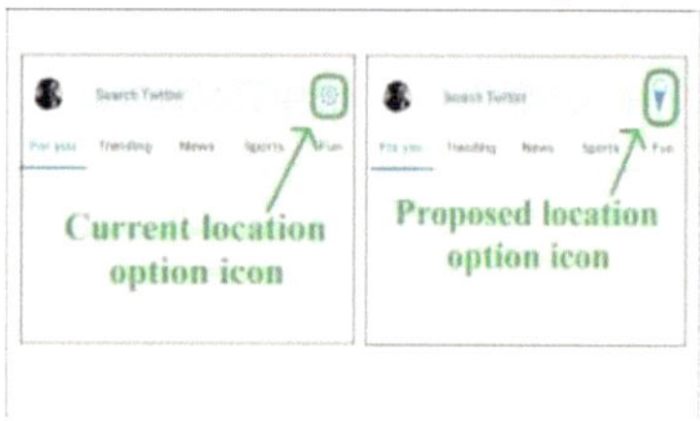

Fig. (26). Location option (a) and (b).

Simplicity and Efficiency of 'List' Function

There is no simple and efficient way to use a frequently used 'List' function in the Twitter app, as discussed in Table **23**. An alternate method is proposed to add users to the desired list without consuming more time. Time is consumed in visiting each user's profile individually and then in adding them to the list. As seen in Fig. (**27a**), a 'Plus' (+) button can be provided for a created list to add new members without leaving that screen. The user can click the 'Plus' button, and then the user's follower list can be displayed. The user can only select the desired users by clicking on related 'Follow' buttons to add the users to the list. Once the user clicks on the 'Plus' button, two sections for followers and suggestions can be displayed. The 'Suggestions' section will be supported or powered by Artificial intelligence (AI). The AI-supported algorithm can process the user's follower list, his / her interests, favorite topics, favorite celebrities, and regular engagement. The user can be provided with suggestions in user categories/user accounts to add to the list. He can also search individually in the search bar for users. As seen in Fig. (**27b**), after clicking the 'Plus' button, the user is provided with followers and suggestions, as seen in Figs. (**28a** and **28b**). The user can click the desired categories and add related user accounts to his list.

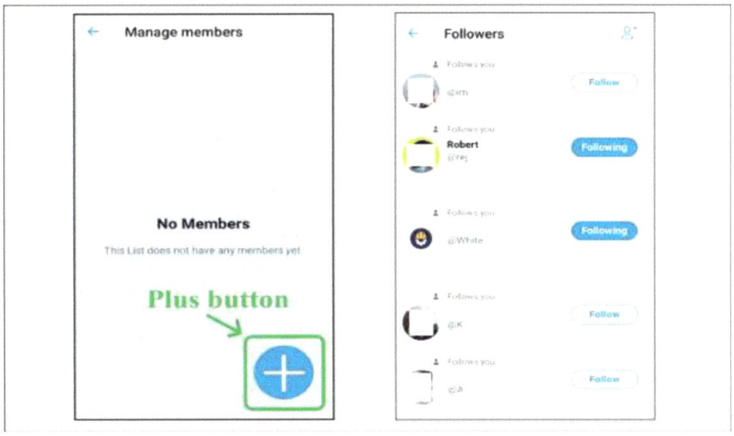

Fig. (27). Adding a user - (a) 'Plus' button and (b) 'Followers' list.

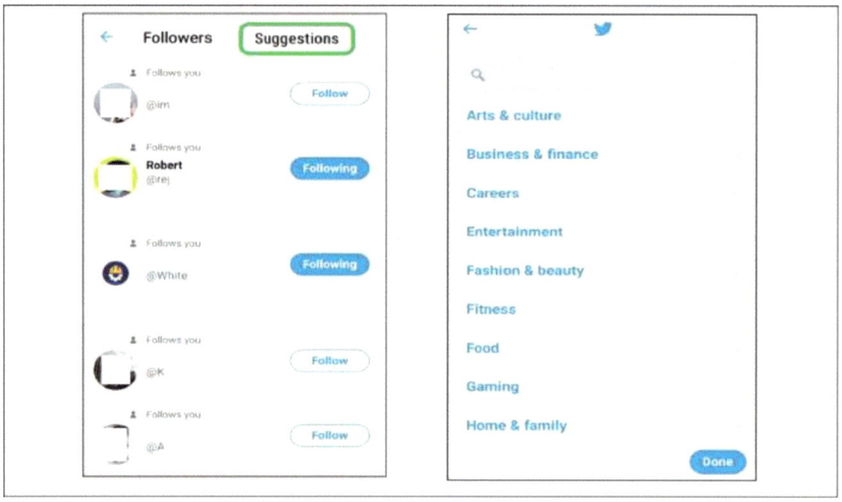

Fig. (28). Followers and suggestion section (a) and various suggestion categories (b).

CONCLUSION

The usability testing of the Twitter app with Indian users leads to identifying several important usability problems. These problems mainly include the ambiguous design of icons, faulty design of buttons, hidden options inside the menu, information overload on screens, and inefficiency with functions.

It is imperative to continuously improve the usability and user experience with the Twitter app. So, few remedies are also proposed for dealing with identified usability problems with the Twitter app. These remedies and related redesign of the Twitter app will improve the user experience of Indian Twitter users. In the future, the awareness about usability problems should be increased, and these problems should be resolved for superior user experience with the Twitter app. Such a positive design effort will surely boost the popularity of the Twitter app among Indian youths.

CONSENT FOR PUBLICATION

Not Applicable.

CONFLICT OF INTEREST

The author confirms that this chapter contents have no conflict of interest.

ACKNOWLEDGEMENT

The authors are thankful to Mr. Siddhant Patil, the B.Tech Industrial intern at the

Center of Excellence in HCI, VIT Pune, INDIA, for UI remarks and questionnaire suggestions. We are also grateful to the students who participated in this usability testing.

REFERENCES

[1] E-commerce Nation Group, "What is Twitter, what is it for and how does this microblogging network work?", ECN, Nov 21, 2018. [Online]. Available: https://www.ecommerce-nation.com/what-is - Twitter-what-is-it-for-and -how-does-this-microblogging-network-work [Accessed 15th Feb. 2020].

[2] S. Kemp, *Global Digital Report 2019,* 2019. Jan 31, 2019. [Online]. Available: https://www.slideshare.net/DataReportal/digital-2019-global-digital-yearbook-january-2019-v01 [Accessed: 15th Feb.2020]

[3] J. Edwards, *Twitter'sDark Pool': IPO Doesn't Mention 651 Million Users Who Abandoned Twitter,* 2013. Business Insider, Nov 6, 2013. [Online]. Available: https://www.businessinsider.in/Twitters-Dark-Pool-IPO-Doesnt-Mention-651-Million-Users-Who-Abandoned-Twitter/articleshow/25330788 .cms [Accessed 15th Feb.2020].

[4] S. Kemp, *Digital 2019: India.* Jan 31,2019. [Online]. Available: https://www.slideshare.net/DataReportal/digital- 2019-india-january-2019-v01 [Accessed: 15th Feb.2020].

[5] R. Mihindukulasuriya, "Why young Indians aren't on Twitter", The Print, Nov 13, 2018. [Online]. Available:https://theprint.in/features/why-young-indians-arent-on- twitter/148907 [Accessed 15th Feb. 2020].

[6] S. Singh, *Twitter's Twin Challenges in India: To increase the user base and make it attractive to advertisers,* 2014. The Economic Times, Mar 30, 2014. [Online]. Available: https://economictimes.indiatimes.com/tech/internet/twitters-twin- challenges-in-india-to-increas- -the-user-base-and-make-it-attractive-to-advertisers/articleshow/3291 8324.cms [Accessed 15th Feb. 2020].

[7] M. Al-khomsan, A. Al-Arjan, A. Al-Amro, and K. Al-Nafjan, "Usability evaluation of Twitter on Android platform for elderly Arab users using morae evaluation tool", In: *2015 10th International Conference for Internet Technology and Secured Transactions (ICITST)*, London, 2015. [http://dx.doi.org/10.1109/ICITST.2015.7412139]

[8] D. Jadhav, G. Bhutkar, and V. Mehta, "Usability evaluation of messenger applications for Android phones using a cognitive walkthrough", In: *11th Asia Pacific Conference on Computer-Human Interaction (APCHI '13)*. Association for Computing Machinery: New York, NY, USA, 2013, pp. 9-18.
[http://dx.doi.org/10.1145/2525194.2525202]

[9] T. Lehutjo, "The usability of mobile Twitter apps", Mar 2013. [Online]. Available: http://wiredspace.wits.ac.za/bitstream/handle/10539/13618/Tshepo_Lehutjo_RR_24Sep2013.pdf [Accessed 20th Feb. 2020].

[10] A. MUSA, "R. JIMOH, " Usability Evaluation of Twitter Micro-Blog Using Heuristic Approach," Annals", *Computer Science Series,* vol. 16, no. 2, pp. 69-76, 2018.

[11] A. Kaikkonen, A. Kekäläinen, M. Cankar, T. Kallio, and A. Kankainen, "Usability testing of mobile applications: a comparison between laboratory and field testing", *J. Usability Stud.,* vol. 1, no. 1, pp. 4-17, 2005.

[12] S. Alvaro, E. Lopez, A. Cabot, L. Marcos, and J. Herraiz, "Identifying Usability Issues in Instant Messaging Apps on iOS and Android Platforms", In: *Mobile Information Systems* vol. 2018. , 2018, p. 19.
[PMID: 2056290]

[13] D. fox, and S. Nidu, *Usability Evaluation of Three Social Networking Sites*. [Online]. Available: https://www.researchgate.net/publication/241642763_Usability_Evaluation_of_Three_Social_Networking _Sites[Accessed Feb 20, 2020].

[14] Anthony, *Solid Vs. Outline Icons: Which Are Faster to Recognize?*. [Online]. Available: https://uxmovement.com/mobile/solid-vs-outline-icons-which-are-faster-to-recognize [Accessed Aug 18 2020].

[15] G. Bhutkar, R. Poovaiah, D. Katre, and S. Karmarkar, "Semiotic analysis combined with usability and ergonomic testing for evaluation of icons in a medical user interface", In: *3rd International Conference on Human-Computer Interaction (India HCI '11)*. Association for Computing Machinery: New York, NY, USA, 2011, pp. 57-67.
[http://dx.doi.org/10.1145/2407796.2407804]

[16] R. Akolkar, and G. Bhutkar, "Usability Evaluation of Tourism Icons in India", In: *Advanced Methodologies and Technologies in Digital Marketing and Entrepreneurship.* IGI Global: CA, 2019, pp. 565-583.
[http://dx.doi.org/10.4018/978-1-5225-7766-9.ch044]

CHAPTER 5

Enhancing Gamified Online Learning User Experience (UX): A Systematic Literature Review of Recent Trends

Abdulsalam S. Mustafa[1,*] and **Kianoosh Karimi**[2]

[1] *College of Graduate Studies, University Tenaga Nasional, Selangor, Malaysia*

[2] *Faculty of Management, University of Tehran, Tehran, Iran*

Abstract: Gamification introduces game elements and game thinking in non-game contexts. Many scholars argue that gamification can potentially be a viable online learning approach to promoting student engagement and learning outcomes in recent years. However, various obstacles impede their practical implementation. As a result, user experience (UX) and user participation may be affected, possibly resulting in high course drop-outs rates. Furthermore, it is unclear which game elements are effective and recognized as the current state-of-the-art gamified online learning research. This study provides a review identifying the game elements introduced in online learning and tested in previous studies from 2017-2020 through a systematic search strategy. By reviewing the literature, we identified the most effective game elements and determined their impact on the learners' user experience. The results show that in 26 of the 34 selected studies, gamified online learning had a significant beneficial effect on user experience, engagement, and completion of courses. Moreover, points, leader boards, levels, badges, and progress bars are the most widely used game elements in the studies. This study's findings may guide the design of more successful gamification interventions for online learning.

Keywords: Adherence, Affordance, Application, Engagement, Education, Game-based, Game elements, Gamification, Gameful design, Innovation, Intervention, Literature review, Motivation, Novelty, Online learning, Platform, Pedagogy, Performance, Technology, User experience.

* **Corresponding author Abdulsalam S. Mustafa:** College of Graduate Studies, University Tenaga Nasional, Selangor, Malaysia; E-mail: abdulsalam.mustafa@nils.gov.ng

Nirmalya Thakur and Parameshachari B.D. (Eds)

INTRODUCTION AND BACKGROUND

In recent decades, the advent of modern technologies such as the high-speed Internet network (5G), cloud computing, the Internet of Things (IoT), and next-generation devices has continued to transform people's lives. This has significantly impacted various domains, such as business, travel, health, and education, and promoted e-learning adoption. The coronavirus (COVID-19) pandemic has created people's need to work and study from home [1]. As a result, we are increasing our over-dependence on information technology in our day-day activities. Education is a crucial area impacted by the pandemic, with about 80 percent of students worldwide affected by COVID-19 [1]. Therefore, classrooms have switched from conventional classrooms to numerous online platforms. Online learning or e-learning relates to utilizing digital technology to provide training and educational resources [2]. Some popular online learning systems include Learning Management Systems (LMS), Moodle, Massive Open Online Courses (MOOC), and Blackboard.

Although online learning institutions have attempted to improve teaching and learning, authors also argue that several online learning systems do not produce the expected results [3, 4]. Essentially, learners' motivation and commitment levels have become a significant hindrance for encouraging online courses' use and completion. Given this, there has been an increase in gamification tools to improve motivation and sustain interest among learners [5]. Gamification is used to modify behaviors in various contexts to achieve behavior outcomes [6]. Education is a critical sector in which gamification is openly explored for its potential to motivate. Hence, it is an essential part of academic performance in an educational setting.

In the specific context of online learning, gamification's impact on user experience (UX) generally relates to motivation and behavioral change [7]. Assuming a user has a poor user experience, they will likely feel discouraged and avoid engaging with the online platform. Although current studies indicate successful gamified interventions, the impact of various game elements on user experience is unclear. Therefore, it is timely to conduct a literature study to establish what we already know thus far and underline multiple future directions. Accordingly, this paper presents a literature review of published works to explain the influential game elements introduced into gamified online learning. The review covers articles published between 2017 and 2020 and their effects on user experience (UX).

The paper is divided into five sections. Section 1 gives a brief overview of gamification and user experience in the education context. Section 2 discusses the current state of gamification in online education and its effect on user experience. Subsequently, Section 3 outlines the review procedure. Next, the results of the analysis are presented in Section 4. Section 5 concludes the article and highlights potential future avenues for research.

GAMIFICATION

Researchers have defined gamification in a multitude of ways. According to Deterding *et al.* [8], gamification uses the game design feature in a non-gaming sense. At the same time, Hamari [9], from a different viewpoint, described gamification as a process of improving a game-like experience-based service to support a user's value. Werbach [10] also took a distinct view of gamification and described it as a process of making tasks more game-like.

Gamification (gamified) is still very much in its early stages and is evolving, dating back to the early twenty-first century. In recent years, several scholars, such as Deterding and colleagues [8], Johnson *et al.* [11], and Landers *et al.* [12], have explored multiple facets of gamification. These facets include design rules [13, 14], psychological and motivational dimensions [15, 16], health and fitness [17 - 19], media [20, 21] and education [22, 23]. As shown in Fig. (**1**), the gamification structured has three layers: mechanics, dynamics, and components [10]. According to the authors [10], mechanics include various behavior and control mechanisms to support interactivity. Dynamics specifies the runtime behavior of the dynamics for inputs and outputs of players over time. Components refer to the specific instantiations of mechanics and dynamics.

HOW GAMIFICATION WORKS

Koepp and colleagues [24] concluded that playing games produce higher dopamine levels in the human brain. The authors also argue that this is correlated with greater motivation, learning, reinforcing current behavior, and focus [24]. They also observed that dopamine generally relates to conditions involving incentives. Typically, rewards or incentives can be either extrinsic or intrinsic and are used to motivate individuals [25]. Extrinsic or tangible rewards include money, goods, discounts, or promotions. Intrinsic or intangible incentives include positive feelings, appreciation, accomplishment, or social interactions [25]. More importantly, extrinsic motivators can produce extrinsic-motivated individuals, encourage non-autotelic behavior, and possibly short-term behavior outcomes [25]. In contrast, intrinsic motivators may lead to hedonic and autotelic behaviors and might be long-term. Hedonic behavior relates to a sense of pleasure, while autotelic involves experiencing a self-contained activity without seeking any potential benefit [26]. In turn, autotelic behaviors engage people entirely (experience a state of flow) and considered the most enjoyable, satisfying, and intense emotional states that individuals experience [27].

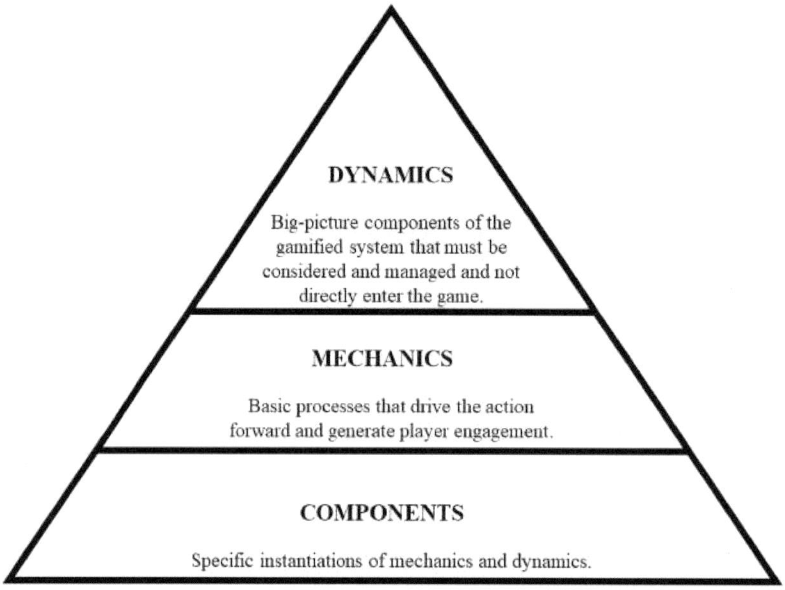

Fig. (1). Classification of game elements [10].

GAMIFIED ONLINE LEARNING

Online learning platforms and web-based apps are becoming increasingly prevalent. Users can access information irrespective of their location [28, 29]. The technological evolution enables more widespread and accessible use of cutting-edge technology. As noted, over 80 percent of students worldwide were affected by the novel COVID-19 [1]. Hence, several academic institutions globally have increased online learning adoption [1], underscoring the value of e-learning. As learning is a continuum, the process requires dedication and motivation to initiate and sustain it. Despite this, some obstacles still exist with the current online learning approach. In particular, one challenge is to sustain the interest of learners and maintain their level of commitment. Given that the popular learning approach is passive and repetitive, users may lose interest and become less involved with time.

Even so, substantial efforts have sought to resolve these challenges through various motivational-based interventions to improve behavioral learning outcomes. Nevertheless, the impact of these interventions was mainly short-term [30]. The novelty effect is another significant problem identified in intervention usage. This phenomenon refers to the initial increase in a novel system's use due to enthusiasm and curiosity [31, 32]. However, studies have observed a decline in user interest overtime after the novelty effect has faded [31, 32]. As a result, this could have a direct effect on student participation and course completion. To this end, a gamification approach could positively affect learning outcomes [6, 30, 33]. Authors have argued that gamification can make a non-game-like task more pleasurable and encourage people to participate in activities while keeping them in a flow state [34, 35]. It follows that, in the specific context of learning and instruction, gamification, similar to games, can be leveraged to promote interaction among learners.

GAMIFICATION AND USER EXPERIENCE (UX)

User experience applies to all forms of end-user engagement with an application or service such as the internet, computer programs, mobile apps, or online platforms [36 - 39]. As identified by [40], user experience has a personal aspect as it deals with the individual's experience and perspective. Users will continue using an app or service if they are satisfied with the user experience and engagement. Ultimately, gamified learning platforms aim to enhance the student learning experience. This can result in improved attendance, engagement, proactiveness, and performance [41].

Literature in the education context shows online learning facilitates active learning, direct feedback, flexibility, study intensity, and easy access to resources [28, 29, 42]. However, if the user does not perceive the application or service as dynamic, challenging, satisfying, or enjoyable, this could negatively affect the user experience [43, 44]. Consequently, a negative user experience may be detrimental to motivation, participation, and continued usage intentions. Similarly, previous studies attest that technology significantly influences students' behavior and their experiences [45]. Thus, it becomes critical to address usability issues throughout the game interface, mechanics, and gameplay [38, 46]. In brief, a successful gamification design enables users to connect with the interface and might encourage them to continue engaging with the system.

The literature shows a few empirical studies on various game elements implemented in the educational context. The results were unclear, making it difficult to conclude the efficacy of these interventions. Simultaneously, some studies show a positive impact of gamification on behavior and performance in the learning environment, while other studies reported negative or neutral effects [40, 41, 47, 48]. Hence, it becomes challenging to successfully deliver a game-based online learning intervention that utilizes user experience to improve student participation and academic performance. Accordingly, the research community needs to investigate further in this context.

RELATED WORKS

As far as gamification analysis in online learning is concerned, evidence [49, 50] shows that this is an under-explored field, and the empirical studies are somewhat lacking. However, several studies explore gamified online educational context [4, 30, 49, 51], research in gamification effects on user experience (UX) in online learning remains limited. This section presents some related studies.

Khalil *et al.* [49] presented one of the few works that systematically reviewed MOOCs' gamification. Their study explored gamification studies in MOOCs, the type of study, hypotheses used, game elements introduced, methods implemented, and the outcomes. Equally important, they highlighted the obstacles encountered by researchers and experts in gamified MOOCs. Their analysis shows that studies on gamification intervention in MOOCs are in their initial stages. Thus, more study involving educational theories is crucial to a deeper understanding of gamification's impact on MOOCs. Urh and colleagues [4] performed a comprehensive study of the gamified framework for higher learning, combining gamification features with e-learning. Their data show that successful integration of gamified e-learning into tertiary education can significantly improve motivation, satisfaction, engagement, and learning.

The experimental research by [51], involving 55 participants, divided into four groups, two experimental and two control study groups, examined gamification's efficacy in an online informatics course. Notably, the gamified course students displayed higher academic performances than those in the non-gamified version. From this perspective, the authors suggest investigating gamified online learning platforms for specific subjects and the effect of certain game elements on motivation and participation. A further relevant study [30] focused on using a meta-analysis approach to assess gamification's impact on psychological, motivational, and behavioral learning outcomes. Their results indicate that gamification, as currently conceptualized in empirical studies, is an effective learning approach. Unfortunately, it fails to identify successful gamification factors, especially in cognitive learning outcomes.

Our analysis aims to examine game elements' effect in gamified online learning on user experience and engagement. In this context, our research questions for this study are:

- What level of education is targeted?
- What topics/subjects are being gamified?
- What combinations of game elements are being implemented?
- What is the influence of Gamification on User Experience (UX)?

REVIEW PROCEDURE

Search Strategy

We comprehensively searched the following databases between June and October 2020: Digital Library, Google Scholar, IEEE Xplore, MDPI, Science Direct, Scopus, Web of Science, and Wiley. The study's primary focus is the gamification of online learning and user experience. We identified relevant literature using the following mixture of search words: "online learning," OR "e-learning," AND "gamify," OR "game *" OR "gamification". Notably, the keywords were retrieved from the paper's metadata (title, abstract, and keywords).

Of the 105 studies reviewed, only 34 met the study criteria. Table **1** provides an overview of the inclusion criteria. We located 82 records *via* database search, with eight additional records from other sources. We then excluded 86 publications that did not meet the inclusion criteria. A forward and backward search identified an additional 15 relevant publications. Overall, the review includes 34 selected articles from 2017 to 2020, as in Table **A1**. This study was conducted and reported in line with the Preferred Reporting Items for Systematic Reviews and Meta-Analyses (PRISMA) Guidelines, illustrated in Fig. (**1**) [52].

Table 1. Study inclusion criteria [6].

1.	The study is available in English.
2.	The study is published on a peer-reviewed platform.
3.	The entire study is available (only the abstract studies are eliminated).
4.	The study applies to the research context: using gamified e-learning platforms to encourage users and improve user experience and user interaction with the system.
5.	The study is empirical, with data obtained from study participants.
6.	The is a clear methodology for the study.

Data Extraction

Following the example of [6], we used a similar approach to structure the analysis of our work in the targeted field. This framework enables us to compare the studies and make firm conclusions [6]. The study focuses on understanding gamification's motivational impact on user experience (UX) in online learning. Accordingly, an intervention is considered effective based on a positive, negative, or neutral (no impact) study outcome. Subsequently, the studies' data include educational level, the academic subject, and the type of gamified learning experience.

Additionally, we included the game elements implemented in the studies. This is because game elements directly influence user experience and engagement [10, 34, 36]. Where possible, we also assessed game elements' effects on student participation and motivation. Our analysis was guided by the following factors: study sample, study length, data collection process, study location, and outcome. The reviewed studies' final framework includes game elements, educational level, academic level, learning activity, study population, study time, data collection, and outcome. Table **A1** illustrates the framework and summary of the articles analyzed.

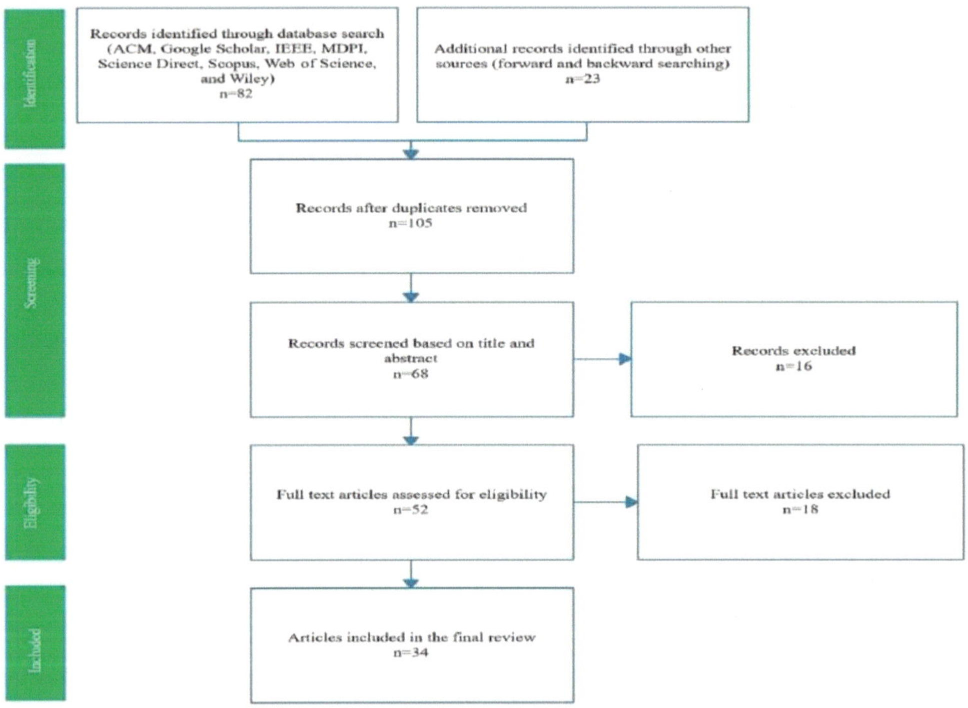

Fig. (2). Flow chart of the literature review process.

ANALYSIS AND RESULTS

The gamification experiments were categorized based on the study sample size, study group number, study period, research location, and the study results. Interestingly, we observed that there is a higher tendency for evidence-based research to use surveys. Moreover, most studies employed experimental or quasi-experimental research designs. These study designs involved two, three, or four study groups: control and experimental groups or gamified and non-gamified groups. Moreover, other studies used a hybrid or mixed-method approach (n=5).

After gathering data from the studies, we then analyzed the type of publications. Fig. (**3**) indicates a higher number of publications in journals (n=23) than in conference proceedings (n=9) and dissertations (n=2). The finding reflects the disparity between the study of [50] on gamification in MOOCs, highlighting that most studies in their analysis were conference proceedings. Next, we identified the number of publications over the time frame (2017-2020), as shown in Fig. (**4**). In detail, we identified seven publications in 2017, fifteen in 2018, eight in 2019, and four in 2020. The drop in the number of publications from 2018 to 2019 is not a clear indication of a lack of academic interest. Besides, since this analysis focus on gamified online learning and user experience, several publications did not meet the inclusion criteria. As such, we excluded them in this analysis. Even then, the literature shows a growing trend in the number of publications incorporating game elements to enhance online learning [50].

The countries in which the studies were carried out was considered in the selected articles. We observed that multiple studies were conducted in USA (n=3), followed by Ecuador (n=2), Croatia (n=2) and Northern Cyprus (n=2). Other study locations include Algeria (n=1), Brazil (n=1), Chile (n=1), Estonia (n=1), Germany (n=1), Greece (n=1), Hong Kong (n=1), New Zealand (n=1), Malaysia (n=1), Mexico (n=1), Lithuania (n=1), Saudi Arabia (n=1), Singapore (n=1), South Korea (n=1), and Turkey (n=1).

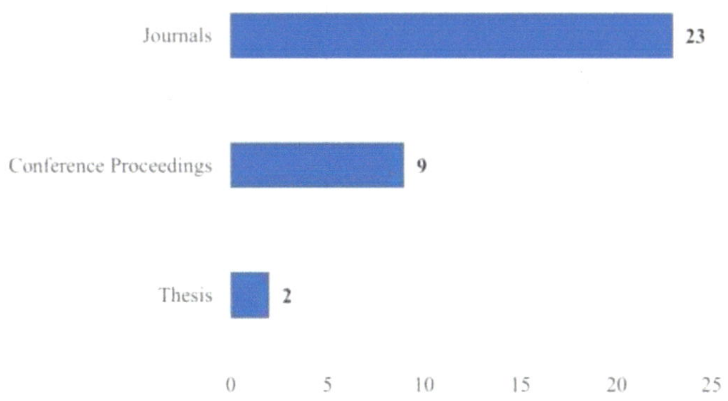

Fig. (3). Types of studies published.

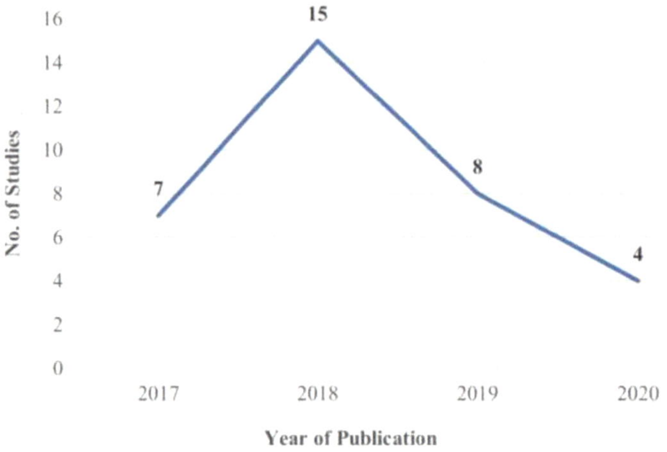

Fig. (4). Timeline of publications.

What Level of Education is Targeted?

Most studies were performed at the university level (23 studies), followed by individual online learning students (7 studies). However, fewer studies were conducted at primary and secondary schools' levels (5 studies). Four studies involved graduate students [59, 65, 66, 73]. Two studies included university instructors [69, 79], and seven studies targeted online learners [55, 57, 58, 60, 62, 67, 75]. Three studies involved secondary school students [64, 76, 82], while two studies targeted primary school students [32, 63]. Besides, one research focused on polytechnic students [54].

These findings provide further evidence that universities' gamification courses are easier to implement as educators can easily incorporate game elements into their specific subjects. Equally, university students are generally more knowledgeable and familiar with online learning. Similarly [6], stated that university students could receive more technical support. Furthermore, university students usually tend to have relevant technical skills to utilize game mechanisms, such as points, badges, and leaderboards (PBL).

What Topics/subjects are being Gamified?

The articles selected gamified several academic courses at different educational levels. For clarity, we grouped these courses into four, including studies with non-specific subjects (Table **2**). Most gamification studies involve several online courses (n=13), followed by computer science and information technology (n=12). Additionally, we identified Mathematics, English, Educational Sciences, Bioinformatics courses in seven engineering studies and MBA in two studies. In line with a previous review [6], we also observed that Information Technology

(IT) courses appear to be much easier to gamify than other subjects. Additionally, IT researchers and experts likely have a better understanding of game design and application.

Generally speaking, the outcome suggests evidence of a rise in the number of online gamified IT courses. Consequently, it may be easier to introduce game elements and novel techniques at various stages of online courses. Another factor could be that the online course platforms are easy to customize. In our analysis, we found that 17 platforms were gamified. The e-learning framework was gamified in nine studies, followed by the LMS model in eight studies. Four studies introduced game-elements in MOOC and flipped learning. Fourteen studies implemented gamified custom platforms. These findings suggest that the e-learning framework and LMS model are likely more adaptive and easier to modify. Some platforms have already embedded similar game features and ideas, making them more compatible with gamification. For example, MOOC platforms such as Coursera, Khan Academy, and Udacity employ game features.

Table 2. Categories of Gamified Online Courses.

Subjects	Number of Studies (%)	Studies
Various Online Courses	13 (38%)	[54, 55, 57 - 60, 64, 67 - 70, 74, 75]
Computer Science and Programming Course	12 (35%)	[53, 56, 62, 66, 79, 77, 71, 73, 78, 81, 83, 85]
Mathematics, English, Educational Science, Biostatistics, MBA	7 (21%)	[32, 61, 63, 72, 79, 80, 82]
Engineering	2 (6%)	[5, 84]

What Combinations of Game Elements are Being Implemented?

In this review, we identified six studies on individual game element's effects. Two studies introduced two game elements, six studies incorporated three game elements, and one research combined four-game elements. As seen in Table **3**, four studies used five-game elements, while the remaining 14 studies used more than five-game elements. A growing number of studies [32, 54] have discovered that gamification's effectiveness is not exclusively based on the number of game elements used but instead on its effects. Indeed, the game elements used in these studies do not always correlate with a positive outcome. Notably, two studies [82, 84] that implemented five-game elements reported neutral outcomes. The first study [82] included points, badges, levels, progress bar, and leader board, while the second study [84] implemented badges, awards, achievements, quest, and experience points. Significantly, two experimental studies involving eleven game elements reported positive [80] and neutral outcomes [58]. Finally, three studies that included badges reported two positive [56, 72] and one adverse [75] effect. Although certain game elements in online learning complement each other, this is not always the case.

Table 3. Combination of game elements in the studies.

Game Elements	Number of Studies (%)	Studies
Leader board only	3 (9%)	[64, 76, 78]
Badges only	3 (9%)	[56, 72, 75]
Point, Leader board	1 (3%)	[54]
Badges, Progress Bar	1 (3%)	[55]
Point, Leader board, Badges	4 (12%)	[59, 68, 70, 71]
Score, Points, Leader board	1 (3%)	[79]
Challenges, Leader board, Badges	1 (3%)	[67]
Points, Leader board, Badges, Levels	1 (3%)	[57]
Points, Badges, Feedback, Challenges, Progress Bar	1 (3%)	[62]
Points, Badges, Levels, Progress Bar, Leader board	1 (3%)	[82]
Badges, Level, Leader board, Virtual Currency, Trading System	1 (3%)	[83]
Badges, Awards, Achievement, Quest, Experience Points	1 (3%)	[84]
Challenges, Leader board, Points, Level, Medal, Unlocking Keys	1 (3%)	[77]
Others (not identified)	2 (6%)	[53, 66]
6 game elements or more	11 (33%)	[32, 58, 60, 61, 63, 65, 69, 73, 74, 80, 85]

We observed that the combination of game elements does not follow a standard criterion. Typically, there is no explanation for the choice of specific game elements in the studies. This suggests that the game design elements implemented in these studies are likely to be selected randomly. It could be generally based on their predominance or based on prior literature. Table **4** illustrates the popular game elements in the reviewed studies. In particular, the seven most commonly used game elements in the studies are Leader board (24 studies), Points (21 studies), Badges (22 studies), Levels (11 studies), Progress Bar (9 studies), Challenges (7 studies), Feedback (7 studies) and Rewards (7 studies).

Indeed, the individual and complementary effects of specific design game elements are not well understood [86]. Even so, evidence shows that gamification's success goes beyond just linking game components to a well-established learning framework [50]. The game elements need to be effectively implemented. Thus, a more detailed study is required to understand better the effects of individual game elements on users' online learning experience and engagement. The game elements need effective implementation. Accordingly, a more detailed study is required to understand better the effects of individual game elements on users' online learning experience and engagement.

Table 4. Most popular game elements in the studies.

Game Elements	Number of Studies (%)	Studies
Leader board	24 (71%)	[32, 54, 57, 59, 61, 63 - 65, 67 - 71, 73, 74, 76 - 83, 85]
Badges	22 (64%)	[55 - 57, 59, 60, 62, 63, 67, 68, 70 - 75, 77, 80 - 85]
Points	21 (62%)	[32, 54, 57, 59 - 63, 65, 68 - 71, 73, 74, 77, 79, 80, 82, 83, 85]
Levels	11 (32%)	[57, 58, 60, 61, 65, 69, 73, 81 - 83, 85]
Progress Bar	9 (26%)	[55, 60, 62, 63, 69, 73, 74, 82, 85]
Challenges	7 (21%)	[61 - 63, 65, 67, 77, 80]
Feedback	7 (21%)	[32, 60 - 62, 80, 85]
Rewards	7 (21%)	[60, 61, 73, 74, 80, 84]

Effectiveness of Gamification on User Experience (UX)?

In gamified online learning, user experience (UX) and interaction are essential to encourage users to continue engaging with the learning platform. For gamification's success in this context, a user experience strategy to promote learning and increase engagement becomes essential. Various online learning platforms demonstrated that gamified online learning could significantly influence students' user experience [60, 63, 65]. However, additional research would help us to confirm this. As illustrated in Tables **3** and **4**, game features such as leaderboard, badges, points, and progress were implemented in the online platforms to improve user experience. The classification of studies following our choice on the reported outcomes' desired accuracy is presented in Table **5**. The data shown in Table **A1** indicates the likelihood of gamification to have a significant beneficial effect on learning outcomes.

Remarkably, of the 34 reviewed studies, 26 (76%) report the beneficial effects of gamification in online learning, while three (9%) show adverse effects. Most empirical works (26 studies) show evidence of positive effects. It underscores gamified online learning's progress towards improving student motivation. This finding, in effect, can also be directly related to improved user experience and engagement.

Our findings do not support previous research in this area. In fact, in contrast with a similar review of [6], we found strong evidence to conclude that gamified online learning offers more positive than adverse effects. Although it might be a rationale to imply that user experience can be improved by simply adding game features to online learning, multiple studies have shown that this is not guaranteed [32, 53, 58, 80, 82]. As a result, there is a need for a novel approach to how game elements can effectively enhance online learners' user experience.

Table 5. Studies based on the outcomes.

Results	Number of Studies (%)	Studies
Positive	26 (76%)	[53, 55 - 57, 59, 60, 62 - 74, 76 - 79, 81, 83, 85]
Negative	3 (9%)	[32, 54, 75]
Inconclusive	5 (15%)	[58, 61, 80, 82, 84]

Table **6** presents five studies found to be inconclusive, with reasons for their inclusion. The authors' assumptions and constraints express this. The rationale for these findings to be inconclusive could be small sample sizes, short duration of the study, non-comparison groups, and limited contexts.

Table 6. Inconclusive studies with rationale for classification.

Study	Reason (data collection/statistical evidence)
[58]	Small sample size (19); Short study period (less than a day).
[61]	Hawthorne effect (biased outcome); No comparison group (non-gamified condition).
[80]	Small sample size (63); Limited context (implemented individual aspect of gamification only).
[82]	Small sample sizes (27+28+21); Limited context (single class).
[84]	Small sample size (41); Limited context (single course implemented).

CONCLUSION

Individuals are encouraged to continue engaging with technologies or services they perceive as interesting, fun, and exciting. Even then, it becomes challenging to adhere to or sustain the usage of technology (app or service). The integration of gamification through game elements into technology could improve the overall user experience and engagement. While this strategy is applied to online learning to enhance user experience and encourage learning, its significant benefits are unclear.

This systematic review analyzed game elements introduced in an online learning context to improve user experience, engagement, and learning outcomes. Of 34 comparative studies, 26 report significant beneficial outcomes. Like [6], we observed an increase in the number of empirical studies on gamification in online learning contexts. Despite the limited number of empirical studies, we found a significant correlation between gamification, student motivation, and user engagement. Our analysis shows that points, leader boards, levels, badges, and progress bars are the most common elements introduced alongside challenges, feedback, and rewards. Thus, while gamification will possibly inspire learning [6, 87], several game elements' integration may not ensure improved academic performance.

There is evidence to suggest that the experimental study design is becoming more widespread in gamification research. Interestingly, 25 studies employed an experimental study design involving gamified and non-gamified groups. This supports the previous finding in the literature [6], highlighting a considerable rise in experimental design for gamification research. Even though our results point to the likelihood that gamification can improve learning experiences [6, 87], there is limited evidence on its long-term impact. Our findings also validate previous studies, attesting that novelty factors can influence gamified interventions over time [34, 35, 88, 89]. In this regard, the beneficial impact of gamification on learning outcomes is, however, not well established.

In brief, our research underlines the importance of gamification's effect on user experience in the online learning context. We have provided further evidence of insufficient empirical evidence to examine gamified online learning's effect on user experience thoroughly. These findings add to the growing body of literature on gamified online learning. The current study was limited because most studies had a small sample size constrained to a single locality. Hence the findings might not represent the larger population. Future randomized controlled trials or experimental studies with a more extensive and more diverse sample population would improve research reliability. Despite the positive outcomes, we found limited evidence of gamification's long-term impact on sustaining learning outcomes. Further longitudinal research help establish the long-term impact of gamification on online learner's user experience and engagement. Also, more rigorous studies will be necessary to evaluate the negative effect of specific game elements on online learners' user experience and engagement. In that case, this will provide a greater understanding of specific game elements to exclude in gamified online learning.

CONSENT FOR PUBLICATION

Not Applicable.

CONFLICT OF INTEREST

The author confirms that this chapter contents have no conflict of interest.

ACKNOWLEDGEMENT

Declared none.

APPENDIX A

Table A1. Study details

Article	Gamified Activity	Game Elements	Sample Size & Demographics	Reported Outcome(s)
[36]	Digital Learning Platform	Competition, Real-time feedback, Individual scores, Other and Group Scores, Individual and Group Performance, Narrative, Collaboration, Leader board, Time Limit	N=54 quasi-experiment 4 group conditions 5 Months Croatia	Inconsistent result. The negative impact in the long term.
[53]	Online Programming Course	Unspecified Game elements	N=201 Gamified and non-gamified groups Two weeks Croatia	Positive effect in the gamified course. A significant beneficial effect on-course experience and user satisfaction.
[54]	Learning Analytics Networked Tutoring System (Learning ANTS)	Point, Leader board	N=67 Experimental Less than one day Singapore	Negative impact on online learning.
[55]	Learning Management System (LMS) Moodle	Badge, Progress Bar	N=32 Mixed Methods 5 Weeks	A significant influence on user satisfaction. The gamified course had a positive effect on student motivation.

(Table A1) cont.....

Article	Gamified Activity	Game Elements	Sample Size & Demographics	Reported Outcome(s)
[56]	Online Learning System	Badges and Meta-badges	N=100 Quasi-experiment pre-test-post-test design 50: Experimental group 50: Control group Six weeks Ecuador	A significant influence on engagement in the gamified group compared to non-gamified.
[57]	Open and Distance Learning (ODL) web	Points, Leader board, Badges, Levels.	N=69 Mixed Methods Turkey	The overall positive effect, especially on leader boards and badges.
[58]	Massive Open Online Courses (MOOCs) Flipped MOOC	Empowerment, Smooth Learning Curves, Communication Channels, Levels, Clues, Goal Indicators, Skills Tree, Guilds, Storytelling, Stimulated Planning.	N=19 Less than one day Estonia	Inconclusive outcome.
[59]	Talen tLMS cloud learning platform (Instructional technology program)	Points, Badges, Leader boards (PBL).	N=47 3 Weeks	A significant beneficial effect on student learning engagement.
[60]	E-learning sites	Avatar, Level, Points, Progress Bar, Rewards, Notification, Mission, Badges.	N=30	Increase motivation and enhance motivation. The majority of participants prefer the reward game element.
[61]	LMS	Objective, Challenge, Feedback, Points, Levels, Reward, Leader board, Platform, Rules, Customise.	N=80 44: Experimental group 36: Control group 16 Weeks	Online gamified activities can have a positive impact. no effect on student engagement
[62]	E-Learning	Points, Badges, Feedback, Challenges, Progress Bar.	N= 175 Experimental and control groups	The learner's motivation increased by 25%, and the drop-out ratio reduced by 26%.
[63]	Pomawin homework App	Challenges, Points, Leader boards, Badges, Achievements, Gifting, Countdown Timer, Progress Bar.	N=53 Mixed methods 2 Weeks	Positive effects with improved students' satisfaction, behavioral intention, and intrinsic motivation.

(Table A1) cont.....

Article	Gamified Activity	Game Elements	Sample Size & Demographics	Reported Outcome(s)
[64]	Minimum Learning Judgement System (Flip Learning)	Leader board	N=30 Pre and post-experiment Seven weeks South Korea	A significant beneficial effect on interest and user experience.
[65]	F-LauReL Teaching forecasting courses	Points, Levels, Challenges, Leader board, Meaningful Story, Time Constraint.	N=261 Experimental Greece	A significant beneficial effect on students' learning performance.
[66]	Online course	Unspecified Game elements.	N=15	Positive influence on the different pleasurable learning experiences.
[67]	MOOC	Challenges, Leader boards, Badges	N=123,124 21 months Mexico	Increased student engagement, course completion, and motivation.
[68]	Zondle platform (Game-based learning website)	Points, Badges, Leader boards (PBL).	N=54 28: Experimental group 26: Control group Eight weeks Malaysia	Positive impact in the experimental group.
[69]	Moodle Gamification Training Platform (MGTP)	Leader board, Bridge, Progress, Points, Level, Chat, Unlocking Content, Completion Tracking	N=375 Three months Northern Cyprus	The gamified platform significantly influenced instructors' participation and behavioral intentions for continued use.
[70]	Peer Wise and Code Write tools	Points, Badges, Leader boards (PBL).	N=6732 Experimental 4 Weeks New Zealand	Badges had a significant impact on engagement. An increase in activity levels and performance.
[71]	A web-based programming learning environment	Points, Badges, Leader board	N=40 Experimental 19: Experimental group 21: Control group Brazil	Significant beneficial effects.
[72]	Online learning environment (admission test)	Badges	N=369 Experimental design Two days	Badges positively influenced engagement.
[73]	LMS Online discussion environment.	Experience Points, Badges, Progress Bars, Level, Leader boards, Award.	N=41 8 Weeks Northern Cyprus	Significant beneficial effect on student engagement.

(Table A1) cont.....

Article	Gamified Activity	Game Elements	Sample Size & Demographics	Reported Outcome(s)
[74]	LMS gEchoLu	Badges, Experience Points, Leader boards, Progress Bar, Reactions, Awards.	N=14 mixed methods design (3 groups) Two months USA	The gamified course had increased user engagement. Significant impact on user experience (more interesting and enjoyable).
[75]	Moodle LMS	Badges	N=159 Experimental (3 groups) 14 Weeks Germany	Badges have a lesser effect on motivation and performance. Over time, students are less intrinsically motivated.
[76]	Moodle LMS	Leader board	N=48 quasi-experimental 23: Gamified group 25: Non-gamified group Saudi Arabia	Significant impact on student completion rates and engagement in the gamified group as compared to the non-gamified group.
[77]	UDPiler Platform	Challenge, Leader board, Points, Medals, Unlocking Keys.	N=817 Quasi-experimental Gamified and non-gamified (3 groups) 4 Months Chile	Overall, moderate effect in the gamified course.
[78]	LMS	Leader board	N=89 quasi experimental Experiment and control Four weeks Ecuador	A significant increase in learning performance.
[79]	E-learning system	Scores, Points, Leader board	N=899 10 Months Algeria	A moderate positive impact on learners' engagement with the system was recorded.
[80]	Wiki spaces open classroom management platform	Challenges, Competitions, Cooperation, Rewards, Feedback, Win States, Achievements, Badges, Gifting, Leader boards, Points.	N=63 quasi-experiment and case study Three groups (21 each group) Six weeks	Positive influence on student's academic achievement. An initial increase in student engagement. No long-term effects were observed.

(Table A1) cont.....

Article	Gamified Activity	Game Elements	Sample Size & Demographics	Reported Outcome(s)
[81]	Gamified Undergraduate Informatic Course	Badges, Level Up, Leader boards, Experience.	N=139 Longitudinal study Ten weeks USA	A significant beneficial effect on learning, achievement, and engagement was observed. A significant influence on user experience (fun and enjoyable).
[82]	Flipped learning	Points, Badges, Levels, Progress Bar, Leader boards.	N=76 Mixed methods 27: Traditional class 28: Gamified flipped 21: Online gamified independent study class Two weeks Hong Kong	Generally inconclusive outcome. A moderate effect of the gamified course on student's achievement and cognitive engagement was observed.
[83]	Moodle Learning Environment	Badges, Levels, Leader board, Virtual Currency, Trading System.	N=172 Experimental 137: Gamified 35: Non-gamified 3 Months Lithuania	There was a considerable improvement in average student scores. A significant influence on user experience and increased intrinsic motivation (fun and interesting).
[84]	Online Course Assessment	Badges, Awards, Achievements, Quest, Experience Points	N=27 Experimental 3 Months USA	No effect on student motivation. Positive effect on user experience (enjoyment).
[85]	Online Learning	Badge, Leader board, Time Constraint, Point, Level, Stages, Feedback, Progress Bar, Competency, Avatar.	N=60 Mixed-Method 30: Gamified group 30: Non-gamified group Malaysia	Significant beneficial effect on motivation and student engagement. All game elements had a positive effect on student's engagement in the gamified group.

REFERENCES

[1] W.C. Chang, and Y. Yano, "How are countries addressing the Covid-19 challenges in education? A snapshot of policy measures", GEM Report. March 2020. [online]. Available from: https://gemreportunesco.wordpress.com/2020/03/24/how-are-countries-addressing-the-covid-19-challenges-in-education-a-snapshot-of-policy-measures/ [Accessed: 10th Oct. 2020].

[2] P. Sun, R.J. Tsai, G. Finger, Y. Chen, and D. Yeh, "What drives a successful e-Learning? An empirical investigation of the critical factors influencing learner satisfaction", *Comput. Educ.,* vol. 50, no. 4, pp. 1183-1202, 2008.
[http://dx.doi.org/10.1016/j.compedu.2006.11.007]

[3] D. Al-Fraihat, M. Joy, and J. Sinclair, "Evaluating E-learning systems success: An empirical study", *Comput. Human Behav.,* vol. 10, pp. 267-286, 2020. [http://dx.doi.org/10.1016/j.chb.2019.08.004]

[4] M. Urh, G. Vukovic, E. Jereb, and R. Pintar, "The model for the introduction of gamification into e-learning in higher education", *Procedia Soc. Behav. Sci.,* vol. 197, no. 25, pp. 388-397, 2015. [http://dx.doi.org/10.1016/j.sbspro.2015.07.154]

[5] R.M. Ryan, and E.L. Deci, "Self-determination theory and the facilitation of intrinsic motivation, social development, and well-being", *Am. Psychol.,* vol. 55, no. 1, pp. 68-78, 2000. [http://dx.doi.org/10.1037/0003-066X.55.1.68] [PMID: 11392867]

[6] D. Dicheva, C. Dichev, G. Agre, and G. Angelova, "Gamification in education: A systematic mapping study", *J. Educ. Technol. Soc.,* vol. 18, no. 3, 2015.

[7] M. Mill, *Changing Users Health Behavior Through Design,* 2017. August 2017. [online]. Available: https://uxdesign.cc/anna-iurchenko-on-changing-users-health-behavior-through-design-fced4dca9be3 [Accessed 18th Oct 2020].

[8] S. Deterding, D. Dixon, R. Khaled, and L. Nacke, "From game design elements to gamefulness", Proc. 15th International Academic MindTrek Conf. Envisioning Future Media Environments (MindTrek 11) [http://dx.doi.org/10.1145/2181037.2181040]

[9] K. Huotari, and J. Hamari, "Defining gamification: a service marketing perspective", In: *Proc. 16th International Academic MindTrek Conference*, 2012, pp. 17-22. [http://dx.doi.org/10.1145/2393132.2393137]

[10] K. Werbach, and D. Hunter, *For the win: How game thinking can revolutionize your business.* Wharton Digital Press: Philadelphia, 2012.

[11] D. Johnson, S. Deterding, K.A. Kuhn, A. Staneva, S. Stoyanov, and L. Hides, "Gamification for health and wellbeing: A systematic review of the literature", *Internet Interv.,* vol. 6, pp. 89-106, 2016. [http://dx.doi.org/10.1016/j.invent.2016.10.002] [PMID: 30135818]

[12] R.N. Landers, K.N. Bauer, and R.C. Callan, "Gamification of task performance with leaderboards: A goal setting experiment", *Comput. Human Behav.,* vol. 71, pp. 508-515, 2017. [http://dx.doi.org/10.1016/j.chb.2015.08.008]

[13] A. Mora, D. Riera, C. Gonzalez, and J. Arnedo-Moreno, "A literature review of gamification design frameworks", In: *7th International Conference on Games and Virtual Worlds for Serious Applications (VS-Games)*, 2015, pp. 1-8. [http://dx.doi.org/10.1109/VS-GAMES.2015.7295760]

[14] D. Aseriskis, and R. Damasevicius, "Gamification patterns for gamification applications", *Procedia Comput. Sci.,* vol. 39, pp. 83-90, 2014. [http://dx.doi.org/10.1016/j.procs.2014.11.013]

[15] K. Karimi, and J. Nickpayam, "Gamification from the viewpoint of motivational theory", *Emerging Science Journal,* vol. 1, no. 1, pp. 34-42, 2017. [http://dx.doi.org/10.28991/esj-2017-01114]

[16] N. Xi, and J. Hamari, "Does gamification satisfy needs? A study on the relationship between gamification features and intrinsic need satisfaction", *Int. J. Inf. Manage.,* vol. 46, pp. 210-221, 2019. [http://dx.doi.org/10.1016/j.ijinfomgt.2018.12.002]

[17] D. Johnson, S. Deterding, K.A. Kuhn, A. Staneva, S. Stoyanov, and L. Hides, "Gamification for health and wellbeing: A systematic review of the literature", *Internet Interv.,* vol. 6, no. 6, pp. 89-106, 2016. [http://dx.doi.org/10.1016/j.invent.2016.10.002] [PMID: 30135818]

[18] K. Huotari, and J. Hamari, "A definition for gamification: anchoring gamification in the service marketing literature", *Electron. Mark.,* vol. 1, no. 27, pp. 21-31, 2017. [http://dx.doi.org/10.1007/s12525-015-0212-z]

[19] J. Koivisto, and J. Hamari, "The rise of motivational information systems: A review of gamification research", *Int. J. Inf. Manage.,* vol. 45, pp. 191-210, 2019. [http://dx.doi.org/10.1016/j.ijinfomgt.2018.10.013]

[20] K. Kianoosh, and S. Salavatian, Audience Engagement as a Competitive Advantage in Public Television: Case of Gamification Use in IRIB IPTV.*Competitiveness in Emerging Markets: Market Dynamics in the Age of Disruptive Technologies.* Springer: Cham, Switzerland, 2018, pp. 391-408.

[21] K. Karimi, and J.G. Ghafari, "The Model of influencing on public-opinion in Cyberspace with the help of Gamification Capabilities", *New Media Studies,* vol. 5, no. 7, pp. 137-172, 2019.

[22] K.R. Christy, and J. Fox, "Leaderboards in a virtual classroom: A test of stereotype threat and social comparison explanations for women's math performance", *Comput. Educ.,* vol. 78, pp. 66-77, 2014. [http://dx.doi.org/10.1016/j.compedu.2014.05.005]

[23] M. Sailer, and M. Sailer, "Gamification of in class activities in flipped classroom lectures", *Br. J. Educ. Technol.,* vol. 52, no. 1, pp. 75-90, 2021. [http://dx.doi.org/10.1111/bjet.12948]

[24] R.M. Ryan, and E.L. Deci, Promoting self-determined school engagement: Motivation, learning, and well-being.*Handbook of Motivation at School.* Routledge: Abingdon, Oxon, 2009, pp. 171-195.

[25] M.J. Koepp, R.N. Gunn, A.D. Lawrence, V.J. Cunningham, A. Dagher, T. Jones, D.J. Brooks, C.J. Bench, and P.M. Grasby, "Evidence for striatal dopamine release during a video game", *Nature,* vol. 393, no. 6682, pp. 266-268, 1998. [http://dx.doi.org/10.1038/30498] [PMID: 9607763]

[26] M. Csikszentmihalyi, *Beyond Boredom and Anxiety.* 2nd ed. Jossey-Bass: San Francisco, 1977.

[27] S. McCallum, "Gamification and serious games for personalized health", In: *9th International Conference on Wearable Micro and Nano Technologies for Personalized Health*, June 26-28, 2012, Amsterdam. IOS Press: Porto, Portugal, 2012.

[28] C. Li, and F. Lalani, "The COVID-19 pandemic has changed education forever. This is how. The World Economic Forum COVID Action Platform", *World Economic Forum.* April 2020. [online]. Available: https://www.weforum.org/agenda/2020/04/coronavirus-education-global-covid19-on-ine-digital-learning/ [Accessed 10th Oct. 2020].

[29] A. Zamfiroiu, and C. Sbora, "Statistical analysis of the behavior for mobile E-learning", *Procedia Econ. Finance,* vol. 10, pp. 237-243, 2014. [http://dx.doi.org/10.1016/S2212-5671(14)00298-6]

[30] M. Sailer, and L. Homner, "The gamification of learning: a meta-analysis", *Educ. Psychol. Rev.,* vol. 32, pp. 77-112, 2020. [http://dx.doi.org/10.1007/s10648-019-09498-w]

[31] J. Hamari, and J. Koivisto, "Working out for likes, An empirical study on social influence in exercise gamification", *Comput. Human Behav.,* vol. 50, pp. 333-347, 2015. [http://dx.doi.org/10.1016/j.chb.2015.04.018]

[32] C.H.H. Tsay, A.K. Kofinas, S.K. Trivedi, and Y. Yang, "Overcoming the novelty effect in online gamified learning systems: An empirical evaluation of student engagement and performance", *J. Comput. Assist. Learn.,* vol. 36, no. 2, pp. 128-146, 2020. [http://dx.doi.org/10.1111/jcal.12385]

[33] L. De-Marcos, A. Dominguez, J. Saenz-de-Navarrete, and C. Pages, "An empirical study comparing gamification and social networking on e-learning", *Comput. Educ.,* vol. 75, pp. 82-91, 2014. [http://dx.doi.org/10.1016/j.compedu.2014.01.012]

[34] G. Zichermann, and C. Cunningham, *Gamification By Design: Implementing Game Mechanics in Web and Mobile apps.* O'Reilly Media: Sebastopol, 2011.

[35] R.N. Landers, "Developing a theory of gamified learning: Linking serious games and gamification of

learning", *Simul. Gaming,* vol. 45, no. 6, pp. 752-768, 2014. [http://dx.doi.org/10.1177/1046878114563660]

[36] T. Jagust, B. Ivica, and S. Hyo-Jeong, "Examining competitive, collaborative and adaptive gamification in young learners' math learning", *Comput. Educ.,* vol. 125, pp. 444-457, 2018. [http://dx.doi.org/10.1016/j.compedu.2018.06.022]

[37] N. Thakur, and C.Y. Han, "An Ambient Intelligence-Based Human Behavior Monitoring Framework for Ubiquitous Environments", *Journal of Information,* vol. 12, no. 2, p. 81, 2021. [http://dx.doi.org/10.3390/info12020081]

[38] G.A. Alkawsi, A.S. Norashikin Ali, Mustafa Y. Baashar, H. Alhussian, A. Alkahtani, S. K. Tiong, and J. Ekanayake, "A hybrid SEM-neural network method for identifying acceptance factors of the smart meters in Malaysia: Challenges perspective", *Alex. Eng. J.,* vol. 60, no. 1, pp. 227-240, 2021. [http://dx.doi.org/10.1016/j.aej.2020.07.002]

[39] N. Thakur, and C.Y. Han, "Methodology for Forecasting User Experience for Smart and Assisted Living in Affect Aware Systems", In: *Proceedings of the 8th International Conference on the Internet of Things (IoT)*, Oct. 15-18, 2018, Santa Barbara, California, 2018. [http://dx.doi.org/10.1145/3277593.3277630]

[40] J. Nielsen, "How many test users in a usability study?", *Nielsen Norman Group.* June 2012. [online]. Available: https://www.nngroup.com/articles/how-many-test-users/ [Accessed 5th Oct 2020].

[41] A. Dominguez, J. Saenz-De-Navarrete, L. De-Marcos, L. Fernandez-Sanz, and C. Pages, *Comput. Educ.,* vol. 63, pp. 380-392, 2013. [http://dx.doi.org/10.1016/j.compedu.2012.12.020]

[42] A. Seifert, A. Schlomann, C. Rietz, and H.R. Schelling, "The use of mobile devices for physical activity tracking in older adults' everyday life", *Digit. Health,* vol. 3, p. 2055207617740088, 2017. [http://dx.doi.org/10.1177/2055207617740088] [PMID: 29942617]

[43] Y.Y. Ng, C.W. Khong, and H. Thwaites, "A review of affective design towards video games", *Procedia Soc. Behav. Sci.,* vol. 51, pp. 687-691, 2012. [http://dx.doi.org/10.1016/j.sbspro.2012.08.225]

[44] J.R. Pagulayan, K. Keeker, D. Wixon, R.L. Romero, and T. Fuller, User-centered design in games.*Handbook for Human-Computer Interaction in Interactive Systems.* Lawrence Erlbaum Associates: New Jersey, 2002, pp. 1-28.

[45] P. Harpur, and M.R. De Villiers, "MUUX-E, a framework of criteria for evaluating the usability, user experience and educational features of m-learning environments", *South African Computer Journal,* vol. 56, no. 1, pp. 1-21, 2015. [http://dx.doi.org/10.18489/sacj.v56i1.240]

[46] M.A. Federoff, "Heuristics and usability guidelines for the creation and evaluation of fun in video games", *Ph.D. thesis,* Indiana University: Bloomington, Indiana, USA, 2002.

[47] S. O'Donovan, J. Gain, and P. Marais, "A case study in the gamification of a university-level games development course", In: *South African Institute for Computer Scientists and Information Technologists Conference*, October 7-9, East London, South Africa. Association for Computing Machinery: New York, 2013.

[48] M. Lister, "Gamification: The effect on student motivation and performance at the post-secondary level", *Issues and Trends in Educational Technology,* vol. 3, no. 2, 2015. [http://dx.doi.org/10.2458/azu_itet_v3i2_lister]

[49] M. Khalil, J. Wong, B. de Koning, M. Ebner, and F. Paas, "Gamification in MOOCs: A Review of the State of the Art", In: *2018 IEEE Global Engineering Education Conference (EDUCON)*, 2018, pp. 1629-1638. [http://dx.doi.org/10.1109/EDUCON.2018.8363430]

[50] N.F. Abu Bakar, A.F. Yusof, N.A. Iahad, and N. Ahmad, "The implementation of gamification in

massive open online courses (MOOC) platform", In: *International Conference on User Science and Engineering*, 2018, pp. 183-193. [http://dx.doi.org/10.1007/978-981-13-1628-9_17]

[51] D. Strmecki, A. Bernik, and D. Radosevic, "Gamification in e-learning: Introducing gamified design elements into e-learning systems", *J. Comput. Sci.,* vol. 11, no. 12, pp. 1108-1117, 2015. [http://dx.doi.org/10.3844/jcssp.2015.1108.1117]

[52] D. Moher, A. Liberati, J. Tetzlaff, and D.G. Altman, PRISMA Group, "Preferred reporting items for systematic reviews and meta-analyses: the PRISMA statement", *Int. J. Surg.,* vol. 8, no. 5, pp. 336-341, 2010. [http://dx.doi.org/10.1016/j.ijsu.2010.02.007] [PMID: 20171303]

[53] A. Bernik, G. Bubas, and D. Radosevic, "Measurement of the effects of e-learning courses gamification on motivation and satisfaction of students", In: *41st International Convention on Information and Communication Technology, Electronics and Microelectronics (MIPRO)*, May 21-25, 2018, Opatija, Croatia, 2018. [http://dx.doi.org/10.23919/MIPRO.2018.8400149]

[54] E. Chan, F. Fui-Hoon Nah, Q. Liu, and Z. Lu, "Effect of gamification on intrinsic motivation", In: *4th International Conference on HCI in Business, Government, and Organizations*, July 9-14, Vancouver, Canada. Springer: Cham, 2018.

[55] M.E. Ortiz Rojas, K. Chiluiza, and M. Valcke, "Gamification in computer programming: Effects on learning, engagement, self-efficacy and intrinsic motivation", In: *11th European Conference on Game-Based Learning (ECGBL)*, October 5-6, 2017, Graz, Austria, 2017.

[56] K. Bovermann, J. Weidlich, and T. Bastiaens, "Online learning readiness and attitudes towards gaming in gamified online learning–a mixed-methods case study", *International Journal of Educational Technology in Higher Education,* vol. 15, no. 1, pp. 1-17, 2018. [http://dx.doi.org/10.1186/s41239-018-0107-0]

[57] R. Klemke, M. Eradze, and A. Antonaci, "The flipped MOOC: using gamification and learning analytics in MOOC design-a conceptual approach", *Educ. Sci. (Basel),* vol. 8, no. 1, pp. 1-13, 2018. [http://dx.doi.org/10.3390/educsci8010025]

[58] C.H. Aydin, and M. Sumer, "Integrating Gamification into Online Learning Sites", In: *Annual Convention of the Association for Educational Communications and Technology Kansas City*, USA, 2018.

[59] D. Alabbasi, "Exploring Graduate Students, Perspectives towards Using Gamification Techniques in Online Learning", *Turk. Online J. Distance Educ.,* vol. 18, no. 3, pp. 180-196, 2017. [http://dx.doi.org/10.17718/tojde.328951]

[60] S.N.M. Mohamad, S. Salam, and N. Bakar, "An analysis of gamification elements in online learning to enhance learning engagement", In: *6th International Conference of Computing and Informatics (ICOCI2017)*, Selangor: Malaysia, 2017.

[61] C. Chen, C. Huang, M. Gribbins, and K. Swan, "Gamify Online Courses with Tools Built into Your Learning Management System (LMS) to Enhance Self-Determined and Active Learning", *Online Learning,* vol. 22, no. 3, pp. 41-54, 2018. [http://dx.doi.org/10.24059/olj.v22i3.1466]

[62] M.A. Hassan, U. Habiba, F. Majeed, and M. Shoaib, "Adaptive gamification in e-learning based on students' learning styles", *Interact. Learn. Environ.,* no. Mar, pp. 1-21, 2019. [http://dx.doi.org/10.1080/10494820.2019.1588745]

[63] A.H.S. Metwally, A.M.F. Yousef, and Y. Wang, "Investigating the effects of gamifying homework on students' perceived satisfaction, behavioral intention, and intrinsic motivation,", *GamiFIN,* pp. 47-57, 2019.

[64] J. Jo, H. Jun, and H. Lim, "A comparative study on gamification of the flipped classroom in

engineering education to enhance the effects of learning", *Comput. Appl. Eng. Educ.,* vol. 26, no. 5, pp. 1626-1640, 2018.
[http://dx.doi.org/10.1002/cae.21992]

[65] N.Z. Legaki, N. Xi, J. Hamari, and V. Assimakopoulos, "Gamification of the future: an experiment on gamifying education of forecasting", In: *52nd Hawaii International Conference on System Sciences*, October 8-11, 2019, Honolulu. University of Hawaii at Manoa: Hawaii, USA, 2019.
[http://dx.doi.org/10.24251/HICSS.2019.219]

[66] S. Abu-Dawood, and T. Tyler-Wood, *Graduate Students' Perceptions Toward Educational Gamification in Online Learning Environments: Society for Information Technology & Teacher Education International Conference*, March 26-30, 2018, San Antonio: USA. Association for the Advancement of Computing in Education (AACE): Waynesville, 2018.

[67] L.M. Romero-Rodriguez, M.S. Ramirez-Montoya, and J.R.V. Gonzalez, "Gamification in MOOCs: Engagement application test in energy sustainability courses", *IEEE Access,* vol. 7, pp. 32093-32101, 2019.
[http://dx.doi.org/10.1109/ACCESS.2019.2903230]

[68] M. Sanmugam, Effects of Gamification on Achievement, Engagement and Intrinsic Motivation among Students of Different Player Traits in Science Learning, 2017.

[69] V. Z., "Vanduhe, M. Nat, and H. F. Hasan, "Continuance Intentions to Use Gamification for Training in Higher Education: Integrating the Technology Acceptance Model (TAM), Social Motivation, and Task Technology Fit (TTF)", *IEEE Access,* vol. 8, pp. 21473-21484, 2020.
[http://dx.doi.org/10.1109/ACCESS.2020.2966179]

[70] P. Denny, "On Using Gamification to Effectively Influence Student Activity in Online Learning Environments", *Ph.D. thesis, University of Auckland, Auckland, New Zealand,* 2017.

[71] R. Smiderle, S.J. Rigo, L.B. Marques, J.A.P. Coelho, and P.A. Jaques, "The impact of gamification on students' learning, engagement and behavior based on their personality traits", *Smart Learning Environments,* vol. 7, no. 1, pp. 1-11, 2020.
[http://dx.doi.org/10.1186/s40561-019-0098-x]

[72] H. Imran, "Evaluation of awarding badges on Student's engagement in Gamified e-learning systems", *Smart Learning Environments,* vol. 6, no. 1, pp. 1-12, 2019.
[http://dx.doi.org/10.1186/s40561-019-0093-2]

[73] H.F. Hasan, M. Nat, and V.Z. Vanduhe, "Gamified collaborative environment in Moodle", *IEEE Access,* vol. 7, pp. 89833-89844, 2019.
[http://dx.doi.org/10.1109/ACCESS.2019.2926622]

[74] L. Ding, E. Er, and M. Orey, "An exploratory study of student engagement in gamified online discussions", *Comput. Educ.,* vol. 120, pp. 213-226, 2018.
[http://dx.doi.org/10.1016/j.compedu.2018.02.007]

[75] E. Kyewski, and N.C. Kramer, "To gamify or not to gamify? An experimental field study of the influence of badges on motivation, activity, and performance in an online learning course", *Comput. Educ.,* vol. 118, pp. 25-37, 2018.
[http://dx.doi.org/10.1016/j.compedu.2017.11.006]

[76] K.M. Almotairi, A. Salha, and M. Meccawy, "The effect of gamification on students engagement: A preliminary study", In: *GamiFIN Conference*, Levi: Finland, 2020.

[77] B. Marin, J. Frez, J. Cruz-Lemus, and M. Genero, "An empirical investigation on the benefits of gamification in programming courses", *ACM Transactions on Computing Education,* vol. 19, no. 1, pp. 1-22, 2018. [TOCE].
[http://dx.doi.org/10.1145/3231709]

[78] M. Ortiz Rojas, K. Chiluiza, and M. Valcke, "Gamification through leaderboards: An empirical study in engineering education", *Comput. Appl. Eng. Educ.,* vol. 27, no. 4, pp. 777-788, 2019.

[http://dx.doi.org/10.1002/cae.12116]

[79] I. Bouchrika, N. Harrati, V. Wanick, and G. Wills, "Exploring the impact of gamification on student engagement and involvement with e-learning systems", *Interact. Learn. Environ.,* no. Jun, pp. 1-14, 2019. [http://dx.doi.org/10.1080/10494820.2019.1623267]

[80] N. Ozdener, "Gamification for enhancing Web 2.0 based educational activities: The case of pre-service grade school teachers using educational Wiki pages", *Telemat. Inform.,* vol. 35, no. 3, pp. 564-578, 2018. [http://dx.doi.org/10.1016/j.tele.2017.04.003]

[81] K. Davis, H. Sridharan, L. Koepke, S. Singh, and R. Boiko, "Learning and engagement in a gamified course: Investigating the effects of student characteristics", *J. Comput. Assist. Learn.,* vol. 34, no. 5, pp. 492-503, 2018. [http://dx.doi.org/10.1111/jcal.12254]

[82] C.K. Lo, and K.F. Hew, "A comparison of flipped learning with gamification, traditional learning, and online independent study: the effects on students' mathematics achievement and cognitive engagement", *Interact. Learn. Environ.,* vol. 28, no. 4, pp. 464-481, 2020. [http://dx.doi.org/10.1080/10494820.2018.1541910]

[83] M. Jurgelaitis, L. Ceponiene, J. Ceponis, and V. Drungilas, "Implementing gamification in a university level UML modeling course: A case study", *Comput. Appl. Eng. Educ.,* vol. 27, no. 2, pp. 332-343, 2019. [http://dx.doi.org/10.1002/cae.22077]

[84] B. Butler, and C. Bodnar, "Establishing the Impact that Gamified Homework Portals Can Have on Students' Academic Motivation", In: *2017 ASEE Annual Conference & Exposition*, Columbus: Ohio, 2017. [http://dx.doi.org/10.18260/1-2--28295]

[85] F.L. Khaleel, N.S. Ashaari, and T.S.M.T. Wook, "The impact of gamification on students learning engagement", *Iran. J. Electr. Comput. Eng.,* vol. 10, no. 5, pp. 4965-4972, 2020. [http://dx.doi.org/10.11591/ijece.v10i5.pp4965-4972]

[86] M. Sailer, J.U. Hense, S.K. Mayr, and H. Mandl, "How gamification motivates: An experimental study of the effects of specific game design elements on psychological need satisfaction", *Comput. Human Behav.,* vol. 69, pp. 371-380, 2017. [http://dx.doi.org/10.1016/j.chb.2016.12.033]

[87] J. Chang, and H. Wei, "Exploring engaging gamification mechanics in massive online open courses", *J. Educ. Technol. Soc.,* vol. 19, no. 2, pp. 177-203, 2016.

[88] A.L. Gremaud, L.J. Carr, J.E. Simmering, N.J. Evans, J.F. Cremer, A.M. Segre, L.A. Polgreen, and P.M. Polgreen, "Gamifying accelerometer use increases physical activity levels of sedentary office workers", *J. Am. Heart Assoc.,* vol. 7, no. 13, pp. 1-13, 2018. [http://dx.doi.org/10.1161/JAHA.117.007735] [PMID: 29967221]

[89] M.D. Hanus, and J. Fox, "Assessing the effects of gamification in the classroom: A longitudinal study on intrinsic motivation, social comparison, satisfaction, effort, and academic performance", *Comput. Educ.,* vol. 80, pp. 152-161, 2015. [http://dx.doi.org/10.1016/j.compedu.2014.08.019]

CHAPTER 6

Applications of HCI in Health Care for Diagnosis of Rheumatoid Arthritis

G.S. Mate[1], **A.K. Kureshi**[1] and **A.N. Banubakode**[1,*]

[1] *JSPM's Rajarshi Shahu College of Engineering, Pune, MMANTC, Malegaon, MET Institute of Computer Science Bandra(W), Mumbai, Maharashtra, India*

Abstract: The human-computer interaction (HCI) is a discipline concerned with the design, evaluation, and implementation of interactive computing systems for human use and the study of major phenomena in the health care system. There is a growing demand for healthcare, and this necessitates the development of healthcare technology. Digital technologies are now playing a major role in delivering healthcare and individuals' health and well-being management experiences. The use of digital technology like digital x-ray and computer interface-based applications makes many tasks easy for doctors and humans. These computer interface system saves time with most accurate results as compared to humans. For health care systems, a computer-developed application is used to save time. It was also used to disseminate doctors' efficiency for critical tasks, which made it easy by computer interface such as diagnosis of a critical disease like rheumatoid arthritis. This research is based on computer applications and their doctors' usage to correct Rhemutoidarthrits in an early stage. This research aims to use the software and identify if it is currently being used to enhance or upgrade the level of diagnosis system for doctors using deep learning methods. The Research analysis of the software is performed by collecting digital x-ray image data. The results of the research share the network-wise details of software for the diagnosis of Rheumatoid arthritis.

Keywords: Abnormal, Automatic Detection, Computer System, Convolutional network, Convolution, Deep Learning, Digital x-ray, Features, Full Connected, Gabor Filter, HCI Design, Human-Computer, Image Preprocessing, Normal, Neural Network, Prediction, Pooling, Rectified, Rheumatoid arthritis, Segmentation.

* **Corresponding author A.N. Banubakode:** JSPM's Rajarshi Shahu College of Engineering, Sr. No 80 New Pune Mumbai Highway, Tathawade, Pune-411033, Maharashtra, India; Tel.: +91 9822 3339 70;
E-mail: gsmate_it@jspmrscoe.edu.in

Nirmalya Thakur and Parameshachari B.D. (Eds)

INTRODUCTION

The implementation of intelligent technologies such as the Internet of Things (IoT) and cloud computing present prospects for advancements in the production of healthcare devices [1]. Along with other sectors, advancements in technology have changed healthcare through electronic health records (EHRs), digital images, wireless sensors, and access to internet information.

Increasing numbers of people own mobile devices from which they access the Internet. Rheumatology and other clinical specialties need to adapt to this changing environment, taking up opportunities that emerge from better digital data and information. As rheumatoid arthritis (R.A.) remains a cornerstone of rheumatology practice, we review these advances in technology and their-opportunities with an R.A. focus.

However, like all new technologies, their introduction adds a learning burden and cognitive load for both patients and healthcare providers (HCPs). Human-computer interaction (HCI) design aims to find solutions to such critical and chronic disease problems. HCI in mobile health (mHealth) devices is a crucial process in the interpretation of health data and dissemination of health services, as it shapes the connection between these devices and both the patients and HCPs

BACKGROUND

The various imaging technologies were studied to evaluate the severity of the disease. But a limitation exists in all the current technologies. The assessment of multiple joints with magnetic resonance imaging (MRI) is time-consuming and too expensive for routine use [2, 3].

For decades, X-ray images have been used to help detect R.A. and monitor bone damage progression [4 - 9]. In early R.A., however, X-rays may appear normal although the disease is active – making the films useful as a baseline but not much help in getting a timely diagnosis and treatment.

Enter modern imaging techniques, including ultrasound and magnetic resonance imaging (MRI), which can reveal early, non-bony signs of R.A. that are invisible on X-ray.

"Both MRI and ultrasound are more sensitive at detecting bone erosion than X-ray. Also, they reveal inflammation, which we could not see directly before and had to rely on blood tests and to use our fingers to feel the joints," says rheumatologist Philip Conaghan, professor of musculoskeletal medicine at the University of Leeds.

That capability has become increasingly important in developing ways to slow the R.A. disease process before severe bone and joint damage occurs, using disease-modifying antirheumatic drugs (DMARDs), including biologics.

Both ultrasound and MRI can detect inflammation of the lining of the joints and tendon abnormalities. Also, MRI detects increased fluid (edema) areas in the bone marrow that is a predictor for bony erosions. While musculoskeletal MRI is quite expensive and requires an experienced radiologist to read, rheumatologists often have access to power Doppler ultrasound in their offices – used most frequently to guide joint aspirations and injections. Many rheumatologists can add ultrasound to their physical exam. Still, quantifiable measures of what distinguishes R.A. from routine ultrasound (or how many joints need to be examined) have been lacking. Fig. (**1**) shows the different existing methods for detecting the R.A.

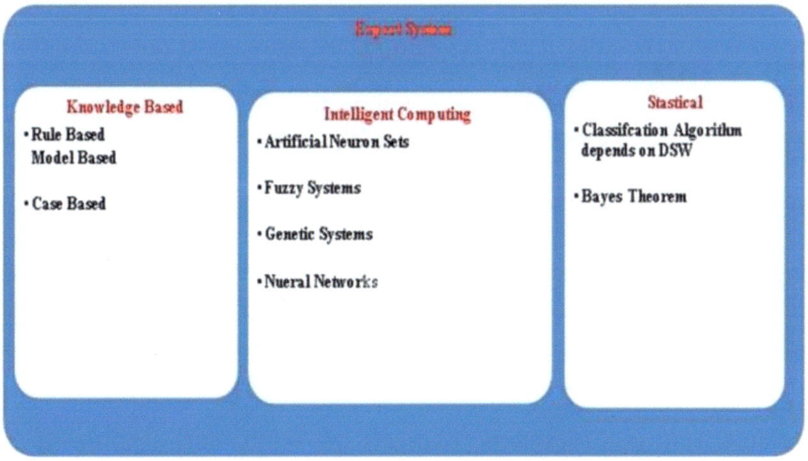

Fig. (1). Existing Different Methods for detecting Rheumatoid Arthritis.

In research presented at the American College of Rheumatology (ACR) annual meeting in November 2012, researchers from Brazil looked at how ultrasound measurements are taken in small, medium, and large joints that could help physicians diagnose R.A. For most joints, they were able to quantify a level of change that distinguished R.A. patients from controls. However, useful ultrasound is not a solo diagnostic test for rheumatoid arthritis.

Patients are typically referred to a rheumatologist by their primary care physician if R.A. is suspected. Rheumatologists use several symptoms and blood tests to determine if R.A. is present. Rheumatologists routinely order radiographs (X-Rays) to help with the diagnosis and record disease progression. Radiographs of the hands and feet have been used consistently for the past half-century to evaluate R.A. disease and the degree of progression [10]. Table **1** shows accuracy by traditional methods for all these approaches.

Table 1. Accuracy by traditional methods.

Type of Input image	Algorithm	Accuracy
Hand x-ray	DTCWT based watershed algorithm	92.9
Hand X-ray	A joint space detection algorithm	96
Hand x-ray	shape LLM	95
Hand Knee x-ray	Backpropagation	82
Hand Knee x-ray	Perception	71

COMPARATIVE STUDY OF EXISTING LITERATURE

HCI: DEFINITION AND CATEGORIZATION

Today, machine learning provides computers with the ability to learn from labeled examples and observations of data and adapt when exposed to new data instead of being explicitly programmed for each task. Researchers are developing computer programs [11, 12] to build models that detect patterns, draw connections, and make predictions from data to construct informed decisions about what to do next. HCI or interaction between humans and machines (HMI) is the syncretic science of computer science, architecture, behavioral science, A.I., and a variety of other topics.

On the primary level, it includes the research of ways and design of new technologies to (better) promote the computers as useful tools. In contrast, on the higher level, it includes the research of intelligent technologies that will adopt the natural ways of interaction between humans and computers, thereby boosting the cause for the computers to become more harmonious as partners. HCI was first used in 1976 [4], and it got famous in the book, The Psychology of Human-Computer Interaction published in 1983 [5]. In 1992, an HCI curriculum was developed by Hewett and other leading HCI educators to serve the needs of the HCI community [6]. In CES 2008, Bill Gates emphasized the role of natural user interface and predicted that how HCI will bring a radical change in the next few years. After that, HCI researchers expounded the definition of a natural HCI by employing different approaches [7 - 9].

In the end, why a system is built can be determined by what the system can do, *i.e.*, how the system's functions can help accomplish the purpose of the system. The functionality of a system is defined by the set of actions or services it provides to its users. Fig. (**2**) shows the transformation of the HCI and Machine Learning Model over the years.

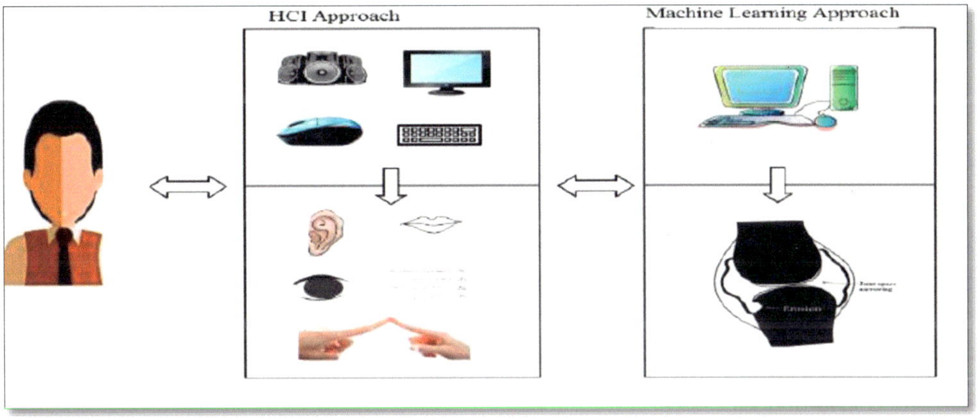

Fig. (2). The Transformation of HCI and Machine Learning Model.

HUMAN-COMPUTER INTERACTION FOR THE R.A. DISABLED

People with disabilities [13, 14] will get enormous benefits from computer assistance. Simply put, technology will increase their contribution to the environment. It is a rich research field with ongoing efforts to develop stable and user-friendly interfaces. These works [15 - 19] target various groups of people with vision, hearing, cognitive and physical disabilities, and the elderly. Standard input devices for general-purpose computers are the keyboard and mouse. Mastering these devices requires fine motor skills and practice. A usability challenge for patients with R.A. is dexterity, movement restriction due to deformities and pain [20].

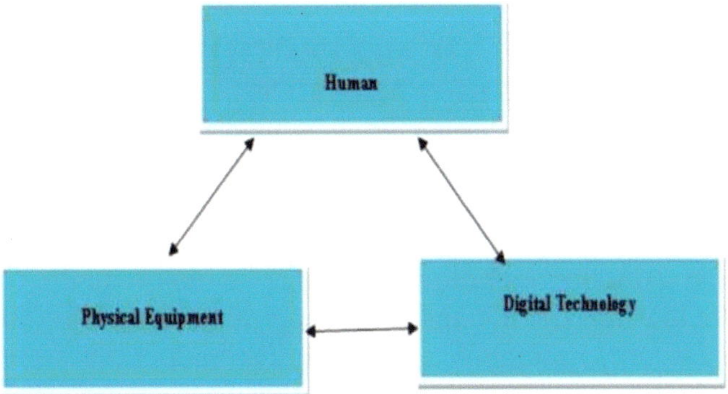

Fig. (3). The relationship between Computers and Physical Devices.

Human hands are complex anatomical structures able to perform delicate motor tasks as well as robust grasping. We need them for day-to-day activities. Most people take them for granted until disaster strikes (*i.e.*, they lose them, or they get diseased). For R.A. patients, losing abilities due to pain and deformities is a reality.

Human hands are complex anatomical structures able to perform delicate motor tasks as well as robust grasping. We need them for day-to-day activities. Most people take them for granted until disaster strikes (*i.e.*, they lose them, or they get diseased). For R.A. patients, losing abilities due to pain and deformities is a reality. To make an impact on the patients' perception of the disease and how treatment choices will impact them, we propose to use a computerized system to classify the hand x-ray images R.A. To do that, we dive into computer graphics and look at current work to classify radiographs to detect the hands correctly automatically. Fig. (**3**) shows the relationship between Computers and Physical Devices.

HCI DESIGN METHODS FOR DETECTING R.A.

The HCI design for devices is complicated by the need for a large variety of interaction modes to support different user roles, tasks, and workflows, the unique features of a healthcare environment for detecting R.A. patients and system functions for multi-threaded, dynamic physiological data collection, which require secure, fast and real-time transmission, reception, storage, and display that are compliant with healthcare frameworks. Designers need to strike a balance between the goal of providing a smooth-running data acquisition platform. Fig. (**4**) shows the user interaction of the proposed system, where the input hand X-ray images are collected from the hospital, and the resolution digital image is 2000pixels×2000pixels.

METHODOLOGY IN AUTOMATIC DETECTION OF HAND X-RAY JOINTS USING HUMAN-CENTERED MACHINE

Preprocessing

Pre-processing is the main step in image analysis that performs image enhancement and noise reduction techniques to improve image quality. The image is enhanced by improving fine details and removing noise from the image. In the rheumatoid arthritis system, enhancement and noise reduction techniques are implemented, producing the best possible results. The enhancement will lead to more prominent edges, and a sharp image such as the tumor noise is obtained will reduce the blurring effect of the image. The original image is resized with 100X100. Error for processing the hand x-ray image is detected, and the same is removed. Fig. (**5**) shows the GUI of the system. It provides six buttons for Training, Input Image, Segmentation, Extract ROI, Gabor filter, Prediction

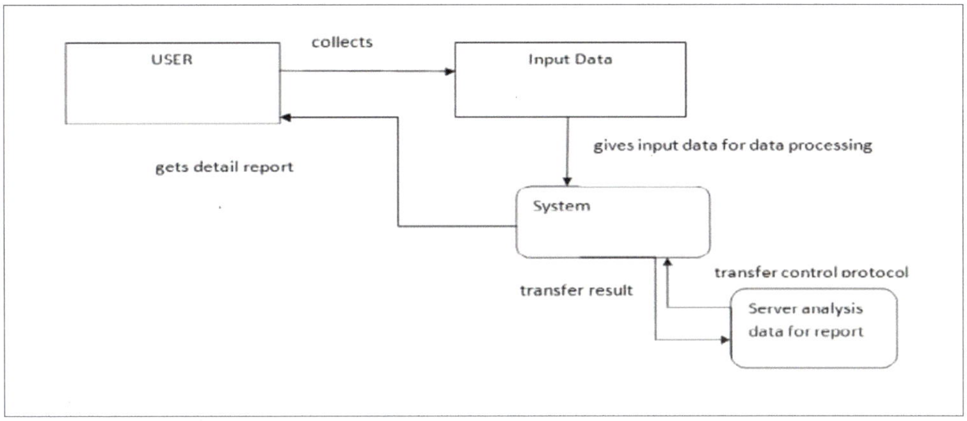

Fig. (4). User Interaction of the Proposed System.

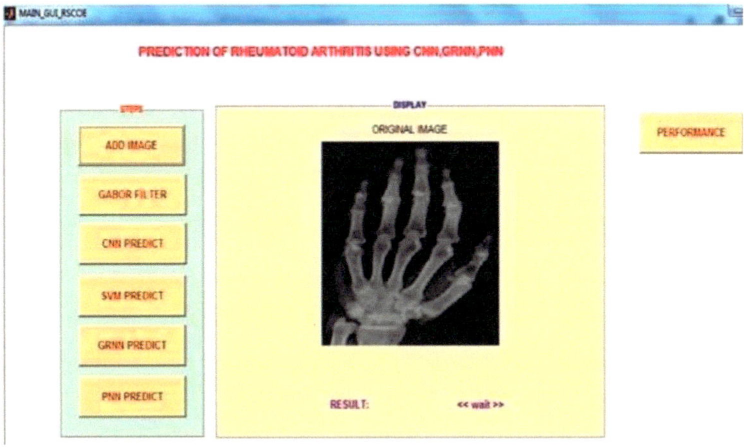

Fig. (5). System Graphical User Interface.

Segmentation

Image segmentation divides the image into homogeneous regions that correspond to different objects in the picture. The image is divided into meaningful areas. The image is segmented using fundamental image features such as intensity, edge, or texture.

Feature Extraction

The extraction of features, shown in Fig. (**6**), is used to extract specific features from preprocessed images of various abnormal categories. This technique removes the high level of components required to classify the targets. Elements are items that are unique in size, shape, composition, location, *etc*. The extraction of features is an essential step in building any classification of patterns and aims to extract the relevant information that characterizes every class. Gabor filter [7] is used to locate the joint position. For 2D signals such as images, the Gaussian kernel's standard deviation depends on the spatial frequency. Φ is the orientation. (x, y) The filter relative to the input signal Gabor filter can be viewed in Equation **1**.

$$g(x,y,\theta,\emptyset) = exp\frac{(-x^2+y^2)}{\sigma^2}.exp\,(2\pi\theta\sqrt{-1}(x\cos\emptyset+y\sin\emptyset)) \quad (1)$$

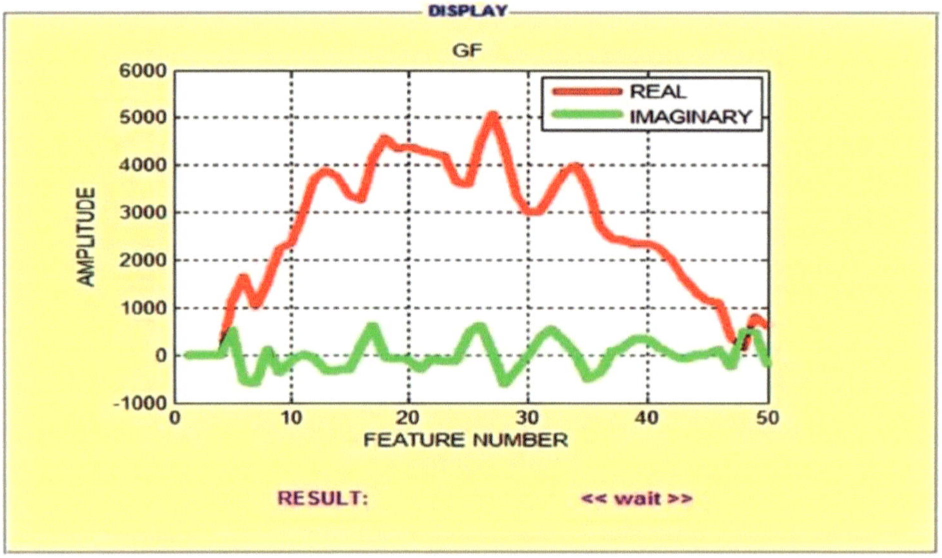

Fig. (6). Feature Extraction from the data.

Prediction

For predicting the class of images, Convolutional Neural Networks have been used. Here, CNN is implemented with convolutional, Pooling, Relu, and Full connected layer. A convolutional neural organization can have tens or many layers that each figure out to identify various picture highlights.

Channels are applied to each preparation picture at multiple goals, and the yield of each convolved image is utilized as the contribution to the following layer. The tracks can begin as essential highlights, for example, brilliance and edges, and increment in multifaceted nature to highlights that interestingly characterize the article. Like other neural organizations, a CNN is made from an information layer, a yield layer, and many concealed layers in the middle.

Feature Learning, Layers, and Classification

These layers perform activities that change the information with the goal of learning highlights explicit to the data. Three of the most well-known layers are convolution, initiation or ReLU, and pooling. Convolution gets the information pictures through many convolutional channels, which initiates specific highlights from the pictures. Rectified straight unit (ReLU) considers quicker and more effective preparation by planning negative qualities to zero and keeping up certain attributes.

This is once alluded to as actuation because lone, enacted highlights are conveyed in the following layer. Pooling rearranges the yield by performing nonlinear down sampling, lessening the number of boundaries that the organization needs to learn. Fig. (**7**) shows the normal and abnormal images of the hand. Fig. (**8**) shows part of an image to be processed, and Fig. (**9**) shows the result of image prediction as normal and abnormal.

Feature /Pattern of Image

This is the selection of one of the filters. Similarly, CNN selects different such filters. Fig. (**10**) outlines the original and contour image selected for testing, and the output of the number of epochs is shown in Fig. (**11**).

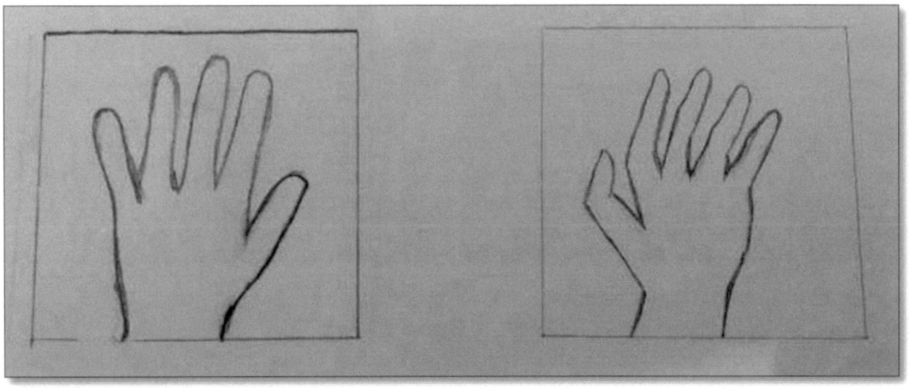

Fig. (7). Normal image Abnormal image.

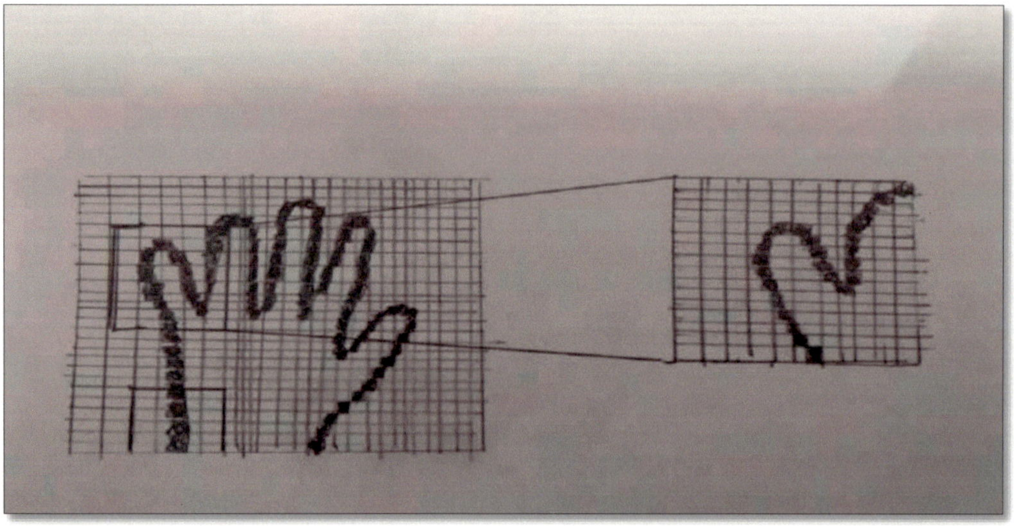

Fig. (8). Part of the image to be processed.

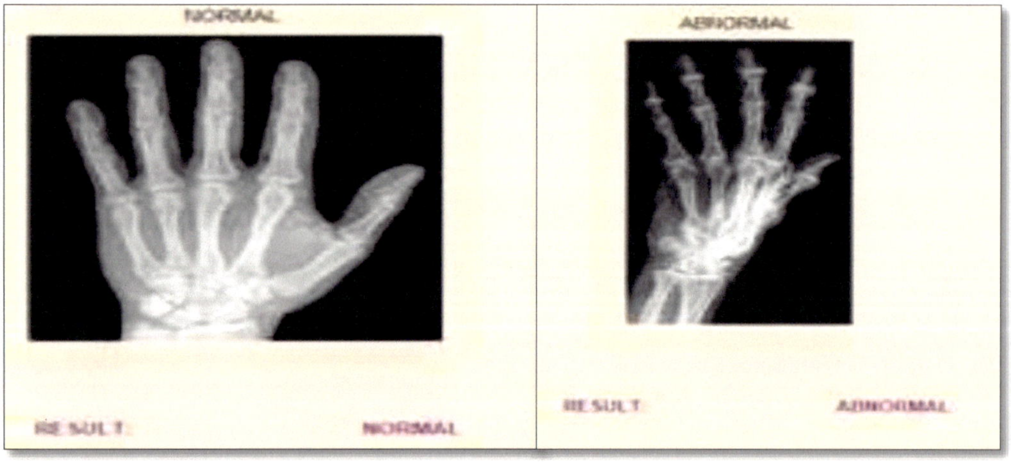

Fig. (9). Result of Image Prediction as Normal and Abnormal.

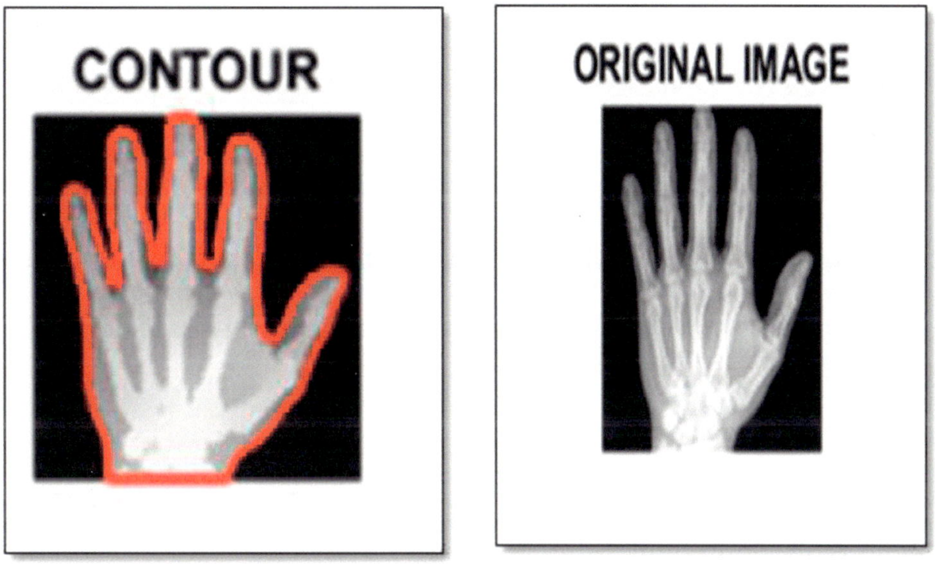

Fig. (10). a) Original Image selected for Testing b) Contour.

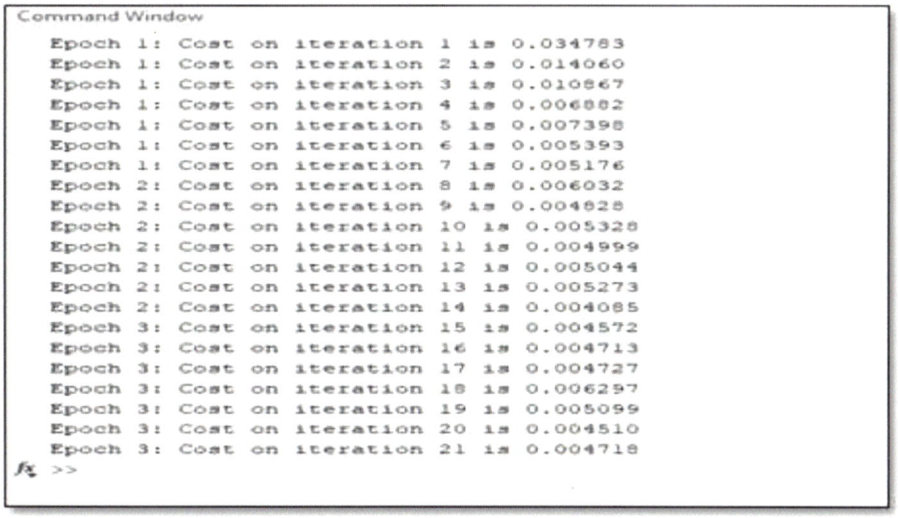

```
Command Window
   Epoch 1: Cost on iteration 1 is 0.034783
   Epoch 1: Cost on iteration 2 is 0.014060
   Epoch 1: Cost on iteration 3 is 0.010867
   Epoch 1: Cost on iteration 4 is 0.006882
   Epoch 1: Cost on iteration 5 is 0.007398
   Epoch 1: Cost on iteration 6 is 0.005393
   Epoch 1: Cost on iteration 7 is 0.005176
   Epoch 2: Cost on iteration 8 is 0.006032
   Epoch 2: Cost on iteration 9 is 0.004828
   Epoch 2: Cost on iteration 10 is 0.005328
   Epoch 2: Cost on iteration 11 is 0.004999
   Epoch 2: Cost on iteration 12 is 0.005044
   Epoch 2: Cost on iteration 13 is 0.005273
   Epoch 2: Cost on iteration 14 is 0.004085
   Epoch 3: Cost on iteration 15 is 0.004572
   Epoch 3: Cost on iteration 16 is 0.004713
   Epoch 3: Cost on iteration 17 is 0.004727
   Epoch 3: Cost on iteration 18 is 0.006297
   Epoch 3: Cost on iteration 19 is 0.005099
   Epoch 3: Cost on iteration 20 is 0.004510
   Epoch 3: Cost on iteration 21 is 0.004718
fx >>
```

Fig. (11). Output of Number of Epochs.

CONCLUDING REMARKS

Including an HCI approach in developing an automatic detection system for Rheumatoid arthritis is critical because good HCI design enhances both the usability and usefulness of the system. HCI design proposed should be delivered with a user-centered design approach and is most effectively supported by the system thinking of a windowing information architecture, consisting of an application with a user-centered approach. This proposed system is designed to develop an intelligent approach to detect rheumatoid arthritis of the hand using image processing techniques and a convolution neural network. The method comprises two main phases. The image processing phase is the first stage in which images are processed using image processing. These techniques include preprocessing, image segmentation, and feature extraction using the Gabor filter. In the second phase, the extracted features being used as inputs for the neural convolution network, which classifies the hand images as normal or abnormal (arthritic). Classification is carried out based on the CNN algorithm, which involves the training of the network with normal and abnormal hand images. The system model accuracy of 94.46%.

FUTURE SCOPE

In this research, we have discussed CNN model in the prediction of hand x-ray for Rheumatoid arthritis. In the future, a more complex model can be implemented, such as Densenet, to improve the recognition rate and increase the accuracy.

CONSENT FOR PUBLICATION

Not Applicable.

CONFLICT OF INTEREST

The authors confirm that this chapter contents have no conflict of interest.

ACKNOWLEDGEMENTS

The authors would like to express appreciation to Dr. Kureshi, A.K. Director, Maulana Mukhtar Ahmad Nadvi Technical Campus, and Malegaon. Dr. S.C. Pati, Dean Research, Rajarshi Shahu College of Engineering, Pune, for their valuable inputs and assistance while carrying out this research.

REFERENCES

[1] C. Doukas, and I. Maglogiannis, "Bringing IoT and cloud computing towards pervasive healthcare", In: *2012 Sixth International Conference on Innovative Mobile and Internet Services in Ubiquitous Computing*, 2012, pp. 922-926. [http://dx.doi.org/10.1109/IMIS.2012.26]

[2] M. Hassanalieragh, "Health monitoring and management using internet-of-things (IoT) sensing with cloud-based processing: Opportunities and challenges", In: *2015 IEEE International Conference on Services Computing*, 2015, pp. 285-292. [http://dx.doi.org/10.1109/SCC.2015.47]

[3] M. Backhaus, T. Kamradt, D. Sandrock, D. Loreck, J. Fritz, K.J. Wolf, H. Raber, B. Hamm, G.R. Burmester, and M. Bollow, "Arthritis of the finger joints: a comprehensive approach comparing conventional radiography, scintigraphy, ultrasound, and contrast-enhanced magnetic resonance imaging", *Arthritis Rheum.,* vol. 42, no. 6, pp. 1232-1245, 1999.

[http://dx.doi.org/10.1002/1529-0131(199906)42:6<1232::AID-ANR21>3.0.CO;2-3] [PMID: 10366117]

[4] B. Martínez-Pérez, I. de la Torre-Díez, and M. López-Coronado, "Mobile health applications for the most prevalent conditions by the World Health Organization: review and analysis", *J. Med. Internet Res.,* vol. 15, no. 6, p. e120, 2013.
[http://dx.doi.org/10.2196/jmir.2600] [PMID: 23770578]

[5] J.H. Carlisle, "Evaluating the impact of office automation on top management communication," "Evaluating the impact of office automation on top management communication",
[http://dx.doi.org/10.1145/1499799.1499885]

[6] S.K. Card, T.P. Moran, and A. Newell, "The keystroke-level model for user performance time with interactive systems", *Commun. ACM,* vol. 23, no. 7, pp. 396-410, 1980.
[http://dx.doi.org/10.1145/358886.358895]

[7] T. Hewett, *ACM SIGCHI Curricula for Human-Computer Interaction.* Association for Computing Machinery, 1992.
[http://dx.doi.org/10.1145/2594128]

[8] G. D'Amico, A. Del Bimbo, F. Dini, L. Landucci, and N. Torpei, Natural Human–Computer Interaction.*Multimedia Interaction and Intelligent User Interfaces.* Springer London: London, 2010, pp. 85-106.
[http://dx.doi.org/10.1007/978-1-84996-507-1_4]

[9] S. Liu, H. Wang, H. Wu, J. Xiong, H. Chen, and J. Zhu, "A model for natural human-computer interaction based on semiotic triangle", *Sci. Sin. Inf.,* vol. 48, no. 4, pp. 466-474, 2018.
[http://dx.doi.org/10.1360/N112017-00214]

[10] K. Kaarela, and H. Kautiainen, "Continuous progression of radiological destruction in seropositive rheumatoid arthritis", *J. Rheumatol.,* vol. 24, no. 7, pp. 1285-1287, 1997.
[PMID: 9228126]

[11] G. Langs, P. Peloschek, H. Bischof, and F. Kainberger, "Automatic quantification of joint space narrowing and erosions in rheumatoid arthritis", *IEEE Trans. Med. Imaging,* vol. 28, no. 1, pp. 151-164, 2009.
[http://dx.doi.org/10.1109/TMI.2008.2004401] [PMID: 19116197]

[12] R. van 't Klooster, E.A. Hendriks, I. Watt, M. Kloppenburg, J.H.C. Reiber, and B.C. Stoel, "Automatic quantification of osteoarthritis in hand radiographs: validation of a new method to measure joint space width", *Osteoarthritis Cartilage,* vol. 16, no. 1, pp. 18-25, 2008.
[http://dx.doi.org/10.1016/j.joca.2007.05.015] [PMID: 17631389]

[13] A. Bielecki, M. Korkosz, and B. Zieliński, "Hand radiographs preprocessing, image representation in the finger regions and joint space width measurements for image interpretation", *Pattern Recognit.,* vol. 41, no. 12, pp. 3786-3798, 2008.
[http://dx.doi.org/10.1016/j.patcog.2008.05.032]

[14] S. Anam, E. Uchino, H. Misawa, and N. Suetake, "Automatic bone boundary detection in hand radiographs by using modified level set method and diffusion filter",
[http://dx.doi.org/10.1109/IWCIA.2013.6624782]

[15] K.K. Leung, M. Holden, N. Saeed, K.J. Brooks, J.B. Buckton, A.A. Williams, S.P. Campbell, K. Changani, D.G. Reid, Y. Zhao, M. Wilde, D. Rueckert, J.V. Hajnal, and D.L. Hill, "Automatic quantification of changes in bone in serial MR images of joints", *IEEE Trans. Med. Imaging,* vol. 25, no. 12, pp. 1617-1626, 2006.
[http://dx.doi.org/10.1109/TMI.2006.884216] [PMID: 17167996]

[16] A. Krizhevsky, I. Sutskever, and G.E. Hinton, "ImageNet classification with deep convolutional neural networks", *Commun. ACM,* vol. 60, no. 6, pp. 84-90, 2017.
[http://dx.doi.org/10.1145/3065386]

[17] S.E. Grigorescu, N. Petkov, and P. Kruizinga, "Comparison of texture features based on Gabor filters", *IEEE Trans. Image Process.,* vol. 11, no. 10, pp. 1160-1167, 2002. [http://dx.doi.org/10.1109/TIP.2002.804262] [PMID: 18249688]

[18] Y. Huo, K.L. Vincken, M.A. Viergever, and F.P. Lafeber, "Automatic joint detection in rheumatoid arthritis hand radiographs", [http://dx.doi.org/10.1109/ISBI.2013.6556428]

[19] K.G. Bhavyashree, "Determination and analysis of arthritis using digital image processing techniques", Iraj.in. [Online]. Available: http://www.iraj.in/journal/journal_file/journal_pdf/1-80-140965751746-49.pdf [Accessed: 10-Ma--2021]

[20] S. Murakami, K. Hatano, J. Tan, H. Kim, and T. Aoki, "Automatic identification of bone erosions in rheumatoid arthritis from hand radiographs based on deep convolutional neural network", *Multimedia Tools Appl.,* vol. 77, no. 9, pp. 10921-10937, 2018. [http://dx.doi.org/10.1007/s11042-017-5449-4]

CHAPTER 7

Optimization Techniques in ANN for Assessing Meteorological Droughts in Dhaka and Chittagong, Bangladesh

M. Hussain[1] and **S.K. Park**[1,*]

[1] *Department of Climate & Energy Systems Engineering, ELTEC College of Engineering, Ewha Woman's University, Seoul, Republic of Korea*

Abstract: Bangladesh significantly depends on seasonal and annual rainfall for agriculture. Yet, there are flash or regional floods and droughts affecting human-lives, properties, and crops that urge low-cost but accurate warning systems in meeting sustainable developments. The paper aims to predict rainfall in Bangladesh by incorporating the Artificial Neural Network with optimizations based on climatology. The study-site is focused on metropolitans: Dhaka (capital) and Chittagong (port) cities and compared with historical evolutions. The experiments include data mining and a statistical approach for trend analyses before modeling. The observation data, *i.e.*, 24-hr accumulated rainfall (mm), is obtained from Bangladesh Meteorological Department (1989 to 2014) and Ogimet (1999 to 2018). September is a neutral and transitional month from monsoon to winter to evaluate drought scenarios. Additionally, in Matlab R2018b, Nonlinear Autoregressive with external input (NARX) is tested with several optimization techniques: Levenberg-Marquardt (LM), Bayesian Regularization (BR), and Scaled-Conjugate Gradient. ANN models show that Chittagong has more rainfall than Dhaka supporting climatological statistics. Specifically, forecasts for Dhaka are 25%, 21%, and 22%, and Chittagong 31%, 30%, and 8%, respectively, using LM, BR, and SCG. The iterations for Chittagong 12, 201, and 10 and Dhaka are 5, 12, and 47, respectively, by LM, BR, and SCG. The results suggest rainfall probabilities in September about 20 to 30% of annual events. The study, particularly for Chittagong in ANN, refers to computational resources and time that are significant to test sensitivities before building a meteorological disaster management tool.

Keywords: Agriculture, Artificial intelligence, Bangladesh, Bayesian Regularization, Computation, Conjugate gradient, Climatology, Development, Economy, Levenberg-Marquardt, Meteorological Droughts, Metropolitans, NARX, Neural Network, Optimization, Prediction, Rainfall, Sustainability.

* **Corresponding author Seon Ki Park:** Hydro-Meteorology Laboratory, Department of Climate & Energy Systems Engineering, Ewha Woman's University, Seoul, South Korea; E-mail: spark@ewha.ac.kr

Nirmalya Thakur and Parameshachari B.D. (Eds)

INTRODUCTION

The 21st century aims to provide comfortable and advanced lifestyles *via* eco-friendly infrastructure and green technology. These developments are leading to the growth of the smart city, smart environment, and disaster management. The role of green infrastructures is also to meet sustainable development goals (SDGs). Various researches illustrate the application of the internet of things (IoT) in developing greener cities, safer environments, and better observations.

For instance, an optimized algorithm using long short-term memory (LSTM) was applied to detect changes in Land-use and Land-cover (LULC) for better environmental management [1]. This modeling system will reduce environmental degradation and secure animal habitats. In other words, IoT application enhances green technology for progressing smart environments. Another current research developed an algorithm to monitor, track, and analyze human behavior (among elderly people) for providing safe healthcare [2]. This study shows that smart city improves lifestyles while continuing the development of applications in information technology. For meeting SDGs, a smart environment is also necessary for better disaster management.

Meteorological disasters, both floods and droughts, have significant impacts on human lives and the environment. Besides economic losses, humans and environmental diversity also suffer from these disastrous effects. Both SDGs and smart city-environment, smart disaster management is growing around the globe. Besides, the government of Bangladesh (GoB) focuses on various actions to enhance smart countries' economic growth and lifestyles. As GoB also declares a slogan "Digital Bangladesh" and SDGs, this initiative shows how Bangladesh aims to enter smart management systems. Eventually, disaster management can boost up using smart technology to save property damages and human losses. In this chapter, the development of a smart meteorological disaster management system is given in the context of Bangladesh.

Rainfall is important for evaluating irrigational costs in an agro-based economy and water infrastructure development and management. Bangladesh, a developing country, significantly depends on rain-fed rivers and groundwater storage for practicing agriculture. However, the country experiences regional and flash floods that frequently affect human-lives, property-damages, and agricultural-products. Furthermore, Bangladesh is a lowland and deltaic country. *Trans*-boundary Mountains with India, Myanmar, and Bhutan complicate the geographical location. Specifically, three major rivers, such as the Ganges, Brahmaputra, and

Meghna, connect to more than 450 channels, rivers, tributaries, streams, and canals around the country flowing to the Bay of Bengal (BoB) and Indian Ocean (IO).

Bangladesh Bureau of Statistics (BBS) states that yearly average rainfall is received 191 and 125 (mm) in 2015 and 2016, respectively comparing from 1981 to 2016 climate data. The variations in season are also found about 210 with 80% relative humidity (RH) in post-monsoon, whereas pre-monsoon, monsoon, winter are 453, 1733, and 44, respectively [3]. This rainfall amount shows how Bangladesh faces floods in the rainy season and droughts in the dry season. Annual rainfall significantly varies in Southeast about 275 and 184 (Chittagong and Teknaf), Southwest about 144 and 185 (Khulna and Sundarbans), Central about 160 and 114 (Dhaka), North about 177 and 180 (Bogra and Rajshahi), Northeast about 269 and 358 (Sylhet and Srimongol) regions in 2015 and 2016 respectively [3]. Station observations signify local situations and their diversity, equally important to note for agricultural and industrial water demands.

In addition to geographical locations, the capital and port city expand to accommodate huge populations for job markets, education, and health- care. The urbanizations and land-use changes eventually have impacts on water storage [4]. For instance, concrete roads and infrastructures poorly support rainfalls to infiltrate recharging the groundwater. This causes metropolitans to experience flash and regional floods along with insufficient warning systems. Since water does not recharge well during monsoon (quick drainages), the groundwater table significantly reduces as over-extraction supports urban lifestyles [4]. Moreover, Bangladesh has sparse observations (only 34 stations), which makes it challenging to forecasting. However, artificial intelligence (AI), mostly machine learning (ML) techniques, can study meteorological variables to efficiently address these challenges.

Investigations of historical evolutions are significant for metropolitans to find any correlation to rainfall climatology and meteorological disasters. Several studies found that backpropagation neural networks (BPNN) are popular in forecasting weather variables like temperature and rainfall. For example [5], found 98% forecasting accuracy for 2001 to 2013 data. A study in [6] showed 99.79% (train) and 94.28% (test) for 1901 to 2000, *i.e.,* 2/3 and 1/3 data used, respectively [7]. concluded the root mean square error (RMSE) of 8.14 and 8.28 respectively for the train: 2005-2009 and for the test: 2010-2014 datasets. Finally [8], performed sensitivity tests for various BPNN and found model E outperformed by yielding a 96.72% efficiency index with 0.71 RMSE. These AI and ML offer a platform for testing Bangladesh rainfall cases.

In the context of a delta, recent developments in artificial neural networks (ANN) provide a possibility for improving rainfall forecasts as a tool in meteorological disaster management. Due to chaotic behaviors in the atmosphere, precipitation forecast is a challenging and computationally expensive task in physics-based numerical weather prediction (NWP) in the tropics. For NWP, sparse observations in tropical regions also weakly validate local predictions. Considering both conditions, AI applications need to test and optimize in estimating weather conditions in tropical regions. Therefore, nonlinear time-series ANN is modeled to predict rainfall and tested optimization techniques for a future [smart] disaster management tool in Bangladesh. The chapter highlights as study-site, data and experimental methodology, results and discussions, and follows by concluding remarks.

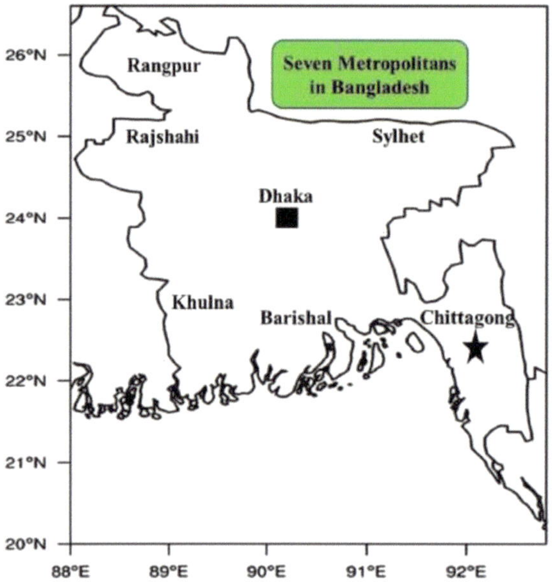

Fig. (1). Study sites: Dhaka (capital, rectangle) and Chittagong (Port, star) Metropolitans, Bangladesh. Modified from [9].

STUDY SITE

The study-site is selected for the biggest metropolitans: Dhaka (capital) and Chittagong (coastal) in Bangladesh (shown in Fig. **1**). Along with the geographical characteristics, the climate in the two cities is easily distinguishable. Moreover, population growth and expansion in these cities are prominently changing over the last few decades. Dhaka (division) is the center city supporting major economic development. It offers extended employments, education, and healthcare. Dhaka (district) is also a hub for businesses and industries, leading to increased population density. Similarly, Chittagong (division) is also recently increasing and expanding. Fig. (**2**) proves how populations significantly increase in both megacities. Though Chittagong district seems lower in population, the port city equally supports large populations and their livelihoods.

Precisely, population growth in Dhaka (district) is exponentially larger than in Chittagong (district) in 2016. These graphs underline how metropolitans in Bangladesh are overcrowded.

The growing population has significantly increased the urban area (UA) in the last few decades. Fig. (**3**) indicates how UA has been extended in both metropolitans since the 1990s. The brown-colored areas in Fig. (**3a**) and red-colored zone in Fig. (**3b**) represent respectively for Dhaka and Chittagong divisions. To note, more than 13 million people live in Dhaka within 1464 sq. km in 2016 [10]. The population density and UA exhaust natural resources such as groundwater and river bodies. The other land-uses changes are also given in Fig. (**3**), where notable transformations are water bodies, forests, agriculture, and rural spaces. The imbalances in UA by industrialized infrastructures hinder natural processes. These eventually threats due to extreme weather events such as flash and regional floods and poor drainage systems in cities.

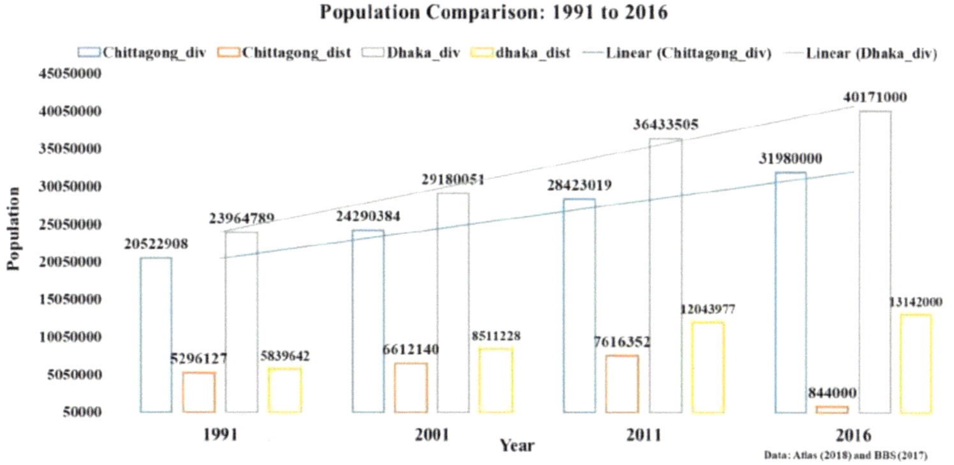

Fig. (2). Population growth in Dhaka and Chittagong Metropolitans, Bangladesh.

Densely populated and extended UA has water demands for various purposes such as drinking water, agricultural, and industrial activities. Bangladesh depends upon rain-fed groundwater recharges and rivers, whereas metropolitans struggle to meet the growing demands. Meanwhile, Bangladesh receives most rainfalls during pre-monsoon and monsoon [3]. These torrential rains flood (regional and flash) in the regions and flow later in the BoB due to its deltaic situations. Yet, post-monsoon and winter record limited rainfall that suffers water scarcity, mostly in agricultural sectors and UA. The above analysis shows how population and UA vary from rural areas, cities, and agro-industrial areas to metropolitans with natural disasters such as floods and droughts. Among these, the key input is rainfall that plays a significant role in water demands and disaster management.

EXPERIMENTAL METHODLOGY

The experiments include data mining by statistical approaches for climatological trends before applying ANN. For both regions (see Fig. **1**), 24-hr accumulated (daily) rainfall (mm) is obtained from Bangladesh Meteorological Department (BMD) and Ogimet, respectively, for 1989 to 2014 and 2015 to 2018. Missing data of Chittagong stations are in 2003, 2005, 2007, and 2013 filling with Ogimet. Ogimet is an open-access source and is found at http://ogimet.com/. The data accessed from Ogimet in 2018. For reducing noises, data normalization is performed by Eq. (1).

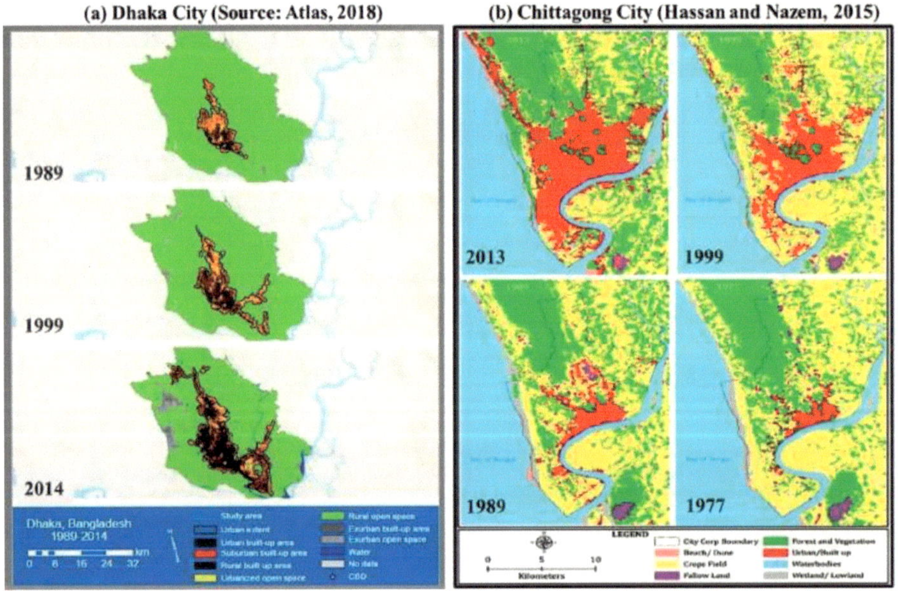

Fig. (3). Metropolitans expansions: (a) Dhaka and (b) Chittagong in Bangladesh. Taken from (a) in [10] and (b) in [11].

Then daily data is averaged for monthly rainfall in September. One can argue for choosing this month. To answer this, after the monsoon, *i.e.,* extreme downpours, September is a transition month to (1) post-monsoon just before (2) winter. After the monsoon, metropolitans and cities might revive from (3) monsoon. However, the question is raised if the monsoon is sufficiently recharging and meeting water demands for metropolitans. As post-monsoon receives relatively lower than other seasonal rainfalls, metropolitans with large populations and UA have many impacts on water scarcity/flood during dry seasons.

The equation for Normalization is from [6]

$$X' = (Xmax - Xmin) * (X - 0.1)/0.8 + Xmin \quad (1)$$

As precipitation is an input for groundwater, water bodies, and UA management, accurate predictions of rainfall events are significant in meteorological disaster management. Climatological analyses are also a part of data pre-processing for applying ML techniques. For predicting rainfall, ANN time-series are tested and examined for optimization techniques (OT). The experimental methodology is summarized in Table **1**. Nonlinear Auto-Regressive with exogenous (NARX) input is well known for a linear system incorporated with additive noises for modeling.

Table 1. Detailed Summary: data information and experimental design.

Data: Rainfall (September)	**Periods**	**Sources**
Stations: Dhaka & Chittagong	1989-2014	BMD
Stations: Dhaka & Chittagong	2015-2018	Ogimet
Missing Values: Chittagong	2003, 05, 07, 13	Ogimet
ANN: NARX (Matlab 2018b)	**IC: Random**	**Experiments**
Hidden Layer (1: 10)	**Time Delay: 2**	**Epoch: 1000**
Levenberg-Marquardt (LM)	Train	630 (75%)
Bayesian Regularization (BR)	Test	135 (15%)
Scaled Conjugate Gradient (SCG)	Prediction	135 (15%)

These are similar characteristics of nonlinear interactions in the atmosphere. Though NARX is regressed to map nonlinear systems, the model's stability is established within nonlinear black-box models [12]. In neural networking, NARX is a recurrent dynamic network, *i.e.,* output feeding back to the input that encloses layers of networks. In Matlab, NARX is formulated based on linear auto-regressive exogenous (ARX) for time-series modeling as discussions and applications are found in [13] and [12].

Optimization techniques (OT) are applied for minimizing any error from chaotic rainfall behaviors. Moreover, initial conditions (IC) in NARX are random division (shown in Table **1**). These might be uncertainties in modeling. Thus, sensitivity tests are important for better prediction accuracy. Fig. (**4**) generalizes the ANN and OT workflow in Matlab. Each OT trains the NARX and stops calculations while meeting a set of conditions. For instance, Levenberg-Marquardt (LM) solves overdetermined systems of nonlinear equations in least-square errors requiring more memories but less computational time [14]. Detailed explanations for LM are given in [15]. Bayesian Regularization (BR) is similar to LM techniques. However, this algorithm might require more time in calculations for limited and nonlinear datasets [16]. Mathematical explanations for BR are discussed in [17] and ANN utilizations in [18]. Scaled Conjugate Gradient (SCG) is a backpropagation algorithm, either feedforward or cascade-forward taking less computational resources [19]. The details of SCG are elaborated in [20].

RESULTS AND DISCUSSIONS

The result sections are discussed with rainfall climatology and NARX predictability for both cities. First, rainfall analyses show a monthly mean rainfall representing both cities in Fig. (**5**). Both cities reveal fluctuations of high and low rainfall events in the 1900s to early 2000s. Moreover, rainfall is ominously reduced more in Dhaka than in Chittagong. The normalized rainfall in Fig. (**6**) indicates a lower amount in the capital than in coastal cities except for two peak rainfall events. Any extreme rainfalls might occur due to tropical cyclones or thunderstorms. To note, extreme events and their effects are also distinct at various periods. Climatological means are scrutinized in long (24 and 12 years) and short (06 years) terms. Dhaka receives lower rainfall than Chittagong consecutively for the last 12 years in September month (shown in Table **2**). The limited rainfall in Dhaka might indirectly cause by urban expansion, *i.e.,* reducing forest and rural areas. Therefore, accurate forecasts are essential for drought management as well as sustainable developments.

Table 2. Rainfall Climatology (1995 to 2018) and ANN Predictability in two metropolitans

Year (Period)	Rain: CR; DR	Model Types:	CR: Chittagong Rainfall Climatology	DR: Dhaka Rainfall Climatology
Y95-18 (24 year)	5.87; 5.89	ANN; OT Condition	Mean Squared Error (MSE = 0 *i.e.* no error)	Regression: 0= random, 1 = close relationship (R)
Y95-06 (12 year)	3.32; 6.31	LM	Epoch: 12	Epoch: 5
Y07-18 (12 year)	8.42; 5.47	R (0-1)	Train: 0.325; Test: 0.318; Valid: 0.291; All: 0.312	Train: 0.242; Test: 0.267; Valid: 0.274; All: 0.249
Y95-00 (06 year)	3.38; 2.28	BR	Epoch: 201	Epoch: 12
Y01-06 (06 year)	3.37; 10.4	R (0-1)	Train: 0.303; Test: 0.335; All: 0.2959	Train: 0.211; Test: 0.235; All: 0.213

(Table 2) cont.....

Year (Period)	Rain: CR; DR	Model Types:	CR: Chittagong Rainfall Climatology	DR: Dhaka Rainfall Climatology
Y07-12 (06 year)	**8.29; 5.40**	SCG	Epoch: 10	Epoch: 47
Y13-18 (06 years)	**8.54; 5.46**	R (0-1)	Train: 0.129; Test: 0.037; Valid: 0.018: All: 0.084	Train: 0.198; Test: 0.477; Valid: 0.189; All: 0.221

ANN modeling results show rainfall occurrences in September for two megacities. In general, time-series, *i.e.,* NARX, show more than 20% rainfall probability in Dhaka and 30% in Chittagong. The detailed modeling for NARX and OT results is in Table **2**. These ANN results suggest that September month has rainfall occurrences around 20 to 30%. Since there is no rainfall event, the model might consider zero value as one of the noises in the datasets. Except for SCG for Chittagong, the ANN predictability is almost consistent for two metropolitans. Specifically, Dhaka shows rainfall events by LM, BR, and SCG about 24.9, 21.3, and 22.1%, whereas Chittagong has 31.2, 29.5, and 8.4%.

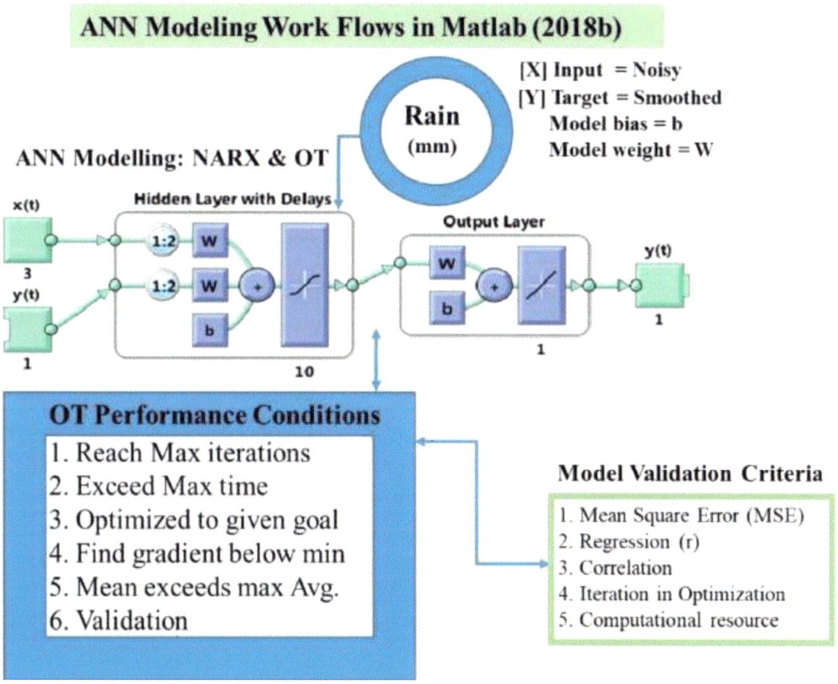

Fig. (4). A general Flowchart for NARX with OT modeling in Matlab 2018b.

Besides model accuracy, the computational resources and time are equally important in numerical predictions. As Bangladesh has sparse and irregular observations, these might result in challenging the performances of ANN. Yet, the architecture of NARX, *i.e.,* model stability in nonlinear dynamic systems, is useful for accepting the above model performances. For enhancing the ANN model, large datasets might be incorporated in improving forecasting quality. Due to lack of data availability, this is now beyond the scope of this chapter. Moreover, the model results are also well compared with climatological trends. Descriptive statistics, *i.e.,* mean, are matched well with predicted correlations. From OT sensitivities, Bayesian Regularization (BR) converges optimum solutions with limited and noisy data in NARX performance.

However, BR might require more computational time and resources (refer to the number of iterations). LM optimizes the NARX predictions estimate faster but might consume more computational resources. Finally, SCG might have caused poor performances for noisy data (for the Chittagong case) and mostly for no rainfall events, *i.e.,* 0 (zero) in integer values. If there is no rainfall event, inputs and outputs in NARX become zeros. As SCG calculates *via* their derivatives, the blank values might create uncertainties at ICs in model predictions.

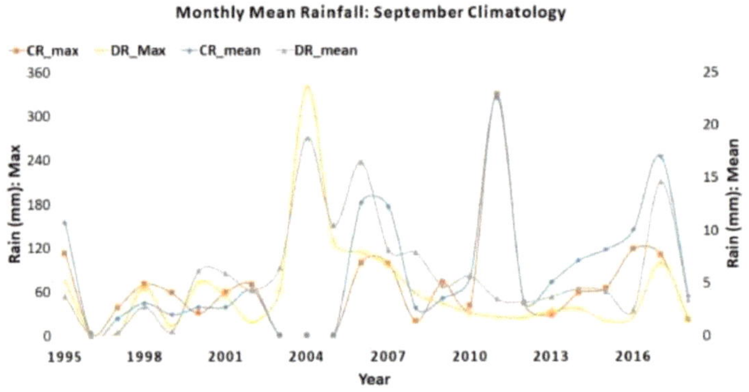

Fig. (5). Rainfall trends (maximum and Mean) in Chittagong (CR) and Dhaka (DR) from 1995 to 2018. (Data: BMD and Ogimet, 2018).

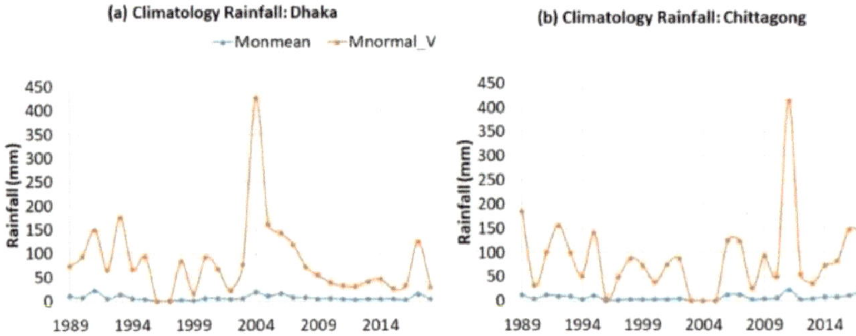

Fig. (6). Monthly mean and normalized rainfall for (a) Dhaka and (b) Chittagong from 1989 to 2018. (Data: BMD and Ogimet, 2018).

CONCLUDING REMARKS

The urban expansions and population growth urge to accurately forecast rainfall events for saving property-damages and resource management. The rainfall (in September) climatology for 29 years (1989 to 2018) showed reductions in rainfall, particularly in Dhaka. Based on observed data, urbanizations, resources, and disaster management are directly influenced by rainfall events. The current research shows how time-series ANN is capable of rainfall predictions. ANN methods performed well to forecast chaotic parameters (30% in Chittagong and 25% in Dhaka). The OT choices show sensitivities yielding better performance by LM> BR> SCG. It also encourages further studies incorporating more events such as flash and regional floods to test sensitivities for rainfall estimations in Bangladesh. Particularly, Chittagong (ANN) forecasts refer to various options in computational resources and time. The results also suggest scrutinizing sensitivity for modeling parameters like the number of iterations and methods. The paper aims to further study more rainfall events for Dhaka and Chittagong, establishing ANN as a great option for a smart disaster management tool.

CONSENT FOR PUBLICATION

Not Applicable.

CONFLICT OF INTEREST

The author confirms that this chapter contents have no conflict of interest.

ACKNOWLEDGEMENTS

The first author likes to show her sincere gratitude to Bangladesh Meteorological Department for providing the requested data. The author also thanks Ewha Woman's University and Samsung Foundation for providing education and research platforms.

REFERENCES

[1] G.B. Rajendran, U.M. Kumarasamy, C. Zarro, P.B. Divakarachari, and S.L. Ullo, "Land-Use and Land-Cover Classification Using a Human Group-Based Particle Swarm Optimization Algorithm with an LSTM Classifier on Hybrid Pre-Processing Remote-Sensing Images", *Remote Sens.,* vol. 12, no. 24, p. 4135, 2020. [http://dx.doi.org/10.3390/rs12244135]

[2] N. Thakur, and C.Y. Han, "An Ambient Intelligence-Based Human Behavior Monitoring Framework for Ubiquitous Environments", *Information (Basel),* vol. 12, no. 2, p. 81, 2021. [http://dx.doi.org/10.3390/info12020081]

[3] BBS, *Bangladesh Statistics.* Bangladesh Bureau of Statistics: Dhaka, Bangladesh, 2017. [Accessed: 10-Mar-2021]

[4] M.M. Hassan, and M.N.I. Nazem, "Examination of land use/land cover changes, urban growth dynamics, and environmental sustainability in Chittagong city, Bangladesh", *Environ. Dev. Sustain.*, vol. 18, no. 3, pp. 697-716, 2015.
[http://dx.doi.org/10.1007/s10668-015-9672-8]

[5] H.D. Purnomo, K.D. Hartomo, and S.Y.J. Prasetyo, "Artificial Neural Network for Monthly Rainfall Rate Prediction", *IOP Conf. Series Mater. Sci. Eng.*, vol. 180, p. 012057, 2017.
[http://dx.doi.org/10.1088/1757-899X/180/1/012057]

[6] E. Vamsidhar, K.V.S.R.P. Varma, P.S. Rao, and R. Satapati, "Prediction of Rainfall Using Backpropagation Neural Network Model", *Int. J. Comput. Sci. Eng.*, vol. 2, no. 4, pp. 1119-1121, 2010.

[7] N.R. Wahyuni, "Adam, W. F. Mahmudy, and A. Iriany, "Modeling Backpropagation Neural Network for Rainfall Prediction in Tengger East Java", In: *Proceedings of the International Conference on Sustainable Information Engineering and Technology (SIET)*, 2017.

[8] N.Q. Hung, M.S. Babel, S. Weesakul, and N.K. Tripathi, "An artificial neural network model for rainfall forecasting in Bangkok, Thailand", *Hydrol. Earth Syst. Sci.*, vol. 13, no. 8, pp. 1413-1425, 2009.
[http://dx.doi.org/10.5194/hess-13-1413-2009]

[9] "Atlas of Urban Expansion-Cities", www.atlasofurbanexpansion.org http://www.atlasofurbanexpansion.org/data[accessed Oct. 20, 2018].

[10] Shlomo Angel and E. Al, Atlas of urban expansion, 2016th ed., vol. 1. United States of America: Lincoln Institute of Land Policy, 2016. [Accessed: 10-Mar-2021].,

[11] B. Ahmed, and Y. A. Rubel, "Understanding the issues involved in urban landslide vulnerability in Chittagong Metropolitan Area, Bangladesh", *MyCOE/SERVIR,* 2013.

[12] H.K. Sahoo, P.K. Dash, and N.P. Rath, "NARX model-based nonlinear dynamic system identification using low complexity neural networks and robust H∞ filter", *Appl. Soft Comput.,* vol. 13, no. 7, pp. 3324-3334, 2013.
[http://dx.doi.org/10.1016/j.asoc.2013.02.007]

[13] Matlab, "Design Time Series NARX Feedback Neural Networks - MATLAB & Simulink", www.mathworks.com [Accessed: 10-Mar-2021]

[14] Matlab, "Train Neural Network Using trainlm Train Function: LM", Mathworks.com https://www.mathworks.com/help/deeplearning/ref/trainlm.html [accessed Oct. 15, 2020].

[15] M. Balda, "LMFsolve.m: Levenberg-Marquardt-Fletcher algorithm for nonlinear least-squares problems", www.mathworks.com [Accessed: 10-Mar-2021]

[16] Matlab, "Bayesian regularization backpropagation - MATLAB trainer", www.mathworks.com https://www.mathworks.com/help/deeplearning/ref/trainbr.html [accessed Oct. 13, 2020].

[17] D.J.C. MacKay, "Bayesian Interpolation", *Neural Comput.,* vol. 4, no. 3, pp. 415-447, 1992.
[http://dx.doi.org/10.1162/neco.1992.4.3.415]

[18] H. Okut, "Bayesian Regularized Neural Networks for Small n Big p Data ", In: *Artificial Neural Networks - Models and Applications, InTech*, 2016, pp. 27-48.
[http://dx.doi.org/10.5772/63256]

[19] Matlab, "Scaled conjugate gradient backpropagation", www.mathworks.com https://www.mathworks.com/help/deeplearning/ref/trainscg.html[accessed Oct. 11, 2020].

[20] M.F. Møller, "A scaled conjugate gradient algorithm for fast supervised learning", *Neural Netw.,* vol. 6, no. 4, pp. 525-533, 1993.
[http://dx.doi.org/10.1016/S0893-6080(05)80056-5]

CHAPTER 8

The Role of EUPs in custom GUIs for Future Integration of HCI-enhancing Devices

Pablo C. Herrera[1,*], José Reátegui[1], Michael Hurtado[1] and Mauricio Loyola[2]

[1] *School of Architecture, Universidad Peruana de Ciencias Aplicadas, Lima, Peru*

[2] *Faculty of Architecture and Urbanism, Universidad de Chile, Santiago, Chile*

Abstract: Although architecture software companies incorporate high-level programming to process the complexity of data, only some End-User Programmers (EUP) manage to customize their GUI to design and integrate smart devices for future smart homes and smart cities. HCI is a source of inspiration to incorporate a large part of the design process into creative flows. In this context, we identify patterns to analyze, interpret, and optimize the work of EUP architects who seek to customize the GUI of their digital design tools. We obtained a set of 16 patterns that reconfigure the interaction of their processes. We programmed the integration of data science in architecture, machine learning, visual and textual programming, Cloud Computing with AWS, and Augmented Reality with Unity. The result is an ecosystem of three platforms that compensate for the shortcomings of computerized design in data-driven design processes, optimizing execution time in an emergency, with perspectives towards Smart and Interconnected Environments. Considering that the GUI is the most important product of HCI research, our analysis and interpretation of the results and their discussion highlight the need to explore personalized GUI solutions promoted by the designers to enrich them, capitalizing on their processes in codes for the reuse and co-design of new interactions.

Keywords: Artificial Intelligence, Architectural Design, Augmented Reality, AWS, AWS Comprehend, AWS Rekognition, Cloud Computing, Computational Design, Design Process, EUP, GUI, HCI, Industry 4.0, IoT, Latin America, Neural Network, Open Data, Unity, Pattern, Visual Programming.

INTRODUCTION

Barricelli *et al.* [1] argue that computational techniques that empower end-users of technologies were born from Human-Computer Interaction (HCI). In the 1990s, Nardi [2] (in the context of End User Computing) explained that people such as chemists, librarians, teachers, architects, and accountants, seriously

* **Corresponding author to Pablo C. Herrera:** School of Architecture, Universidad Peruana de Ciencias Aplicadas, Lima, Perú; E-mail: pablo.herrera@upc.edu.pe

Nirmalya Thakur and Parameshachari B.D. (Eds)

wanted to use computers level because they often failed to get the applications they wanted. However, they were not interested in becoming professional programmers or "contract programmers or in-house programmers to write the few programs they will need" [2]. In architecture, Gantt and Nardi [3] named them Gardeners. In the same context, Burry [4] justified this practice due to the lack of specific tools to solve some design problems, forcing architects to create their macros in the software of their choice. At the end of the first decade of the 21st century, the evolution of Computation Theories and Technologies in Architectural Design [5] allowed architects to develop their tools [6] above other professionals such as industrial designers [7].

As demonstrated [8], End-User Programming (EUP) introduced a new scenario in the HCI because it brought users closer to personalizing, expanding, and/or combining resources for other contexts of needs and usage, to the point that the EUP along with Graphical User Interfaces (GUI) became convergent technologies.

Research in the context of Smart Home of connected objects and Smart Cities initiatives is driven towards hyper-connected urban environments, promoting that intelligent systems adapt to the work and daily needs of users who interact with defined parameters and in a context-specific to achieve a goal [9]. In this context, interactions are captured and processed in databases [10], or human behavior is analyzed during the interaction of those actions [11]. Di Nardo *et al.* [12] stated that the data of these interactions originated from the Internet of Things (IoT) and Cyber-Physical Systems (CPS) in the context of the Fourth Industrial Revolution: Big Data and analytics, Robot-assisted production, self-driving logistics vehicles, augmented reality, and additive manufacturing. EUPs in the Fourth Industrial revolution context [12], [13] revealed solutions to different modes of interaction because they allowed adapting tools and workplaces to the needs and user preferences [14].

Scupelli [15] proposed that commercially available IoT systems could empower non-programmers to sense user activity, control smart things, test their configuration, and make it easier for end-users to customize their work environment. Sailer [16] showed how researchers from the Space Syntax group discovered that the configuration of a space system significantly explains the movement flows but shows limitations when the interaction and co-presence of participants are highly controlled. Therefore, the movement flows prevent following the configuration proposed by the users. Brich *et al.* [17] stated that scheduling notations and rule-based process-oriented configuration could be used by end-users for effective scheduling, rather than just focusing on the configuration. For this reason, EUP designers proposed solutions such as activity connectivity, which implies a set of parameters (integration, choice, control value, and entropy) that would allow the configuration of the living quarters for the elderly [18]. Designers can thus know all the variables to optimize their design over time, improving users' quality of life, unlike only those who configure their environment, without knowing the variables that govern the design.

The System Mapping Study (2000-2017) [1] showed that the solutions proposed by the EUPs focused on making programming an easy activity for non-programming expert users, but at the same time, "to design novel techniques that foster end users' participation in system modification and shaping over time without requiring a high cognitive effort." Reisinger *et al.* [19] argued that the use of End-User Programming addressed different solutions from simple to complex in the context of smart homes. From an opposite context, we consider Harrison [20], quoted by Barricelli *et al.* [1], who doubts the value of the EUP in the correction, maintenance, and security that can be configured in the products. In our experience, this statement is critical when the end-user has not been part of the product creation process. On the contrary, designers who were part of the process have more opportunities to enhance their work as EUP. Therefore, in this research, we focus on programming for the End-User of the process (such as designers and architects) and not on programming for the product's End-User. The inclusion of EUP and customization from the design process becomes an important basis for integrating them into devices that improve and promote the sustainability of HCI towards Smart and interconnected environments. The model proposed for the End-User of the design process integrates different professionals who co-design (and program) the solution simultaneously. This process is constantly reviewed, with a code that promotes participatory design using a common visual programming language. Raymond [21] evidenced that in a digital context and the socialization of information, "the greater the number of reviewers, the easier the errors in a problem will be found," allowing advancing and integrating sub-processes to enhance the model. This could answer Kronman and Zingerle [22] in the context of the internet of other people's things: How are citizens involved in co-design collaborations with private corporations and the public sector to build better cities? A starting point, which is the subject of this research, is to return to the process code. Action between the 1960s and 1980s was limited by programming languages that did not manage to separate themselves from academic research and make sustained incursions into the practice. Our model is emerging as a space for integration and continuous improvement, allowing the HCI to strengthen its life cycle from the workgroup that produces it to enrich the product's user experience.

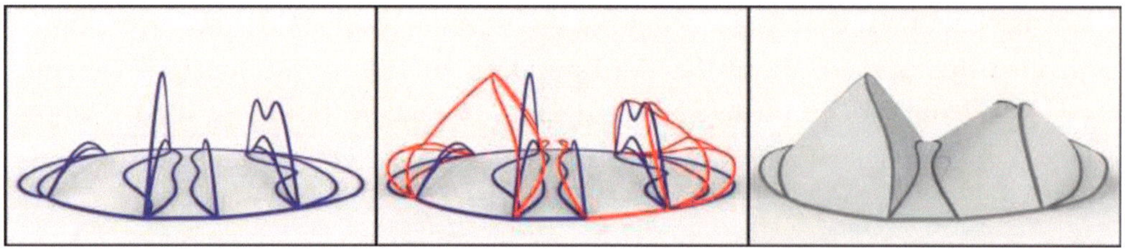

Fig. (1). Evolution of the representation of a design using computerized tools. (Authors).

In this research, we believe that technology will continue to be an important ally if open access techniques are used. Their results are not rigid artifacts using techniques that eliminate process steps. In hand or digital drawing (the most important interfaces for architects to demonstrate the solution to a design problem), the information is not reused from the original interface because the result is only a representation (Fig. **1**), where we lose the history of the design process for future modifications and reuse.

Raymond [21] associated this process with constructing a cathedral, where the solution only belongs to those who produce it. On the contrary, when we codify the process, we expose the origin and development, evidencing mistakes and successes. This observation is known as Linus's Law, and it is the origin of the working model of the Linux© operating system created by Linus Torvalds. As shown by Sennett [23], "the source code is constantly evolving and is not a finished or fixed object, because it maintains a reciprocal relationship between solution and problem discovery." This characterization is not new because it is part of one of the construction processes supported by computerized digital technologies, which is monitoring, life cycle, and maintenance in the context of Facility and Asset Management [24] however, it is not directly related to the EUP, as proposed by this research.

Thus, in this research, the customization of technological tools is promoted, based on the practice of computational design in architecture, to become an important ally in the face of variable and unpredictable scenarios. For instance, it could focus on designing during an epidemic like COVID-19, which does not demand a passive design practice but a responsive one in the context of co-design [25] and distributed production [26].

Our theoretical framework reviewed the advancement of automation, the current complexity of architecture, the stability that open design environments offer EUP, and the technologies of Industry 4.0. However, technology is not the only variable that motivates this architectural research, distinguishing it from other generations of EUP. Sollohub [27] evidenced millennial behaviors, characteristics, and predisposition to link to more technologies and methods to architecture, like those proposed in this research. Millennial architects are characterized by digital natives, showing skills for exploratory learning, establishing networks with friends, desiring personalization, and customization, and being open to change and experiment. With this introduction, we consider a strong context requiring actions from academia and the profession to go beyond the current GUI that designers and architects use.

AUTOMATION AND COMPLEXITY IN ARCHITECTURAL DESIGN

Control techniques in the development of complex products are not new. Automation, data processing, value analysis, and standardization in design appeared systematically in the 1960s. As indicated [28], this produced a lower degree of freedom in selecting components to perform specific work, restricting the introduction of new or special materials. Baudrillard [29] argues that an object will be susceptible to redesign if it is not automated. On the contrary, "automatism always embodies the risk of arresting technical advance (...) which exiles man to the irresponsibility of a mere spectator".

Faced with the challenge of solving the complexity of contemporary architecture [30], which demands a high level of innovation, quick solutions, and low cost [31], we add the production of large amounts of data that begin to replace traditional drawings, creating new flows in the materialization of the architecture [32]. This complex context forces us to think about new tools promoted by the EUPs because they can save the code of the final product reconfiguration process.

According to [33], in the 21st century, digital technologies in architecture are still computerized or computational. As demonstrated in [34], the computerized architecture produces a large amount of complex information but is very unmanageable and limited only to form representation. Therefore, automation and computerized digital processes are not a widespread answer to customizing or configuring GUIs by end-users, especially when designing during emergencies. Time is a factor of consideration. The degree of automatization of professions was studied by Frey and Osborne [35] and demonstrated a probability factor in which occupations could be not computerized (0) or computerized (1). In the context of automating architecture-related activities, Celani *et al.* [36] did not include "Architectural and Engineering Managers (0.017)" in their analysis but did select eight occupations from "Architects, Except Landscape and Naval (0.018)" to "Model Makers, Wood (0.96)". In the selection, drafters and technicians linked to architecture and civil engineering represented the most computerized employments because they produce more routines. Therefore Celani *et al.* [36] conclude that the Future of the Architect's Employment "will not be competing against computers (a competition they can't win), but rather taking better advantage of it." In our research, we demonstrated that EUPs represent a powerful resource for HCI improvement in smart homes and cities, because they can introduce new solutions once they are sensitized to an ecosystem in which data flow can be managed for design and user behavior.

END-USER PROGRAMMERS AND COMPUTATIONAL DESIGN IN ARCHITECTURE

For years there were unsuccessful attempts to use programming in Computer-Aided Design since the 1980s. This led architecture students to live the simulation of their reality [37, 23], because the software worked immediately after installation, without any modification or configuration [38].

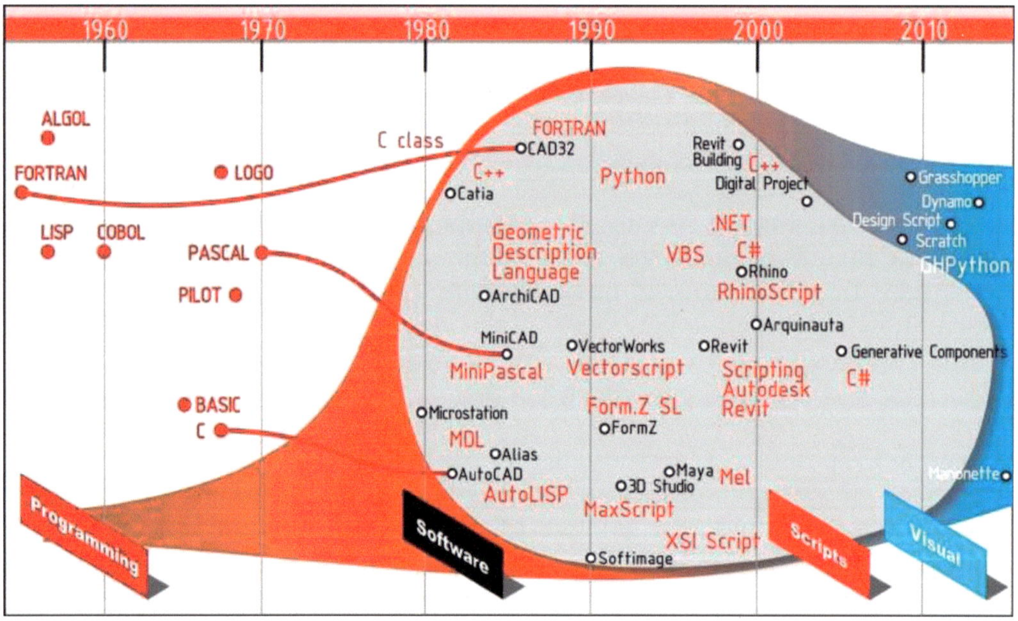

Fig. (2). High-level languages available in architecture and design software. (Authors).

Although companies standardized solutions with the introduction of software in the 1980s, developers incorporated a high-level language into design software in the face of the impossibility of offering all possible conventions to design problems (Fig. **2**). This allowed customizing processes or reusing existing ones, depending on the circumstances to be solved and the demand for the users' needs. Through these languages, we develop the research to manage to move the data in each of its stages.

Engineering developed technologies that offer architects opportunities to enhance their processes without the end-users being trained in software or computer engineering from its different specialties. Therefore, we distance ourselves from the GUIs of computerized technologies, and we do not directly use the software but drive programming and computational processes at the level of EUP

Computational exploration in architecture using emerging technology is not recent. It was promoted from the teaching of architecture in the northern hemisphere, in master's programs such as MIT's "Design and Computation" (1989) and the Architectural Association's "Emergent Technologies and Design" (2001). These computational methods were linked to improving the representation interface and tools and techniques that originated from mathematical approaches from software programming such as Generative Components of Bentley Systems and Rhinoceros of McNeel Associates [39]. The academy responded to a demand from the profession [40] that had begun to deploy computer design equipment in the main architectural offices of the Northern Hemisphere [41] because GUI limitations continue to be a problem for customization solutions in the context of Industry 4.0.

INDUSTRY 4.0 IN ARCHITECTURAL DESIGN

In 2012, the German government created the concept of Industry 4.0 [42], transforming industries from digitization technologies to customized products [43], and the construction industry was no exception, including the architectural topics on emerging digital technologies [44]. The production of data on devices that allow setting up an architectural or urban space makes it necessary to complement computational processes linked to the concepts proposed by Maskuriy and co-workers [45] in the context of Cyber-Physical Systems (CPS), IoT, Internet of Services (IoS), Artificial Intelligence (AI), Big Data and Smart Production.

In this research, we propose a set of patterns that integrates data science, artificial intelligence, design at different scales, communication and storage from cloud services, verification and testing using augmented reality to co-design and reduce response and decision time in a health emergency public. This implementation explains a context for future integration with IoT devices, making it easier for the designer to customize their tools to meet the specific needs of end-users.

METHODS

We agree that to face an era where Big Data, Cloud Computing, and Artificial Intelligence technologies are increasingly used [46], the creation and testing of GUI and APIs must be promoted. Therefore, this research aimed to create and program connections to exchange data in three design environments with a different scenario than architects or designers in the spatial configuration of the projects they face. This allows you to integrate the different skills of EUPs into the creation of your tools. To select the programming environments for EUP, we rely on a review of the literature and historical trends of the digital tools used in the design stage for future implementation in the architectural community in a scalable way. The ecosystem is composed of three platforms (Fig. **3**): (A) Design: In this platform, we used visual programming software for design (Grasshopper in Rhinoceros) as a parametric modeling environment for the project. On the (B) Backend service platform: We use the services of an Application Programming Interface (API) on Amazon Web Services (AWS) and (C) Peer Review: We create a workspace to remotely access design changes (Augmented Reality using a cross-platform game engine developed by Unity Technologies).

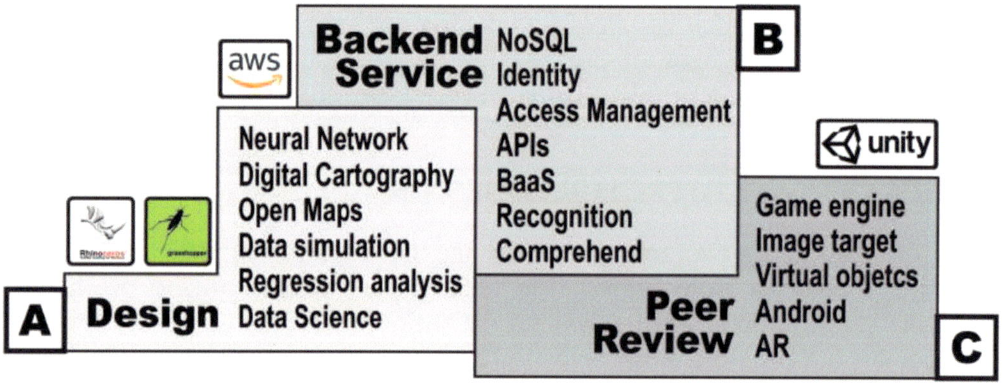

Fig. (3). Environment platforms and techniques: (A) Design; (B) Backend Service; (C) Collaborative Design.

The modulation allows you to change the design software, the cloud service, or the augmented reality interface, depending on the needs of the EUP at any time of the process. However, the most important consideration is that the three platforms coincide in the same programming language so that the data flow immediately.

Table 1. Structure that determines the set of patterns in the ecosystem.

Design			Back End Service		Peer Review
Data Science	**Data Sources**	**Design**	**Cloud Storage**	**Artificial Intelligence**	**Augmented Reality**
Pattern 1	Patterns 2 - 10	Patterns 11 - 12	Pattern 13	Patterns 14 - 15	Pattern 16

From Table **1**, six groups of techniques distributed on the platforms were developed: (A1) Data Science, (A2) Data sources, (A3) Design, (B1) Cloud Storage, (B2) Artificial Intelligence in AWS, and (C) Augmented Reality and within them a group of 16 patterns. Techniques follow a path in the proposed process' ecosystem (Fig. **4**).

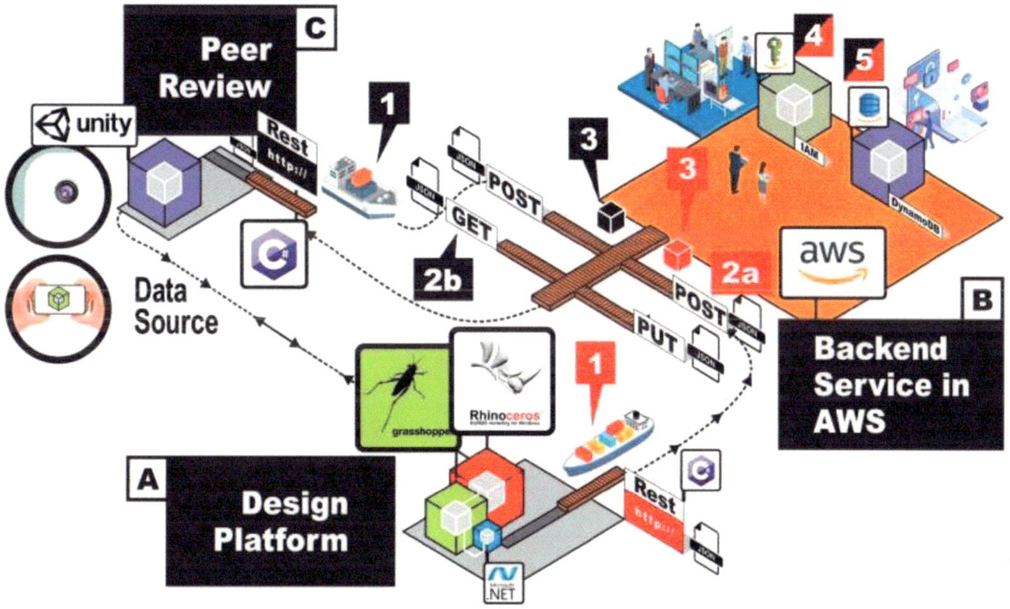

Fig. (4). Ecosystem Path: (1) Prepare JSON Message; (2a) Post information; (2b) Get information; (3) Serverless; (4) Credentials validation (AWS IAM); (5) Post and Get Information from AWS.

The following text is the selection criteria for each programming environment for the three platforms.

Design Platform

We analyze the limitations of creating new software for design because historically, the software uses high-level languages (Fig. **2**), facilitating the use and reuse of existing conventions, routines, and skills in existing digital design tools. For this reason, we use existing software that allowed us to program and reuse the code in the different design stages. It incorporates a high-level textual or visual programming language to personalize the processes and customization by the user. The design software that uses (i) a GUI with established tools for design, (ii) a textual programming language, and (iii) a visual programming language is Rhinoceros. This software uses a mathematical model to represent spline-based complex geometries based on non-uniform rationales from its own GUI. It also incorporates textual programming (VB Script, Python, JavaScript, C ++, NET) and visual programming (VBA, VB.NET, C #, Visual Studio). The programming language transversal to all environments was C#, mainly because Rhinoceros uses .NET like Unity; in both cases, .NET is one of the cores of their systems.

Backend service in Amazon Web Services (AWS)

In historical comparisons, Kotas *et al.* [47] argue that cloud providers continually improve their offerings. Many factors (a type of connection, service fee, *etc.*) make it difficult to establish criteria to compare and decide on a cloud platform.

Therefore, in our critical analysis, the selection decision was made by trends in research published by the IEEE. The three most referenced platforms in IEEE Xplore began to be published in 2005: Google Cloud (2010), Microsoft Azure (2009), and AWS (2005). Of the total (1,116 publications), the number of case studies has been led annually by AWS (41%), followed by Google Cloud (31%) and MS Azure (27%). (Table **2**).

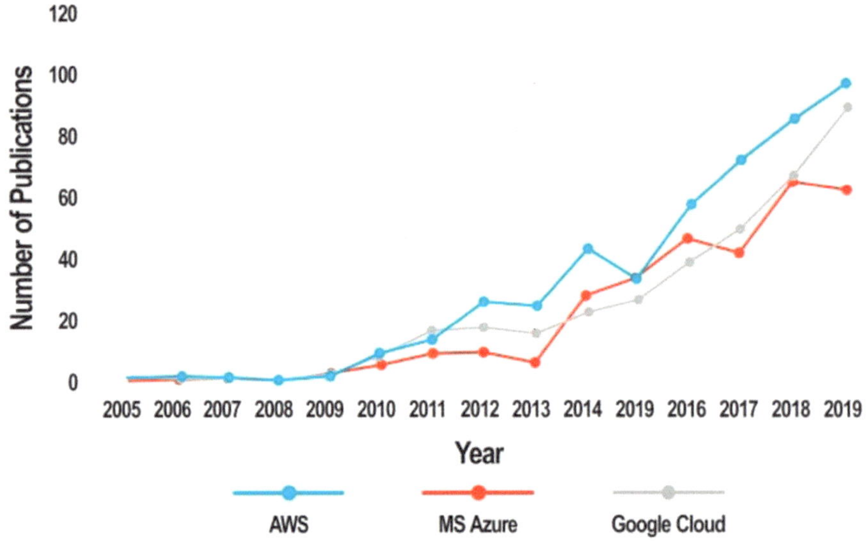

Table 2. IEEE Publications (2005-19) with Case Studies on AWS, MS Azure, and Google Cloud.

The process begins by creating the permissions and identities in AWS IAM, used by the serverless functions of the AWS Lambda service. These functions allow entering and extracting information from the database and the image repository using Artificial Intelligence resources. These serverless functions are activated from the AWS API Gateway service when orders arrive at the server from grasshopper or the mobile application.

Peer Review

This ecosystem requires a system to create highly customizable augmented reality applications with APIs connected to AWS. Considering that users would be EUP, the learning curve was minimized to connect with the Android mobile operating system. Unity uses C# and optimizes the export to Android, better responding to other platforms such as Unreal, which uses C ++, making it more difficult for its incorporation to a EUP context.

The method for organizing the case study was based on the research of Woodbury [48] that establishes the structure of the pattern for parametric design, based on the work of Christopher Alexander [49]. The answers to these four questions are flexible ideas that, in addition to the Name that identifies the pattern, develop four questions (Table **3**). This structure will improve or reduce the methods in the process according to the needs of the project. Each is self-sufficient and functions as the particular solution to a specific problem in the process.

Table 3. Questions that configure the structure of each of the 16 patterns of the process.

(1)	(2)	(3)	(4)
What	**Why**	**When**	**How**
The goal behind the pattern	States the reasons to use this pattern	Describes a scenario comprising a problem context	Explains how to adopt the pattern to solve the given problem

For the development of the ecosystem of the case study, a work team was formed made up of five professionals with academic degrees in mathematics, industrial design, and architecture with academic and professional experience in digital technologies from eight to twenty years. Indistinctly, the team has skills in computational design techniques, digital fabrication, and programming in Unity, APIs in AWS, data science, and augmented reality.

The discussion of this ecosystem was presented in a seminar/workshop on artificial intelligence, and computational design in architecture design conducted online in July 2020 in which 20 architects from 5 countries voluntarily participated (7 from Peru, four from Brazil, four from Chile, three from Argentina, two from Mexico and one from Bolivia).

CASE STUDY

This research sought to respond to the complex task of choosing from the total public spaces of a city those that meet the spatial conditions to be transformed into a point of intervention in design, which at the same time could be visualized remotely by other health specialists or designers.

DESIGN PLATFORM (A)

Data Science (A1)

Pattern 1. Information: (1) What: Introduces estimations, linear, multivariate, and nonlinear regressions, socializing basic concepts and procedures necessary for EUP on data science. (2) Why: The interaction of people in a building or public space produces large volumes of data that must be used to promote redesign. (3) When: Before development to familiarize ourselves with future procedures. (4) How: Through LunchBox [50] to communicate daily, generate a large amount of georeferenced data stored on a web mapping service. As such, they are an important source of data, that by analyzing them, we understand the behavior of a population that is extremely important in the design process.

There are two proposals for cartographic services in the private sector, Google Maps, and OpenStreetMap (OSM). The first one in its free version has limitations to download all the data. Still, its information is more complete because the data entry is carried out by the same company, traveling the world at different time intervals. On the other hand, OSM is an open software project where we can download cartographic information for free. However, as the information providers are the users, there are large areas of the territory where there is no information, especially in the planet's southern hemisphere.

Considering that this model seeks to integrate into open databases because not only its use is democratized but also because it allows the community itself to be responsible for its verification, we decided to use the visual interface of OpenStreetMap OSM [51] and its open geodata, which starts the development of Pattern 2.

Pattern 2. Source Cartography (1) What: Open geodata cartography is used to extract cadastral information for the design project. (2) Why: the context is unavoidable to establish the constraints of the geometry parameters. (3) When: Given the limitations of obtaining cadastre sources due to the limitations of an emergency, open data is the main source of information (4) How: OSM is used, and the information is exported using visual programming with ELK [52] for Grasshopper in Rhinoceros.

We used ELK, a plug-in for grasshopper, to import the geodata that allowed us to load the OSM files. From its interface, we obtained information about public spaces, urban areas, bus stops, roads, *etc*. From these categories, we extracted information about areas and the number of access points to each public space to organize the information for pattern 3.

Pattern 3. Spatial Heat map simulation: (1) What: Data visualization technique represents a phenomenon using colors over a geographical region considering data. (2) Why: It is the best option to visualize data that has a geographic location. (3) When: After loading the OSM data using ELK, it was necessary to represent the infectious foci and their influence. (4) How: From the Configurbanist [53], a plug-in for grasshopper, we use the "relative neighbor" object to visualize areas of the map with the highest infection rate.

With data from public spaces. The construction of the interface had to incorporate techniques to select the most suitable public space for its intervention. We consider that, unlike traditional design methods, where a software interface allows access to data through a device such as a mouse, in this model, the intervention is through code. Therefore, we established three selection criteria: (1) Public space area. (2) Access points. (3) Infection index. For the calculation of areas, we use the Grasshopper "Area" component, while to visualize the infection rates through a heat map, we use the Cheetah plug-in, Configurbanist. This plug-in will allow us to work in two ways: proximity and neighborhood. Its vicinity component was used to visualize the infectious foci.

Pattern 4. Shortest paths network alternatives: (1) What: Topological technique allowed finding the shortest distance from each public space to the access points. (2) Why: One of the important variables of the model is accessibility. Topological techniques allow you to measure connectivity and integration. (3) When loading the OSM data, we needed to get the shortest distance from each public space to an access point. (4) How: Taking the access points and public spaces' locations, we use the "short walk" component to obtain the smallest distance between them.

Although Cheetah, the Configurbanist, allows us to calculate the shortest distance between two points on a map, the computational cost of using this component was too high because we had to calculate the distance from all bus stops to public spaces on the map. It was then that the shortest walk [54] plug-in emerged as an alternative to find the solution to the distance problem because it is based on a topology calculator and the A* search algorithm [55], optimizing the time of the result.

Pattern 5: Extract geometry by type: (1) What: Characteristics extraction exercise for creating typologies. (2) Why: We want to obtain possible public spaces that can be intervened, for which it is necessary to extract characteristics that allow us to compare them. (3) When: After obtaining all the characteristics for each public space. (4) How: Based on the area of each public space, its accessibility, and its infection rate, we build a typology that allows us to manually establish suitable spaces and then automate the choice in future steps.

We are looking for a method to identify public spaces with a "large" or configurable area according to a range of values. That once had a "greater" number of access points, with a low infection rate in the area. This problem requires establishing valuation ranges because terms such as "large" or "greater" lack precision. This type of problem led us to use artificial neural networks.

Pattern 6: Neural Network (1) What: Mathematical model with inputs and outputs that tries to imitate neurons when making decisions when faced with a problem. (2) Why: This type of technique allows solving complex estimation and classification problems. (3) When defining the data for the specific area, accessibility, and infection rate associated with each public space. (4) How: Using a Neural component from LunchBox, the training of a neural network was programmed to select public spaces considering data such as area, accessibility, and infection rate based on previous options target work.

The data stored in lists were chosen to use a neural network model belonging to the LunchBox plug-in. We use the NEURAL component from the Lunchbox interface that represents our neural network with a single output. This model allowed us to classify public spaces into two groups, those suitable for intervention and those not suitable. The greatest advantage of using this type of model is that it allows us to find classification functions by assessing the contribution of each of the characteristics originating in each iteration.

Pattern 7. Classification problems: (1) What: They are problems with data necessary to their classification according to their characteristics. (2) Why: Because the intervention of suitable public space is very complex due to the number of possibilities, this intervention is a classification problem. (3) When defining the data on area, accessibility, and infection rate for each public space, the suitable space is identified. (4) How: Using artificial neural networks to optimize the efficiency of the method when training is required.

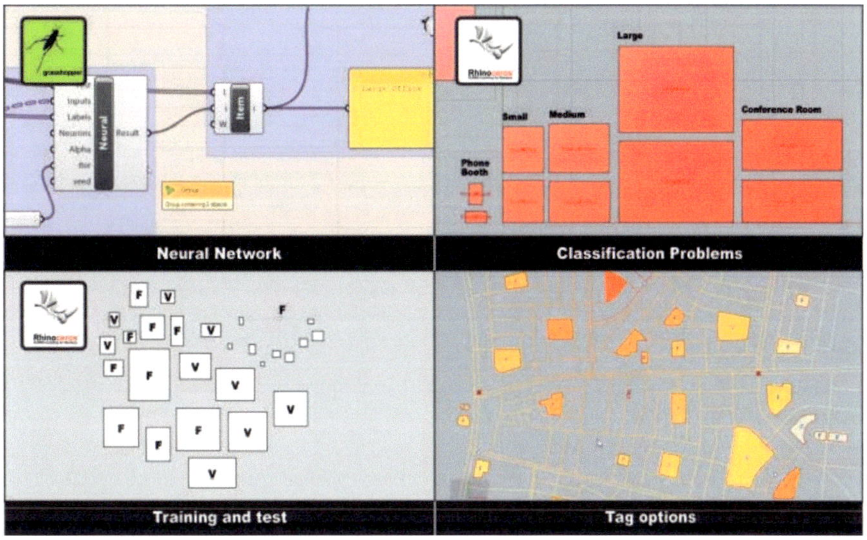

Fig. (5). Images on the neural network training process, data labeling, and selection using Lunchbox in Grasshopper.

With this model, we find the appropriate assessment for each characteristic, considering that real problems have more parameters (some interdependent). This type of approach is more efficient than models that seek to establish an analytical classification function.

Pattern 8. Training and test: (1) What: Work routines with neural networks. (2) Why: The neural networks for classification will require a training phase and a test phase. (3) When: After determining the suitable public spaces of our training data, we will use the neural network so that the algorithm automatically labels the test data. (4) How: After training the neural network with properly labeled public space data, we continue to evaluate the real data model (Fig. **5**). We consider the aspect of training data in our work with neural networks. Due to LunchBox's neural network limitation and the use of the same amount of input and training data, we produce a greater number of results for training. We established policies for training data based on the three types of characteristics of Pattern 6 (Fig. **6**).

Pattern 9. Tag options (1) What: Activity allows assigning labels to a database for training a neural network. (2) Why: Neural networks only work with numerical values. (3) When: Once we have training data on relevant public spaces for its intervention. (4) How: There are two ways of labeling. The first one can be manual or automated. The second one requires a definition in grasshopper to build the data.

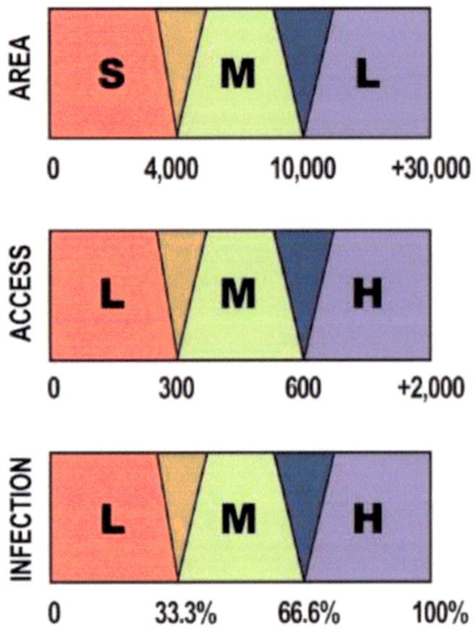

Area	Access	Index	Value
L	H	H	F
L	H	M	F
L	H	L	V
L	M	H	F
L	M	M	V
L	M	L	V
L	L	H	F
L	L	M	V
L	L	L	V
M	H	H	F
M	H	M	F
M	H	L	F
M	M	H	F
M	M	M	V
M	M	L	V
M	L	H	F
M	L	M	V
M	L	L	V
S	H	H	F
S	H	M	F
S	H	L	F
S	M	H	F
S	M	M	F
S	M	L	F
S	L	H	F
S	L	M	F
S	L	L	F

Fig. (6). Table with the policies used for training the neural network.

Pattern 10. Park Selection: (1) What: Decision-based on neural networks that evaluate the best public space for the intervention. (2) Why: To know the suitable public spaces to modulate the design in a park. (3) When: After the neural network evaluated the suitable spaces. (4) How: The programming of the LunchBox Neural object results in the labeling of the test information, classifying the data into two groups: pass and fail.

Design (A3)

Pattern 11. Parametric Design: (1) What: Process for defining modulation parameters and circulation restrictions and social distancing. (2) Why: These are data that will constantly change and modify the design (3) When: by analyzing the proposals based on the data source previously worked with the artificial intelligence engine (4) How: It is done by including components that allow the generation of polyhedron for the stands, and then extract their data such as position and dimensions.

Pattern 12. Data Export to AWS: (1) What: Development of code that prepares the data sent to AWS considering the URLs of the endpoints in the APIs. (2) Why: When sending data to AWS it is necessary to format it through code development in C #. (3) When: To outsource data and generate interoperability between computer systems. (4) How: Develop the cloud service in AWS producing the Endpoints in the API Gateway service.

For the development of the algorithm and preparation of the data, the architecture/structure of the Grasshopper component and its information export protocols were considered. The below diagram illustrates the data flow considered for sending the data.

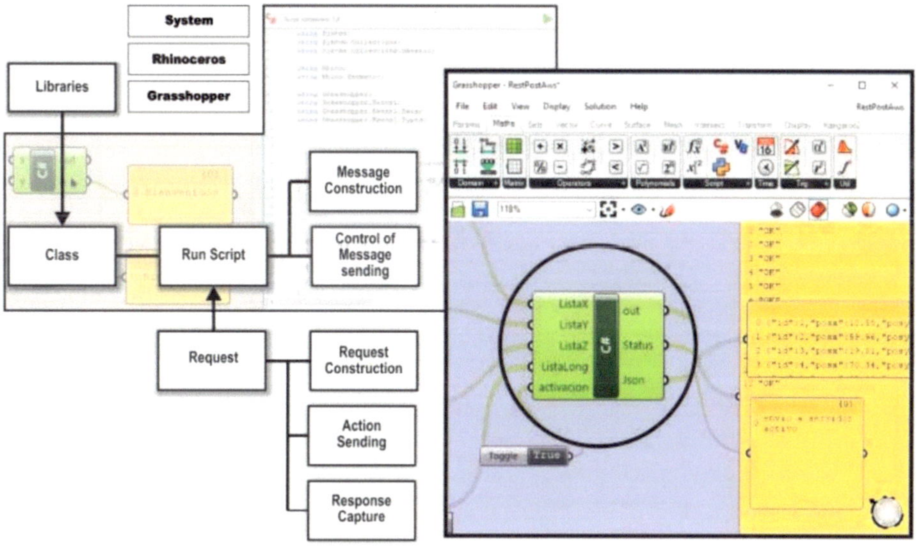

Fig. (7). **(A)** Front End Code for analysis with AWS Comprehend. **(B)** Frontend Code for send data to AWS DynamoDB.

This process allows you to send referential coordinates of design geometry from grasshopper, images of pedestrian dynamics in urban space, text records resulting from surveys, and stroke drawings to AWS. Considering that the script architecture in the Grasshopper components receives data from three types of inputs: Item Access, List Access, and Tree Access, the data type or geometry of the input (integers, decimal, objects such as curves, points, among others) was identified and the script was created in the Grasshopper C# component, by customizing your inputs and outputs.

Within the script, existing kernels were imported into the system in the form of .NET, Rhinoceros, and Grasshopper libraries to manage data and geometry. The data was exported in JSON format by building its parts from the string data type, inserting the numeric data as variables into the message once converted to strings (Fig. **8**). Finally, an ID was defined for each geometry point to carry out the shipment in an agile and orderly manner. A protocol and shipping address, format, message, and communication conditions were developed. The "HTTP Request" library was used for the message, and the "HTTP Response" was used to receive the server's response. POST was used as a Rest method for sending data and for analytics scripts using artificial intelligence. This procedure was also used for Unity 3D.

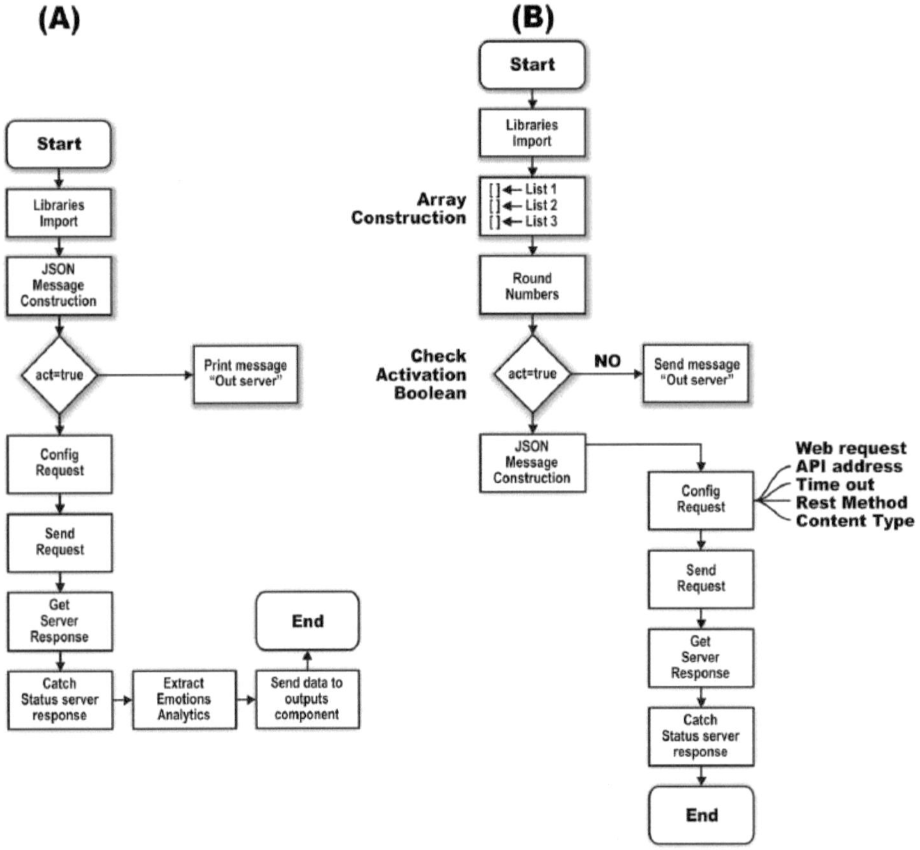

Fig. (8). Algorithmic architecture in Grasshopper's C# component.

BACKEND SERVICE IN AMAZON WEB SERVICES (B)

Cloud Storage (B1)

Pattern 13. AWS Backend: (1) What: Microservices connection to support a server in the cloud using NoSQL Databases (DynamoDB), Object Storage (simple storage service-S3), Serverless Functions (Lambda), external exposure (API

Gateway), identity and permission management (AWS IAM), and the use of artificial intelligence (AWS Rekognition, AWS Comprehend) (2) Why: To store and analyze data on AWS. (3) When: Once the data has been sent from grasshopper to be consumed by the mobile application or artificial intelligence. (4) Creating an access role towards the database, the repository, and the cognitive services with AWS IAM assigning the role to the serverless function to execute the tasks coming from the API Gateway endpoints.

The integrity and security represented by the use of cloud computing were considered a priority, so roles were created to manage access to services across the account, including database entry protocols, unstructured data repository, AWS Comprehend, AWS Rekognition, and the server instance that included building and training a neural network with AWS Sage Maker. To customize information management and microservices access policies, we used the JSON format and used the protocols suggested by AWS.

The first microservice created was the NoSQL database with AWS DynamoDB, thereby increasing the agility to develop the Backend solution. This step defines the Hash Key for the database tables in coordination with the message sent from the grasshopper. To complete the creation of the database, local tests with unit tests were required, and the type of security role was defined for writing and reading records to the database.

The second microservice used was AWS Lambda to create serverless functions, taking advantage of the compute advantage of this service is not relying on powered server instances, drastically reducing the cost of the computational solution. Assigned tasks with an Execute Authorized Role previously defined in AWS IAM were run in this microservice. Finally, the serverless script was built with specific roles for each microservice, using the NodeJS development language and its trigger from the API Gateway service.

The third microservice used allowed the development of APIs for the different types of communication. The AWS API Gateway microservice was used, with the HTTP protocol, differentiating each API by the verbs present in Rest and by the microservice to which it points.

We use this development path for unstructured data repository services and Artificial Intelligence microservices. The API Gateway integrated orders to the server and serverless functions, managing data that came from the Gateway to target microservices and thus be consumed.

Artificial Intelligence in AWS (B2)

Amazon Web Services provides its users with services at different levels of appropriation. From ready-to-use services, such as AWS Rekognition and Comprehend, to those for creating, training, and refining our neural network through TensorFlow frameworks. Although the service exists, the programming procedure is mandatory to configure the requirement according to our design needs. Real-time design experiences using AWS are limited to Product End-User. The object changes according to specific value ranges but without the possibility of introducing new parameters or design constraints. Therefore, we explore using AWS as an End-User solution for the process.

Pattern 14. AWS Rekognition: (1) What: AWS out-of-the-box microservice that identifies participants and objects in images and videos (2) Why: Intervention in public spaces requires checking social distancing, recording activities, counting people, facial analysis to optimize the design spatial distribution solution. (3) When: Every time we need the information to improve the design, we resort to the data registered from the original location (4) How: It works on-demand and accesses it.

AWS Rekognition is a service that uses an existing artificial intelligence engine that allows us to perform image analysis, showing the number of recognized people, emotions, age, gender, the distance that exists between participants through a triangulation script created in a serverless function.

From grasshopper, we prepare the submission by encoding the image in a Base64 string. This string was decoded on AWS by a serverless function, saved to the repository, then extracted and parsed, reducing the latency time to produce the response. The same serverless code encodes the AWS Rekognition response and sends the server response to the grasshopper. The image analytics solution is on-demand, and the number of images does billing. If there is no use of the service, it generates no cost and reduces the risk in the sustainability of the computing solution.

Pattern 15. AWS Comprehend: (1) What: AWS microservice for processing natural language using machine learning to identify data and find connections in blocks of text. (2) Why: It allows us to know the feelings associated with the text, keywords. (3) When: Its use is related to converting the surveys and audio transcripts of interviews to objective data of the feelings to be consumed in the definitions from grasshopper. (4) How: works on demand and is managed by a serverless function activated from the API.

AWS Comprehend is a microservice that identifies language, keywords, subjects, and verbs in a block of text, recognizing the feelings associated with each. It is a service run on-demand without having to power on a server instance to run it.

From grasshopper, we enter the parsed text in the JSON message as part of the content string. Using the API, we directed this content using a serverless function to the AWS Comprehend microservice and got a response associated with the feelings in the text. The texts come from different sources, such as a survey in urban space to make the feeling of one or more users of space objective. The data set processed allows us to identify patterns that show neutral, positive, or negative feelings.

PEER REVIEW (C)

Augmented Reality (C1)

Pattern 16. Unity3D-Vuforia Connection: (1) What: Unity 3D is a mobile application development system that incorporates external solutions such as Vuforia for augmented reality. (2) Why: Because it facilitates quick decisions, oriented to the 3D visualization of each change made in the design platform (Rhinoceros and Grasshopper) using dynamic data from AWS. (3) When: To externalize the results of the Grasshopper definition. (4) Create a project in Unity3D and a traceable objective on the Vuforia website, and then integrate it into Unity, also link the objects to be displayed with the data brought from AWS.

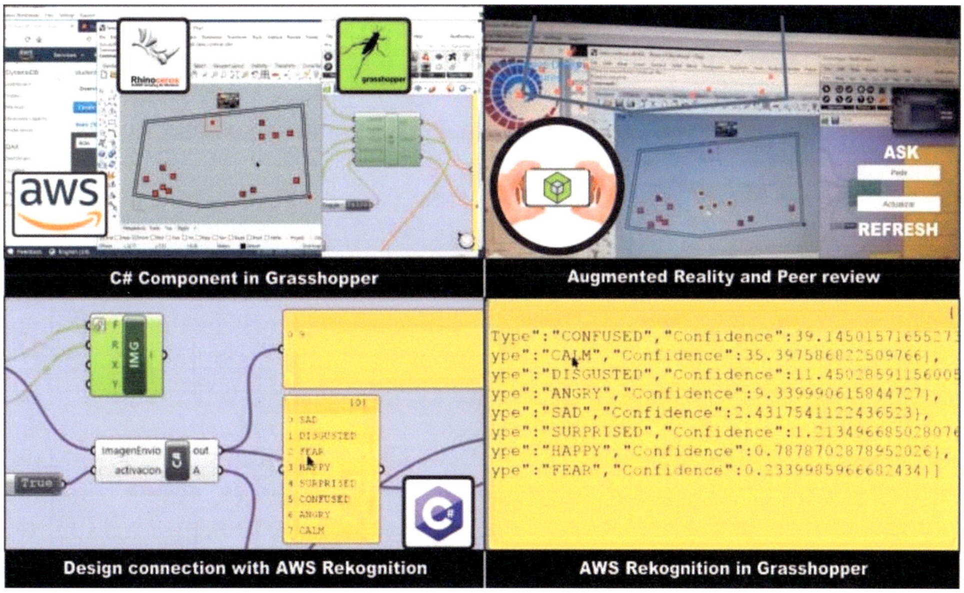

Fig. (9). Customization of tools that drive the flow of design data to the visualization platform.

It was necessary to create an application that fits the need to manage and visualize data from geometry in grasshopper to a device that runs augmented reality. Remote viewing allowed specialists outside the project to review the modifications or propose changes to the process. These changes were due to regulatory circumstances in each location facilitating the customization of the project to different user realities. We decided to use Unity 3D because it uses the C# programming language that uses grasshopper and streamlines code transfer. Another factor is that Unity integrates with Vuforia's augmented reality solutions, increasing development speed for situations where response time is critical. This integration resulted from using an objective image to recognize the position and scale of digital objects in grasshopper that are displayed on the device to interact with physical reality. The integration of EUP into the co-design of the application allowed us to consume APIs in AWS to visualize the data of the consumed project geometry from a database.

With the data, our app rebuilt digital objects dependent on the trackable target (Fig. **9**) so that Vuforia can find and position them through image recognition. Our team visualized the changes produced in the grasshopper and the participants located in six countries from the application.

For this solution, we consider the effect produced by the scale (of the architectural or urban project), the coordinate systems (produced by grasshopper), and the rotation system (of digital objects). Here it is important to consider that Unity has a global coordinate system that configures the scale of objects and when defining the objective tracked by Vuforia, a new coordinate system is established because the digital objects that will be affected by digital tracking will be dependent on coordinates, scale, and rotation of the trackable digital object. Each geometry state change requires a request for data to the server located in the database.

CONCLUDING REMARKS

GUI customization is necessary because existing solutions do not have enough parameters and data processing logic. These could allow us high flexibility for design and connection with other technologies requiring work formats and data type. Besides, the amount of computing resources in library code format or third-party servers through APIs is higher than those available with a GUI.

If we use IoT technologies, it is advisable to have an information broker hosted on a server that allows us to manage orders to the database, states, action triggers, connectivity management, and security. It must also be able to support HTTP or MQTT connections, and from which one can extract information to be exposed in Grasshopper or M2M connections. We recommend developing serverless computing functions for data management, internal logic, or gateways to use this broker. IoT connects end devices with an intermediary, for this reason, the role of EUPs in the design of GUIs for HCI-enhancing devices is important because it involves other aspects besides design, such as the management of the communication protocol with WI-FI using routers, GSM / GPRS from 2G to 5G networks, developing the processor and hardware control software.

IoT devices represent a way for obtaining a massive amount of information, enabling the training of artificial intelligence systems based on neural networks. After achieving data processing with Big Data tools, these networks can be hosted on remote servers or edge devices, creating autonomous machines and fog computing. If the compute capacity for processing this data exceeds what edge devices can perform, you need to use remote servers, with processors optimized for these tasks, whether CPU, GPU, or TPU. More processing power can be requested remotely from quantum computing servers with QPU processors. For all these cases, it is necessary to develop new codes that allow us to use the computing capacity of computers in other regions of the world.

In this research, it was found that design and its complexity are more than a creative discipline. It also revealed the mission of integrating social, economic, psychological, and biological requirements that are generally not part of the traditional/passive design, which uses technical requirements, material, shape, color, volume, and space in a project. This experience demonstrates an evolution towards responsive and computational design with autonomous learning, using computational solutions that offer multiple and unpredictable results with artificial intelligence techniques for the future of GUIs for HCI-enhancing devices.

In the discussion session with the 20 participants from five countries, it was highlighted that this model allowed us to understand how subjective data can be turned into objective information to be added to a design proposal, which is not possible directly using computational tools. Likewise, this model was perceived as innovative since it contextualizes the design proposal based on direct information from users and not from an average or typical user. In the discussion, expert users in visual programming perceived that the geometric response or sometimes aesthetic result of the computational design is complemented by incorporating emotions and particularities of the users or the environment. From a traditional/passive design, the data produced by a design team generates a workflow that does not support rapid decision-making. The method proposed in this research allows reducing the time in decision-making as well as generating an approach towards subjective characteristics present in the architectural-urban space.

CONSENT FOR PUBLICATION

Not Applicable.

CONFLICT OF INTEREST

The author confirms that this chapter contents have no conflict of interest.

ACKNOWLEDGEMENTS

This research has been developed by the Computational Design Research Group of the Universidad Peruana de Ciencias Aplicadas (UPC), which includes professors Pedro Arteaga and Darío Sánchez who contributed to the development of the codes and proposals in the design project. This investigation was supported by the Research Incentive Annual Contest (project C-002-2020), Research Department of the UPC. We would like to thank Dr. Matias del Campo, from Taubman College - University of Michigan, for the invitation to the DigitalFUTURES WORLD workshops, organized by Tongji University, as well as the 20 participants of the "Responsive Design for Emergency" team for their ideas and reflections.

REFERENCES

[1] B. Barricelli, F. Cassano, D. Foglic, and A. Piccinno, "End-user development, end-user programming, and end-user software engineering: A systematic mapping study", *J. Syst. Softw.*, vol. 149, pp. 101-137, 2019. [http://dx.doi.org/10.1016/j.jss.2018.11.041]

[2] B. Nardi, *A Small Matter of Programming.* MIT Press: Cambridge, MA, 1993. [http://dx.doi.org/10.7551/mitpress/1020.001.0001]

[3] M. Gantt, and B. Nardi, "Gardeners and gurus: Patterns of cooperation among CAD users", In: *Proc. SIGCHI Conf. on Human Factors in Computing Systems*, 1992, pp. 107-117. [http://dx.doi.org/10.1145/142750.142767]

[4] M. Burry, "Narrowing the Gap Between CAAD and Computer Programming", In: *Proc. Computer-Aided Architectural Design Research in Asia (CAADRIA 1997)*, 1997, pp. 491-498.

[5] G. Celani, U. Bruscato, and P.C. Herrera, "Incorporating Computational Theories and Technologies in Architectural Design", *Int. J. Archit. Comput.*, vol. 7, no. 4, pp. I-vi, 2009. [http://dx.doi.org/10.1260/1478-0771.7.4.i]

[6] J. da Silva, A. Mussi, T. Da Silva, and P. Zardo, "Designers of the XXI century: BIM software programming and the development of new competencies", In: *Proc. XXII Conf. Sociedad Iberoamericana de Gráfica Digital*, pp. 538-545. [http://dx.doi.org/10.5151/sigradi2018-1444]

[7] P.C. Herrera, "Scripting and Digital Fabrication in Artisanal Processes: The Case of South America", In: *Proc. Int. Conf. Cross Americas: Probing Disglobal Networks* , 2016, pp. 357-362.

[8] A.B. Raposo, L.P. Magalhães, and C.S. de Souza, "Users´ Perceptions of Integrated GUI + EUP Communicative Environments", In: *Anais do II IHC - Workshop sobre Fatores Humanos em Sistemas Computacionais (CD-ROM)*, 1999.

[9] N. Thakur, and C.Y. Han, A Multilayered Contextually Intelligent Activity Recognition Framework for Smart Home.*Human Interaction, Emerging Technologies, and Future Applications III. Advances in Intelligent Systems and Computing.* Springer: Cham, Switzerland, 2021, pp. 278-283. [http://dx.doi.org/10.1007/978-3-030-55307-4_42]

[10] N. Thakur, and C.Y. Han, "A Context-Driven Complex Activity Framework for Smart Home", In: *Proc. IEEE 9th Annual Information Technology, Electronics and Mobile Communication Conf.*, 2018, pp. 801-806. [http://dx.doi.org/10.1109/IEMCON.2018.8615079]

[11] N. Thakur, and C.Y. Han, "A Context-Driven Indoor Localization Framework for Assisted Living in Smart Homes," In HCI Int. 2020. Late-Breaking Papers: Universal Access and Inclusive Design, Cham, Switzerland: Springer, 2021, pp.387-400.,

[12] M. Di Nardo, D. Forino, and T. Murino, "The evolution of man-machine interaction: the role of the human in Industry 4.0 paradigm", *Prod. Manuf. Res.*, vol. 8, no. 1, pp. 20-34, 2020. [http://dx.doi.org/10.1080/21693277.2020.1737592]

[13] F. Paterno, V. Wulf, Ed., *New Perspectives in End-User Development.* Springer Int. Publishing: Cham, 2017. [http://dx.doi.org/10.1007/978-3-319-60291-2]

[14] D. Fogli, and A. Piccino, End-User Development in Industry 4.0: Challenges and Opportunities.*End-User Development.* Springer: Cham, Switzerland, 2019, pp. 230-233.Lecture Notes in Computer Science [http://dx.doi.org/10.1007/978-3-030-24781-2_21]

[15] P. Scupelli, Creative Workplace Alchemies: Individual Workspaces and Collaboration Hotspots.*Architecture and Interaction.* Springer: Cham, 2016, pp. 85-111. [http://dx.doi.org/10.1007/978-3-319-30028-3_5]

[16] K. Sailer, "Movement in workplace environments: configurational or programmed", In: *Proc. 6th Int. Space Syntax Symp*, 2007, pp. 068_1-068_14.

[17] J. Brich, M. Walch, M. Rietzler, M. Weber, and F. Schaub, "Exploring End-User Programming Needs in Home Automation", *ACM Trans. Comput. Hum. Interact.,* vol. 24, no. 2, pp. 1-35, 2017. [http://dx.doi.org/10.1145/3057858]

[18] Y. Mariana, A. Triwardhani, and M. Djimantoro, "The study of space configuration using space syntax analysis Case study: an elderly housing", In: *The Int. Conf. on Eco Engineering Development*, 2017. [http://dx.doi.org/10.1088/1755-1315/109/1/012048]

[19] M. Reisinger, J. Schrammel, and P. Fröhlich, "Visual end-user programming in smart homes: Complexity and performance", In: *Proc. IEEE Symp. on Visual Languages and Human-Centric Computing*, 2017, pp. 331-332. [http://dx.doi.org/10.1109/VLHCC.2017.8103495]

[20] W. Harrison, From the Editor: The Dangers of End-User Programming [http://dx.doi.org/10.1109/MS.2004.13]

[21] E. Raymond, *The Cathedral & the Bazaar.* O'Reilly Media Inc.: Sebastopol, 1999. [http://dx.doi.org/10.1007/s12130-999-1026-0]

[22] L. Kronman, A. Zingerle, Ed., *The Internet of Other People's Things. Dealing with pathologies of a digital world*, 2018.

[23] R. Sennett, *The Craftman.* Yale University Press: New Haven, 2008.

[24] R. Sacks, and Ch. Eastman, *Lee, Ghang and P. Teichholz, "BIM Handbook. A Guide to Building Information Modeling For Owners, Designers, Engineers, Contractors, and Facility Managers.* John Wiley: Hoboken, 2018. [http://dx.doi.org/10.1002/9781119287568]

[25] E. Manzini, "Design in a changing, connected world", *Strategic Design Research Journal,* vol. 13, no. 1, pp. 1-5, 2014.

[26] C. Kohtala, "Addressing sustainability in research on distributed production: an integrated literature review", *J. Clean. Prod.,* vol. 106, pp. 654-668, 2015. [http://dx.doi.org/10.1016/j.jclepro.2014.09.039]

[27] D. Sollohub, *Millennials in Architecture. Generations, Disruption, and the Legacy of a Profession.* University of Texas Press: Austin, 2019.

[28] R. Kaplan, "The fundamentals of insulating motors", In: *Proc. 1960 Nat. Conf. on the Application of Electrical Insulation*, Chicago: USA, 1960. [http://dx.doi.org/10.1109/ENCAEI.1960.7466619]

[29] J. Baudrillard, *The System of Objects.* Verso: London, 2005.

[30] G. Schmitt, *Information Architecture. Basis and Future of CAAD.* Birkhauser: Basel, 1999.

[31] R. Deutsch, *Superusers: Design Technology Specialists and the Future of Practice.* John Wiley: London, 2017.

[32] P. Bernstein, *Architecture, Design, Data: Practice Competency in the Era of Computation.* Birkhauser: Basel, 2018. [http://dx.doi.org/10.1515/9783035610444]

[33] K. Terzidis, *Algorithmic Architecture.* Architectural Press: London, 2006. [http://dx.doi.org/10.4324/9780080461298]

[34] A. Koutamanis, "On the Management of Visual Design Documentation", In: *Proc. 19th Education and research in Computer Aided Architectural Design in Europe Conf.*, 2001, pp. 124-130.

[35] C. Frey, and M. Osborne, "The Future of Employment: How susceptible are jobs to computerization?", *Technol. Forecast. Soc. Change,* vol. 114, pp. 254-280, 2017. [http://dx.doi.org/10.1016/j.techfore.2016.08.019]

[36] G. Celani, S. Maycon, D. Lenz, and A. Macedo, The Future of the Architect's Employment To Which Extent Can Architectural Design Be Computerised?

[37] S. Turkle, *Simulations and its Discontents.* MIT Press: Cambridge, MA, 2009. [http://dx.doi.org/10.7551/mitpress/8200.001.0001]

[38] S. Turkle, *Life on the Screen. Identity in the Age of the Internet.* MIT Press: Cambridge, MA, 1995.

[39] M. Hensel, A. Menges, and M. Weinstock, *Emergent Technologies and Design. Towards a biological paradigm for architecture.* Routledge: New York, 2010.

[40] P. Yuan, A. Menges, and N. Leach, *Digital Fabrication.* Tongji University Press: Shangai, 2018.

[41] B. Peters, and X. De Kestelier, "The building of algorithmic thought", *Architectural Design,* vol. 83, no. 2, pp. 8-15, 2013. [http://dx.doi.org/10.1002/ad.1545]

[42] G. Celani, "Shortcut to the Fourth Industrial Revolution: The case of Latin America", *Int. J. Archit. Comput.,* vol. 18, no. 4, pp. 320-334, 2020. [http://dx.doi.org/10.1177/1478077120942193]

[43] A. Rojko, "Industry 4.0 concept: background and overview", *Int J Interact Mob Technol,* vol. 11, no. 5, pp. 77-90, 2017. [http://dx.doi.org/10.3991/ijim.v11i5.7072]

[44] P.C. Herrera, and F. Braida, "Digital Technologies in Latin American Architecture A Literature Review from the Third to the Fourth Industrial Revolution", In: *Proc. 32nd Education and research in Computer Aided Architectural Design in Europe and 23rd Sociedad Iberoamericana de Grafica Digital Conf.*, 2019, pp. 431-440.

[45] R. Maskuriy, A. Selamat, P. Maresova, O. Krejcar, and O. Olalekan, "Industry 4.0 for the Construction Industry: Review of Management Perspective", *Economies,* vol. 7, no. 68, 2019. [http://dx.doi.org/10.3390/economies7030068]

[46] X. Bao, Z. Wang, and X. Chen, A Flexible and Efficient Approach to Component Test in Time-Critical Scenarios.*Reuse in Big Data Era, Lectures Notes in Computer Science.* Springer: Cham, Switzerland, 2019, pp. 3-13. [http://dx.doi.org/10.1007/978-3-030-22888-0_1]

[47] C. Kotas, T. Naughton, and N. Imam, "A comparison of Amazon Web Services and Microsoft Azure cloud platforms for high-performance computing", In: *Proc. IEEE Int. Conf. on Consumer Electronics*, 2018, pp. 1-4. [http://dx.doi.org/10.1109/ICCE.2018.8326349]

[48] R. Woodbury, *Elements of Parametric Design.* Routledge: New York, 2010.

[49] C. Alexander, *The Timeless Way of Building.* Oxford University Press: Oxford, 1979.

[50] LunchBox, *Computational design tools for Grasshopper and Dynamo.,* 2020. Oct. 2020. [Online]. Available from: https://provingground.io/tools/lunchbox/ [Accessed: 11st Oct. 2020]

[51] OpenStreetMap (OSM), October 2020. [Online]. Available: https://www.openstreetmap.org/ [Accessed: 11st Oct. 2020]

[52] ELK, "Tools to generate a map and topographical surfaces using open source data from OSM and USGS", Oct. 2020. [Online]. Available from: https://www.food4rhino.com/app/elk [Accessed: 11st Oct. 2020]

[53] CONFIGURBANIST, Oct. 2020. [Online]. Available from: https://sites.google.com/site/pirou-znourian/configurbanist [Accessed: 11st Oct. 2020]

[54] SHORTEST WALK, October 2020. [Online]. Available from: https://www.food4rhino.com/app/shortest-walk-gh [Accessed: 11th Oct. 2020]

[55] P.E. Hart, N.J. Nilsson, and B. Raphael, "A Formal Basis for the Heuristic Determination of Minimum Cost Paths", *IEEE Transactions on Systems Science and Cybernetics,* vol. 4, no. 2, pp. 100-107, 1968. [http://dx.doi.org/10.1109/TSSC.1968.300136]

SUBJECT INDEX

A

B

Nirmalya Thakur and Parameshachari B.D. (Eds)

C

D

E

F

G

H

I

L

M

N

O

P

R

S

T

Made in the USA
Las Vegas, NV
03 November 2026

57422837R00105